The Politics of Intersectionality

The Politics of Intersectionality series builds on the long-standing insights of intersectionality theory from a vast variety of disciplinary perspectives. As a globally utilitzed analytical framework for understanding issues of social justice, Leslie McCall, Mary Hawkesworth, and others argue that intersectionality is arguably the most important theoretical contribution of women's and gender studies to date. Indeed the imprint of intersectional analysis can be easily found on innovations in equality legislation, human rights, and development discourses.

The history of what is now called "intersectional thinking" is long. In fact, prior to its mainstreaming, intersectionality analysis was carried for many years mainly by black and other racialized women who, from their situated gaze, perceived as absurd, not just misleading, any attempt by feminists and others to homogenize women's situation, particularly in conceptualizing such situations as analogous to that of racialized others. As Brah and Phoenix point out, many black feminists fulfilled significant roles in the development of intersectional analysis, such as the Combahee River Collective, the black lesbian feminist organization from Boston, who pointed out the need of developing an integrated analysis and practice based upon the fact that major systems of oppression interlock rather than operate separately. However the term "intersectionality" itself emerged nominally from the field of critical legal studies, where critical race feminist Kimberle Williams Crenshaw wrote two pathbreaking articles, "Demarginalizing the Intersection of Race and Sex: A Critique of Antidiscrimination Doctrine, Feminist Theory and Antiracist Politics" and "Mapping the Margins: Intersectionality, Identity Politics, and Violence against Women of Color." At nearly the same time, social theorist Patricia Hill Collins was preparing her landmark work, *Black Feminist Thought: Knowledge, Consciousness and the Politics of Empowerment*, which characterized intersections of race, class, and gender as mutually reinforcing sites of power relations.

Both Crenshaw and Collins gave the name "intersectionality" to a far larger and more ethnically diverse trajectory of work, now global in nature, that speaks truth to power sited differentially rather than centralized in a single locus. What could also be called intersectional analysis was in fact developing at roughly the same time among European and postcolonial feminists, including, for example, Anthias and Yuval-Davis (1983; 1992); Brah (1996); Essed (1991); Ifekwunigwe (1999); Lutz (1991); Meekosha, and Min-ha (1989). Indeed it seems, in a manner parallel to that which Sandra Harding characterizes the evolution of standpoint theory, that intersectionality was an idea whose time had come precisely because of the plethora of authors working independently across the globe to make vastly similar sets of claims. Around the world, those interested in a more comprehensive and transformative approach to social justice—whether sociologists, legal scholars, feminist theorists, policy makers, or human rights advocates—have used the language and tenets of intersectionality to more effectively articulate injustice and advocate for positive social change.

The books in this series represent an interrogation of intersectionality at various levels of analysis. They unabashedly foreground the politics of intersectionality in a way that is designed to both honor the legacy of earlier scholarship and activism as well as to push the boundaries of intersectionality's value to the academy and most importantly to the world. We interpret the series title, The Politics of Intersectionality, in two general ways:

First, we emphasize the politics of intersectionality, broadly conceived; that is to say we include debates among scholars regarding the proper conceptualization and application of the term "intersectionality" as part and parcel of the series' intellectual project. Is intersectionality a paradigm? Is intersectionality a normative political (specifically feminist) project? Is it a method or epistemological approach? Is it (merely) a concept with limited applicability beyond multiply marginalized populations? Our own idiosyncratic answers to these questions are far less important than the open dialogue we seek by including them within the scholarly discourse generated by the series.

What this means pragmatically is that rather than dictatorially denote an extant definition of intersectionality and impose it on every author's manuscript, as series editors our task has been to meaningfully push each author to grapple with their own conceptualization of intersectionality and facilitate their interaction with an ever-growing body of global scholarship, policy, and advocacy work as they render such a conceptualization transparent to readers, reflexive as befits the best feminist work, and committed to rigorous standards of quality no matter the subject, the method, or the conclusions. As editors we have taken such an active role precisely because grappling with the politics of intersectionality demands our adherence to the normative standards of transparency, reflexivity, and speaking to multiple sites of power for which intersectionality is not only known but lauded as the gold standard. It is our honor to build this area of scholarship across false boundaries of theory and praxis; artificially distinct academic disciplines; and the semipermeable line between scholarship and activism.

No less importantly we emphasize politics to mean, well, *politics*, whether everyday senses of justice; so-called formal politics of social movements, campaigns, elections, policy, and government institutions; or personal politics of identity, community, and activism across a broad swath of the world. While this general conceptualization of politics lends itself to the social sciences, we define social sciences in a broad way that again seeks to unite theoretical concerns (whether normative or positive) with interpretive and empirical approaches across an array of topics far too numerous to list in their entirety.

The second way we interpret the series title—simultaneously, as one might expect of intersectionality scholars—is with an emphasis on the word intersectionality. That is, the books in this series neither depend solely on 20-year-old articulations of intersectionality, nor do they adhere to one particular theoretical or methodological approach to study intersectionality; they are steeped in a rich literature of both substantive and analytical depth that in the twenty-first century reaches around the world. This is not your professor's "women of color" or "race-class-gender" series of the late twentieth century. Indeed an emphasis on up-to-date engagement with the best and brightest global thinking on intersectionality has been the single most exacting standard we have imposed on the editing process. As series editors we seek to develop manuscripts that aspire to a level of sophistication about intersectionality as a body of research that is in fact worthy of the intellectual, political, and personal risks taken by so many of its earliest interlocutors in voicing and naming this work. We thus relate to intersectionality as both methodological and analytical tools that are firmly rooted in the epistemological tradition of the feminist situated gaze but do not necessarily prioritize discussion of gender relations over other cross-cutting social, economic, and political power relations.

Series Editors:

Ange-Marie Hancock, University of Southern California
Nira Yuval-Davis, University of East London

Also in the series:

Solidarity Politics for Millennials
Ange-Marie Hancock

Social Change and Intersectional Activism: The Spirit of Social Movement
Sharon Doetsch-Kidder

Urban Black Women and the Politics of Resistance
Zenzele Isoke

Gender Equality, Intersectionality and Diversity in Europe
Lise Rolandsen Agustin

Situating Intersectionality: Politics, Policy, and Power
Edited by Angelia R. Wilson

Crossing Boundaries during Peace and Conflict: Transforming Identity in Chiapas and in Northern Ireland
Melanie Hoewer

Crossing Boundaries during Peace and Conflict

Transforming Identity in Chiapas and in Northern Ireland

Melanie Hoewer

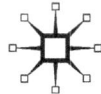

CROSSING BOUNDARIES DURING PEACE AND CONFLICT
Copyright © Melanie Hoewer, 2014.
Softcover reprint of the hardcover 1st edition 2014 978-1-137-38286-3
All rights reserved.

First published in 2014 by
PALGRAVE MACMILLAN®
in the United States—a division of St. Martin's Press LLC,
175 Fifth Avenue, New York, NY 10010.

Where this book is distributed in the UK, Europe and the rest of the world, this is by Palgrave Macmillan, a division of Macmillan Publishers Limited, registered in England, company number 785998, of Houndmills, Basingstoke, Hampshire RG21 6XS.

Palgrave Macmillan is the global academic imprint of the above companies and has companies and representatives throughout the world.

Palgrave® and Macmillan® are registered trademarks in the United States, the United Kingdom, Europe and other countries.

ISBN 978-1-349-48020-3   ISBN 978-1-137-46874-1 (eBook)
DOI 10.1057/9781137468741
Library of Congress Cataloging-in-Publication Data

Crossing boundaries during peace and conflict : transforming identity in Chiapas and in Northern Ireland / by Melanie Hoewer.
    pages cm
    Includes bibliographical references and index.

    1. Identity politics—Mexico—Chipas. 2. Identity politics—Northern Ireland. 3. Ethnic conflict—Mexico—Chipas. 4. Ethnic conflict—Northern Ireland. 5. Chiapas (Mexico)—Ethnic relations. 6. Northern Ireland—Ethnic relations. I. Title.

F1256.C896 2014
305.800972'75—dc23   2014017523

A catalogue record of the book is available from the British Library.

Design by Newgen Knowledge Works (P) Ltd., Chennai, India.

First edition: November 2014

10 9 8 7 6 5 4 3 2 1

Contents

List of Figures ix

Foreword xi

Introduction 1

Part I Addressing Complexity and Difference: A Theoretical and Practical Framework

1 Identity in Transition: Concept, Context, and Complexity 7

2 Addressing Complexity and Difference in Research Methodology 29

Part II The Voices

3 From the Margin to the Center: Female Narratives of Ethno-National Mobilization 47

4 The Meaning of Contentious Peace: A Multilayered Approach to Conflict Settlement 97

Part III Connecting Voices: Lessons from Collective Identity Processes

5 Connecting Boundary Processes during Episodes of Mobilization and Demobilization 149

6 Lessons Learned from Listening to Women's Voices in Peace and Conflict Situations 171

Notes 179

Bibliography 195

Index 219

Figures

3.1	Map of our community conflict	49
4.1	Map of the community of dreams	109
4.2	Action plan toward change	116

Foreword

This research has been a journey, a journey that began a long time ago when I listened as a child to my grandfathers' and grandmothers' stories about the Second World War. I vividly remember sitting on long winter evenings in my grandmothers' kitchen and learning about their experiences of war and peace, which were so strikingly different than the war stories my grandfathers told. It was precisely in those "listening spaces" that the seeds for this research project were sown. I was lucky to have my grandmothers still around when I began to plan this project and benefited very much from their wonderful support. However, they have all passed by now and I am writing these lines in loving memory of them and their different voices.

My journey has allowed me not only to pursue my childhood interest in learning about different experiences of women during armed conflict and its aftermath, but also to reflect on my own activism path and gain a deeper understanding on how activisms work. In other words, being an activist and having worked as an activist in civil society organizations, I have developed an interest in learning about the way solidarity amongst people develops. Having shifted myself in my activism pathway from a more general campaigning about human rights to a stronger focus on women's rights and peace building, I set out to learn more about the connection between peace and conflict, identity and activism.

My experience of growing up in a border region and living for many years outside the nation state I was born into has constantly informed my interest in intersecting identity categories and their social construction. My activism has provided a space to reflect about identity from my own perspective as a woman from a particular background (nation, ethnicity, race, class, age, educational, and etc.); the awareness of the intersection of identity categories and inequalities developed in particular during my work with indigenous and nonindigenous women and men in Chiapas. It was through the wonderful activists in this region in the south of Mexico that I was introduced first to the practice of intersectionality and later learned about the theory.

Actively listening to the different experiences of female activists in periods of armed conflict and its aftermath connects my interest in peace and conflict, identity processes, and different activisms of women. I hope that my analysis of the way female activists perceive and position themselves during conflict and conflict settlement processes contributes to finding ways to create a more sustainable and just peace.

I owe a special debt of gratitude to the many women and activists in Northern Ireland and in Mexico who graciously agreed to work with me and to share their stories with me and from whom I learnt so much about their important work. Their enthusiasm and friendship were truly inspiring and energizing.

I would further like to thank, Prof. Jennifer Todd, Prof. Nira Yuval Davis, Prof. John Coakley, and Dr. Tobias Theiler for their guidance, critical insight, and unwavering encouragement. I would like to extend my heartfelt appreciation to the faculty, staff, and friends in the School of Politics and International Relations in University College Dublin, in particular Ciaran O'Driscoll for helping with the bibliography, to my friends in Ireland, Mexico, Germany, and in other parts of the world, especially to Louise Beirne, Catherine Joyce, Francis O'Rourke, Dr. Roja Fazaeli, and Joel Hanisek for dedicating many hours to this work and providing great advice, to Dr. Xochitl Leyva Solano, Prof. Cynthia Enloe, Prof. Jil Vickers, Dr. Ernesto Vazquez, Dr. Katherine O'Donnell, Dr. Pamela Scully, and the wonderful women of *Sibéal* for great discussions and encouragement and my family for their love and support.

This research was made possible through the generous financial support of the Department of Foreign Affairs and Trade Conflict Resolution Unit in Ireland and the UCD College of Human Science.

It was further facilitated by the UCD John Hume Institute for Global Irish Studies, CIESAS Sureste (San Cristóbal de las Casas, Chiapas, Mexico), Marina Pagés and colleagues in SIPAZ (San Cristóbal de las Casas, Chiapas, Mexico), Maria del Carmen and colleagues in CODIMUJ (San Cristóbal de las Casas,

Chiapas, Mexico), Sara Duque Sosa and colleagues in SERAPAZ (Ocosingo, Chiapas, Mexico), Toribia Hernández and colleagues in the Centro de Derechos Humanos Fray Pedro de la Nada (Ocosingo, Chiapas, Mexico), Shirley Graham and colleagues in Hanna's House, Lisa Moody, Claire Hackett, and colleagues in the Falls Community Council, Eibhlín Glenholmes and colleagues in TarAnall, Dr. Margaret Ward and colleagues in the Women's Resource and Development Agency; thank you so very much for graciously providing me with the space and tools necessary to complete my research.

Finally, a very special thank you to my partner, Seán Shanagher, who has shared this journey with me, the exciting and the difficult moments.

Introduction

Dealing with change and conflicting identities has become a central element in our increasingly complex, globalized world. Many books have been written about ethnic groups in conflict, addressing questions of motivations for becoming violent or setting out to find the right recipe for peaceful cohabitation of people from different ethnic or national groups. However, we still lack in understanding how processes of social change, such as ethno-national conflict and conflict settlement processes interact with identity change and in what way shifts in different identity categories, such as ethnicity, nationality, race, gender, class, and the like are interconnected. In particular, listening to women who have experienced ethno-national conflict and its aftermath raises many questions about our understanding of what happens with individuals in situations of social change.

Periods of ethno-national mobilization are typically portrayed as momentums in which already existing unequal gender structures and meanings are reaffirmed. Women's narratives from Chiapas and from Northern Ireland show a need for questioning whether this picture is possibly overessentialized and where we might find opportunities for social and symbolic transformations during phases of ethno-national conflict and settlement processes.

Mobilization processes that started against the state structure, particularly against the marginalization of their communities, became, for many female activists, spaces for having their female voices included in the wider community struggle and for changing community traditions that institutionalized gender inequality. By finding their voices and including their experiences in the struggle, women's lives begin to change and they in turn begin to change. In my inductive, comparative study, I address the following set of questions:

a. Has identity change within gender and ethnic categories actually taken place within the ethno-national mobilization and demobilization processes in Chiapas and Northern Ireland?

b. If so, how do these processes of change interrelate? and finally,
c. What are the differences between the two case studies?

As "the most innovative insights are discovered at the boundaries of disciplines" (Hall & Lamont, 2013, p. 50), this research incorporates richer conceptions of social relations into the comparative analyses of identity processes during peace and conflict through a more intensive dialogue of political science with sociology. I address the complexity of intersecting identity processes during episodes of peace and conflict by using a methodology that allows me to gain an in-depth understanding of historical processes and individual motivation (della Porta, 2008, p. 202). My qualitative, active-participative research strategy and interpretative approach allows me to actively listen to the voices or the "objects" of my research and to gain a more in-depth understanding of their experiences, perceptions, and perspectives. These voices have not only informed but are at the heart of this research project; therefore I begin the presentation of my findings from this research in Chapters 3 and 4 by letting those voices come to the fore by telling a story. The stories that open each sub-chapter are compiled of different voices in order to comply with research ethics. I promised all research participants to use their responses anonymously, and telling a story of many voices and using pseudonyms instead of real names allows me to present their voices without identifying them.

What can we learn about identity change in peace and conflict situations though a comparative analysis of female activists' collective identity narratives? The analysis of women's stories from Chiapas and Northern Ireland not only provides an innovative model for examining the interconnection of different processes of identity, social change, and academic scholarship but also has potential policy impact. The in-depth analysis of the different levels of change in peace and conflict situations contributes to further development of more inclusive models for conflict resolution processes.

This monograph first introduces the framework for this research by embedding the research question into the contemporary academic debate on identity and intersectionality in social (de)mobilizations and then introducing the research methodology. The heart piece of the monograph is the presentation of findings from the collective identity narratives from Chiapas and Northern Ireland, portraying the experiences, perceptions, and positioning of the voices that have informed this research. This is followed by the evaluation of general trends and lessons learned from connecting the findings from this empirical research.

I

Addressing Complexity and Difference: A Theoretical and Practical Framework

1

IDENTITY IN TRANSITION: CONCEPT, CONTEXT, AND COMPLEXITY

INTRODUCTION

Why is it important to look at the interconnection of identity categories in processes of social change? And how do the making and change of gender, ethnic, and other identity categories intersect during periods of conflict and conflict settlement? Setting the conceptual framework, this chapter addresses existing gaps in the study of ethno-national conflict and conflict settlement. It does so by highlighting the need to explore the making and change of intersecting identity categories during these processes. Women's experiences are largely written out of official narratives of ethno-national conflicts to protect the "manliness" of armed conflict based on a hegemonic (heterosexual) masculinity (Cohn, 2013, p. 23). Feminist research has highlighted that this exclusion prevents conflict societies from being transformed into peaceful ones (Cohn, 2013; Enloe, 2002; Kronsell & Svedberg, 2012). Not only does the exclusion of women's experiences of conflict avert from understanding and unlocking social dynamics and discourses that fuel injustice, inequality, and violence, but it also does not take account of the fact that identity categories are not static and change during periods of ethno-national conflict. Building on findings of identity change during peace and conflict (Hoewer, 2013; Mitchell, 2006; Todd, 2005, 2007), my research primarily focuses on the way the making and change of ethnic and gender identity intersects during periods of ethno-national contention and conflict settlement. First, I ask if and how identity changes, second, I reveal the intersection of gender and ethnic identity change, and finally, I explore the connection between identity and social change in a comparative fashion.

The concept of identity has gained a certain prominence in social science research on race, gender, ethnicity, and class. In comparative politics, *identity* plays an important role in work on nationalism and ethnic conflict (Horowitz, 1985). In international relations, the idea of "state identity" is at the center of constructivist critiques of realism and the analysis of state sovereignty (Wendt, 2004). Further, identity is a focus of many studies of gender, sexuality, nationality, ethnicity, and culture in political theory (Anthias, 2006; Alsop, Fitzsimons, & Lennon, 2002; Todd, 2005). Feminist research on ethno-national conflict has highlighted issues arising from the gendered image of national identity, which predominantly focuses on women as mothers and men as warriors and protectors of women and children.[1] First, the positioning of women in the role of a mother and portraying them as "naturally peaceful" does not reflect the actual reality of ethno-national conflict; it ignores the fact that some women fight in ethno-national movements and support militarized violence (Ruddick, 1989, p. 176). Second, being represented as reproducers and as the embodiment of the ethno-national collective, women acquire political meaning as targets of violence (Jayawardena, 1986; Yuval-Davis, 1997). Finally, the way motherhood and peacefulness are rooted deeply in women's gender identity and turn women into natural peacemakers (Cohn & Jacobson, 2013, p. 111) obscures women's agency. The naturalization of women's peacefulness depoliticizes their activism in the public sphere and excludes them from peace talks and other political decision making (Waylen, 2000). In order to enhance the understanding of peace and conflict and contribute to the development of sustainable peace, I will critically explore these public perceptions of gender and ethnic identity. This monograph enhances understanding of peace and conflict by listening to and learning from women's perceptions, perspectives, and experiences of ethno-national mobilization and conflict settlement in Chiapas and in Northern Ireland.

Part I of this research sets out to provide a theoretical framework and a methodology for an analysis of identity change in peace and conflict situations that allows us to acknowledge and address the complexity of those processes. Chapter 1 introduces identity as key concept and ethnicity and gender as central boundaries, highlighting the significance of intersectional analysis of boundaries during ethno-national conflicts and peace processes. The chapter also addresses challenges in the application of the concept of intersectionality to policy analysis and research practice (McCall, 2005; Yuval-Davis, 2006). It does so by further developing Michelle Lamont's boundary approach (Lamont, 2012; Lamont & Molnar, 2002) and proposing a multilayered analysis of the ways in which different identity shifts are interrelated with objectified social changes. The second part of chapter 1 outlines the author's positioning toward and within the research, the research design, and methodology. It introduces an innovative active participatory research approach created for this project.

Intersectionality and Difference

The assumption that men and women are socially constructed by the operation of material and social structures grounds this analysis of changes in gender and ethnic identity in peace and conflict processes. My research builds on existing criticism of theories of international relations in the particular field of ethno-national conflict and its inscribed preferences for masculinity and for a particular form of sexual difference (Sluga, 2000, p. 17). In order to address these criticisms, we need to look at not only the ethnic or national, but also the gendered and class perspectives in the interpretation and analysis of ethno-national conflict and peace processes. Providing a framework for doing so, intersectional analysis of social divisions has come to occupy a central space in both academic research and in policy analysis. Intersectionality analysis provides the opportunity to shine a light on the different characters of social structures, such as gender, ethnicity, race, sexuality, age, generation, and the like, and the way these structures impact processes of identification. Applying an intersectional framework to the in-depth research of the way female activists interrelate gender and ethnic identity in peace and conflict situations contributes to the operationalization of the analysis of complex processes and structures.

Intersectionality is a term invented by feminist scholars to capture the complex interplay of social forces that affect the lives of women and men as members of particular races, classes, ethnicities, and nationalities, with different sexual orientations, and from different generations (Crenshaw, 1991; Hill Collins, 1990; Yuval-Davis, 2006), and which places some individuals in disadvantaged positions. The concept of intersectionality suggests that these above-mentioned processes of oppression are specific, but at the same time interrelated. Originally, the focus of intersectionality was the problematic dynamics evolving from the construction of difference and from the "solidarities of sameness" during processes of social mobilization against discrimination.

Within indigenous struggles, as in Chiapas, the so called white, Western feminist approach of equality to notions on indigeneity often leads to controversy, as equality within a Western context is often understood by indigenous women as *sameness*. Therefore, many indigenous women criticize feminism as a "white," "Western" concept, for assuming homogenized feminist or "gender interests" (Molyneux, 2001), and for not allowing us to look at distinctions within the category "women" (Leigh, 2009).

On the other hand, a strong focus on ethnicity and group rights ignores intragroup differences. In the context of gendered power structures, the omission of difference is problematic, as the discrimination that many women experience is shaped by other dimensions such as race, class, sexuality, age, and so on. Defining the relationship between gender and ethnicity or race as antagonistic often leads to the perception that a focus on gender equality is dividing, obscuring, and weakening the strength of an ethnonational movement (Leigh, 2009, p. 81; Yuval-Davis, 1997) The asymmetry between men and women in different social, political, economic, and cultural contexts impacts the way in which feminist approaches are developed in this context.

Feminist efforts to politicize experiences of women and antiracist efforts to politicize experiences of people belonging to particular ethnic groups often seem to occur on mutually exclusive terrains. Although racism and sexism intersect in the lives of people, they seldom do in feminist and antiracist practices or in policies for the transformation of ethno-national conflicts (McCall, 2005, p. 1773). Hence, if political practices only tackle one side of a social identity, for instance, either "woman" or "Catholic/indigenous," they transfer the identity of a Catholic or indigenous woman to a location that resists telling the full story of women's lived experiences within ethnic boundaries.

"Praxis has been a key site of intersectional critique and intervention" (Cho et al., 2013, p. 786). While the term has been used since the 1980s, some feminist activisms have long placed an intersectional approach at the core of their social mobilizations. For instance, during the 1960s and 1970s, Chicana feminist mobilizations focused on issues of race, nation, gender, sexuality, and class, providing the basis for a "both/and" rather than an "either/or" approach to social identities (Blackwell, 2011, p. 208).

The intersectionality approach has been developed within a wider feminist attempt to de-essentialize categories of analysis. Anti-essentialism in the late 1980s was driven by the concerns of women of color that women's experiences were not only overlooked by men, but also by the feminist mainstream that mainly focused on white women (Hunter, 1996).[2] Intersectionality urges us to take into consideration the complexities of social dynamics and inequality, to question the term women as a basis for unity, and to place greater emphasis on existing differences between women (Mohanty, 1992, p. 85).

Feminist scholars address the problem of intersectionality by drawing on the common analogue many feminists are using between the situation of women and the situation of ethnonational minorities. Following hooks (1981), the lack of acknowledging difference implies that all women are white and all blacks are men. Acknowledging difference was a central aspect of the black women's movement, which set out to deconstruct the categories of both women and "blacks" and to develop an analysis of the intersectionality of various social divisions, most often—but not exclusively—focusing on gender, race, and class.[3] This idea has found its way into the policy agenda of the United Nations, as is evident in the resolution on the human rights of women at the 58th session of the UN Commission on Human Rights, which recognized "the importance of examining the intersection of multiple forms of discrimination, including their root causes from a gender perspective" (Resolution E/CN.4/2002/L.59, as cited in Yuval-Davis, 2006, p. 194).

Any attempt to essentialize ethnicity, gender, age, sexuality, or working classness as specific forms of concrete oppression inevitably creates narratives and categories that reflect hegemonic discourses of identity politics; it further obscures experiences of the members at the margin of the specific group by constructing a homogenized "right way" of group belonging (Yuval-Davis, 2006, p. 195). The ignorance of complexity and of existing differences becomes problematic, when experiences of conflict by Catholic or indigenous people who are of a particular gender—mostly male—determine conflict resolution policies.

The question is: how do we think intersectionally and how do we do intersectionality? At the core of intersectionality analysis is the adoption of an intersectional way of thinking about how sameness and difference are constructed in relation to power. Second, we need to look at categories of identification as fluid and permanently changing, of creating and being created by existing power dynamics. (Cho et al., 2013, p. 795) Third, we have to explore how intersectionality works as a multilevel process (Marx Ferree, 2009) on cognitive processes and the development of feminist agency.

We need to pay attention to the homogenizing incentive in academic scholarship, and indeed in academic feminist research. Clarity is often achieved at the expense of visibility, agency, and identity of those represented. Focusing on the way different identity categories and social structures intersect enables us to bring together gender and ethnicity. It provides a framework to look at different identities and experiences, for example, at the particular situation of indigenous women in Chiapas and Catholic, working-class republican women in Northern Ireland.

Considering the possibility that different backgrounds, such as ethnicity, nationality, age, class, sexuality, and the like might shape the interests of women differently (Mihesuah, 2003, p. 5) is central to the formation of women's "strategic gender interests" (Molyneux, 1985, p. 43).

The concept of strategic gender interests acknowledges the impossibility to generalize about women. Being derived deductively from the analysis of women's subordination, it further focuses on alternative and more satisfying sets of arrangements to existing unequal power structures (Molyneux, 2001, p. 43). The notion of women's interests is based on the presumption that all women share a set of interests; some of those interests evolve from women's traditional gender roles, others challenge the existing gender hierarchy. The distinction here is between "practical" and "strategic" (Molyneux, 1985) or "feminine" and "feminist" (Alvarez, 1990) gender interest. I use this categorization to reveal a shift between the moment women from marginalized communities organize in defense of their community and the moment when they consciously and strategically campaign against unequal gender structures within and across the boundaries of their communities. This research looks at the evolving shared strategic gender interests in social mobilizations as evidence for the triggering of the gender boundary. Gender interests and the highlighting of the gender boundary does not evolve in a vacuum, but intersects with other boundary processes.

Recognizing the different boundaries that intersect within women's diverse politics of belonging (Yuval-Davis, 2011) opens a space for women's activism to evolve across ethnic and class boundaries. It requires the acceptance that women are rooted in their own identity but at the same time can shift in order to take part in an intercultural dialogue with women who share their gender interests, but have different identities. This transversal activism is determined by the way the ethno-national boundary is highlighted in the community (Yuval-Davis, 1997).

My research contributes to a better understanding of the complexities of identity categories and the way they are affected by mechanisms of mobilization in different sequences and dimensions of conflict and peace processes. Intersectionality is centrally linked to the analysis of power, yet discussing categories of identity versus structures of inequality is a significant challenge to intersectionality (Cho et al., 2013, p. 797). Instead of placing them in opposition, we need to analyze power structures and identity processes in connection.

In feminist studies, the salience of identity categories is often interpreted as a product of power relationships, which are embedded and reproduced through historical discourses (Butler, 1990). Defining women as the "other" reveals an important dichotomy that impacts upon the labelling of social practices as male and female (Epstein, 1988; Gerson & Peiss, 1985) and positions women in the private and men in the public realm. This brings to light a power distinction between men and women, which leads to the marginalization of the latter by the dominance of the male group in order to control or restrict women's access to resources and to positions of power. The possibility of shifting gender identity plays a significant role for understanding possible power shifts in pursuing a more equal society and a sustainable peace.

Feminist research has identified opportunities and difficulties in applying the concept of intersectionality to policy analysis and research practice (McCall, 2005; Yuval-Davis, 2006, 2011); for instance Choo and Ferree critically remarked that the concept is often used without explaining what it entails (2010, p. 130). Further, the aim for completeness at the expense of clarity of analysis reveals a challenge in applying an intersectional research approach (McCall, 2005, p. 1778).

The debate as to which categories to include in intersectional analysis[4] reveals a lack of conceptual coherence of intersectionality. Further, there is a need to include perspectives to problematize relationships of power and to take account of the way inequalities are multiple determined (Choo & Ferree, 2010, p. 131). My research further develops this analytical framework by exploring how social change, collective identity categories, and political values are created and the way in which they interrelate and affect each other in peace and conflict situations. One cannot assume the same effect or constellation at any moment of social mobilization and demobilization. The investigation of identity perceptions within the specific social, political, and economic processes at different time periods and at different levels of peace and conflict is essential.

Although ethnic and gender boundaries are not static, they are "anchor" points for the analysis of identity formation and change. The nature of the relationship between collective identity categories, the way in which these different categories are changing, and how changes in these categories (ethnicity/gender) are intersecting is central to this analysis.

The examination of the intersection of processes of identity formation and change will enhance the understanding of the way in which shifts on one level (ethnic) impact upon identity perceptions on another level (gender) and vice versa. The question is, why is it important to explore identity processes during conflict? As this research focuses on the process of the formation and change of collective identity categories, both the intersubjective and the objectified dimensions of identity processes are important. The concept of boundaries is suitable for this analysis, as it permits us first, to illustrate the intersection of different identity categories (ethnic and gender), and second, to reveal how changes at the intersubjective level (symbolic boundary) are translated into objectified differences (social boundary).

DEFINING IDENTITY—GENDERED AND ETHICIZED ASPECTS

Why Identity?

Identity and gender are often neglected aspects in political scientists' research on peace and conflict, which is mostly grounded on rational choice and neorealism theories looking at interest as the central motivation for action. However, exploring individual behavior, the framework for social action and social change during peace and conflict, requires both the notion of identity and of interest.

Rational-choice approaches put the "security dilemma" at the heart of conflict (Jervis, 1978; Posen, 1993) and advocate a strong central state as the main solution to the increasing feeling of insecurity in situations of anarchy created during armed conflict. However, this does not explain the outbreak of ethnonational conflict in societies like Chiapas and Northern Ireland, where central authority is relatively strong (Crawford, 1998). The neorealist security dilemma approach fails to explain how states might even exacerbate ethnic conflict through discriminatory laws, institutions, and practices (Rose, 2000). Being uncritical of the gendered problems of the traditional state, the rational choice and neorealist research approaches further reemphasize unequal gender structures (Enloe, 2002).

Purely interest-based approaches do not explain why preconditions for intense conflict, such as ethnic group inequalities, produce high conflict in some places, but very little in others (Miller, 1992). Rational-choice-based analysis of conflict does not offer adequate answers to questions of a normative nature and fails to provide a useful tool to analyze structures and meanings of inequalities, which are deeply entrenched in the society and play a significant role in violent conflicts (Hansen, 2001, p. 57).

The intersection of ethnicity and gender needs to be at the very heart of what constitutes and creates security and insecurity for both women and men during ethno-national conflict. However, scholarly literature to date has not sufficiently explored these linkages. Therefore, the application of realism to explain individual behavior, particularly in relation to gender or ethnic inequality within the context of peace and conflict situations, will result in the reinforcement and legitimization of these same unequal structures; as such an analysis fails to go beyond the surface.

However, rather than developing a separate research agenda or dismiss the existing paradigms in the studies of peace and conflict, we need to show courage and develop new research that challenges traditional structures and parameters of academic scholarship in the area. It is important to ask *how* and *why* does the study of intersecting identity categories matter in situations of peace and conflict.

Rather than placing identity in opposition to interest, we can interrelate the two approaches by looking at interest as culturally and socially composed in a particular time and space (Somers, 1994, p. 624).[5] Social interactions are core elements of social life, which are institutionally structured and mediated through both individual identity perceptions and interests (McAdam, Tilly & Tarrow, 2001). Interests are always framed from an identity perspective. Therefore, an analysis of the deeply entrenched and interrelated gender and ethnic aspects of ethno-national conflict is only possible when looking into the intersection of different interests and identity categories at different moments of peace and conflict situations.

The Concept of Identity

The concept of identity has gained a certain prominence in social science research on race, gender, ethnicity, or class. In comparative politics, "identity" plays an important role in work on nationalism and ethnic conflict (Horowitz, 1985). In international relations, the idea of "state identity" is at the center of constructivist critiques of realism and the analysis of state sovereignty (Wendt, 2004). Further, identity is a focus of many studies of gender, sexuality, nationality, ethnicity, and culture in political theory (Alsop et al., 2002; Anthias, 2006; Todd, 2005). In academic literature, it is often assumed that there is a common understanding of the term, which is not the case. The following part will outline the *meaning* of identity in this research project.

Identity has its roots in the Latin word "idem" (the same) and has found its way into the English language in the sixteenth century. It was not until the 1950s that the term identity gained some prominence within social sciences. The International Encyclopaedia of the Social Sciences from 1968 includes a definition of "identity psychosocial"; another entry refers to "identification, political." The Oxford English Dictionary (OED) defines the term within a philosophical context as

> the sameness of a person or a thing at all times or in all circumstances, the condition or the fact that a person or thing is itself and not something else; individuality, personality. *Personal Identity (in Psychology)*, the condition or fact of remaining the same person throughout the various phases of existence; continuity of the personality.

The meaning of identity, as it is currently applied, is not well captured by these dictionary definitions. Identity has to be seen as a process located *in the core of the individual* and yet also *in the core of his/her communal culture* (Erikson, 1968, p. 22; Fearon, 1999, p. 4). Identity is always personally assumed and socially ascribed; therefore identity is always both individual and social (Jenkins, 2008). However, analyzing the intersection of ethnic and gender identity requires us to interrelate individual and social identity, to look at self-reported identification of individuals, and at the way individuals intersect the different identity categories available to them.

How can we interrelate the individual and social aspect of identity? We can do so by understanding collective identity categories as embedded in the individual "habitus" (Bourdieu, 1984). As such, collective identity categories find expression not only in collective action, but also in the "subtler signs of individual distinction" (Todd, 2005, p. 434). On the one hand, identity is relatively stable; it is internalized in earliest childhood and contains a "set of cumulative, superimposed meanings, dispositions, and modes of perception embodied in the individual" (Todd, 2005, p. 434).On the other hand, identity can and does change; while identity categories can be salient, they are at the same time permeable (Wimmer, 2008, p. 989). Therefore we need to take account of the fact that the extent of group solidarity is variable (Ashmore, Deaux & McLaughlin-Volpe, 2004, p. 94).

The content and meaning of identity is central to understanding *how* individuals interrelate ethnic, gender, and class categories in more or less united, or more or less differentiated, ways in terms of key values, concepts of rationality, standards of valuation, and so on. Identity includes self-attributed characteristics, political ideology, and developmental narratives. The content of identity refers to the extent to which traits and dispositions that are associated with a social category are endorsed as self-descriptive by a member of that category (Ashmore et al., 2004, p. 14).

The social construction of identity is rooted in social practice, which provides time and space to experience and internalize distinctions and boundaries. Social interactions and relations are the core aspects of social life. They are institutionally and environmentally structured and mediated through individual perceptions, self-categorizations, interests, and strategic calculations (McAdam et al., 2001, p. 57–8).

In processes of social practice, collective identity categories such as gender and ethnicity are interrelated in interpretation, meanings, and values. The focus has changed through recent developments of the constructivist research agenda from the "categories of identification" to a discussion of the meanings and contents of identity categories (Cornell, 1996; Jenkins, 2008; Todd, 2005). Personal narratives allow us to reveal the mentally represented story that an individual person has developed regarding the "self" and the social category in question.

In this research, I focus on the *collective identity story* (or, story of me as a member of my group), not on the *group story* (or, story of my group). While the *group story* narrates the ideology of a movement, the *collective identity story* provides a framework for a more objective analysis of the implications of existing power structures on identity formation. Looking at thoughts and feelings about the past, present, and future of "group membership" from an individual perspective allows us to understand the importance of a particular identity for the person telling the story (Ashmore et al., 2004). The collective identity narratives reveal changes in the degree of the "'connectedness" (Brubaker & Cooper, 2004, p. 19) and in the meaning female activists attribute to group membership at different moments of intersecting social mobilization processes.

While a comprehensive body of research already exists on group narratives, far less academic work has been dedicated so far to analyzing ways in which collective identity stories can be understood. Questions arising in this context are: How do certain identities become important for individuals? How are they triggered? How and when do identities lose their significance?

Individuals vary in the way they experience the sense of belonging within a particular identity category in different situations and at different moments in time. In order to make sense of the differing contents and processes of collective identification, I will look at collective identity in historical time. This enables me to trace patterns of change and to explore how the individual frames identity contents in each phase of the conflict and conflict settlement process. Retracing patterns of change reveals the interrelation between intentionality, institutions, and interactions. Such an approach is essential for analyzing how actors frame their claim, their opponents, and their identity. (McAdam et al., 2001, p. 126)

Within mobilization processes, an identity category becomes important and political when people make public claims on the basis of this identity (McAdam et al., 2001, p. 134). In ethno-national mobilization processes the ethnic identity category becomes highlighted as the most important category within the collective identity story. Triggering the ethnic category unites people in their right to voice collective demands. However, the salience of the identity category or the level of group belonging occurring within these processes varies as there is no uniform sense of group belonging. Acknowledging the existence of different social divisions (ethnicity, class, or gender) allows us to explore *how* concrete experiences of oppression are constructed in interaction with other social divisions (Yuval-Davis, 1997, p. 195). Following Brubaker (Brubaker & Cooper, 2004, Brubaker, Feischmidt, Fox & Grancea, 2006), we need to problematize the relationship between a category and a group in order to explore the various meanings of this group solidarity. In order to explore the meaning of identity, more qualitative forms of inquiry are required in this research, namely semi-structured in-depth interviews to elicit detailed individual and historical narratives of time and place.

De-Essentializing Identity

Definitions of ethnic identity are contested in the social sciences.[6] Many different approaches, frameworks, and definitions of the term have led to questioning the use of the term identity (Brubaker & Cooper, 2004). Feminist scholarship[7] has criticized how primordialist notions of "the nation" present the national community in the mobilization of myths of common ancestry as a natural extension of family and kinship relations; this reinforces the sexual division of labor in the family as a natural phenomenon. The focus on women's role as mothers, biological reproducers of the nation, and those responsible for its cultural reproduction nourishes the perception of "womanhood" as a locus of national honor in ethno-national mobilizations (Yuval-Davis, 1997, p. 45), which in many cases prepared the ground for using rape as a weapon of war.

In this context, the primordialist notion of identity as a "stable marker of sameness or difference" (Anthias, 2006, p. 20) has been particularly criticized. Primordialist self-definitions of ethnic communities represent the in-group perspective of the interaction between religious elements, norms and traditions, bloodline, language, and ethnicity. Certain images, cults, customs, events, values, and so on form a repository of the ethnic culture, which is drawn upon selectively by different generations of the community (Smith, 1986, p. 38) and play a significant role in mobilization processes. Common ancestry, language, and religion are important aspects in analyzing felt kinship ties and national bounds; these aspects are the material that glues people together and allows for the genesis of a group feeling (Connor, 1994, p. 75, 145). However, the question of defining elements of identity is far from clear.

Notions of equality, justice, and self-determination play a significant role in identifications of indigenous women in Chiapas and republican Irish Catholic women in Northern Ireland. While these notions shape the norms, traditions, and the meaning of the community in both cases, they differ in their content and context. Inherent tensions between demands for gender justice and group rights of a particular cultural community become visible in the attempt of female indigenous activists in Chiapas to change norms and traditions and in different prioritizations of women's and community concerns in Northern Ireland. This shows limitations in analyzing mobilization processes based on an essentialist notion of ethnicity.

The feminist critique on the primordialist notion of ethnic identity shows the need for an intersectional analysis of ethnic and gender identity in social mobilization and conflict settlement. Looking at the intersection of ethicized and gendered processes in peace and conflict situations reveals possibilities for changes in both ethnic and gender identity, which contests the primordial assumption of identity as stabile and fixed. The primordialist approach explains the continuous existence and permanency of some elements of the "identity package" (Todd, 2005). However, it fails to account for the coexistence and interrelated changes of different identity categories within a wider socioeconomic and political context. Therefore, the analysis of the interconnection of shifts in socially constructed identity categories (gender and ethnicity) requires going beyond the primordialist answer.

I understand identity as socially constructed rather than as a constant element of reality,[8] but will move beyond the "soft constructivist" approach, which fails to provide conceptual coherence, constants, and continuity. Although we need to problematize the epistemological and ontological dimension of the concept of identity, we can still use identity as a socially meaningful concept. Brubaker et al. (2006) argue that, unless triggered through particular events or activities, ethnic boundaries remain silent. In their study of the Romanian town Cluj, they show the need to examine more closely how ethnic distinctions are triggered in certain events, in particular, the role that ethno-political entrepreneurs play in "group-making" or "group-mobilizing" processes (Brubaker et al., 2006). Brubaker's approach is useful for understanding the complexity of ethnicization processes. However, we need to go beyond this approach to explore the intersection of different identity categories in peace and conflict by looking at identification as a process as narrated by individuals with an aim of coherence and consistency.

The analysis of the social construction of gender provides a framework to understand how gender is formed and given meaning by the social structure of the society. Individuals are defined as men or women according to the particular positions that they are allocated in the social order (Alsop et al., 2002).

The intersection of different identities such as gender, ethnicity, class, sexuality, and age facilitates understanding the meaning of those differences in processes of social change. However, the analysis of men and women's different experiences and perceptions of conflict and peace requires asking where and how they are positioned differently in their society and for the way in which different power hierarchies are structured.

Constructivists agree that "masculinity" and "femininity" are socially constructed, but gender meanings are not only located in the relational structures of people's lives. Gender further functions as a "set of ways of thinking, images, categories and beliefs which inform how we experience understand and represent ourselves as men and women (and) a familiar set of metaphors, dichotomies and values which structure ways of thinking about other aspects of the world, including war and security" (Cohn & Ruddick, 2004, p. 5).

The sexualized and genderized symbols of national identity are based on the differing roles given to men, active "constructors and promoters of the state" and women, passive "guardians of traditional values" (Cusack, 2000, p. 546). Gender in this context not only intersects with other identity categories, such as ethnicity, it is also a primary way of signifying power structures in society (Cohn, 2013, p. 15, Scott, 1986).

Postcolonial feminist research reveals how in postcolonial societies ethnic and racial power hierarchies are legitimized through the feminization of the subordinated "other" (McClintock, 1993). Looking at the mestizo myth in the development of Mexican nationalism, Natividad Gutiérrez Chong (2007) highlights the uses of sexuality and gender as mechanisms for excluding certain ethnicities and creating racisms, which control collective identity.

The notion of boundaries provides a framework to explore the intersection of different identity categories and the dynamic between social change and shifts at the intersubjective, symbolic level.

Boundaries and Categories of Identification

In recent years, scholarly literature on social or collective identity has been concentrated on the formation of the opposition of "us and them" as the main focus for understanding the world. Looking at processes of identity formation and change through the lens of boundary crossing or shifting has become a significant tool for identity analysis. Within this context, an important theoretical perspective focuses on power relations as a key factor in the development of boundaries and identifies changing power relations as a central incentive for shifts in identity categories.[9] Some episodes of contentious politics (Chiapas, Northern Ireland) trigger the ethnic boundary; the ethnicization process leads to shifts in perceptions at the subjective, symbolic level, which becomes translated into objectified changes in social positioning.

In my analysis of collective identity stories, I will show how the politicization and contestation of institutionalized and intersecting unequal power relations (class/gender/ethnicity) impact on symbolic resources; and vice versa, I will reveal how shifts of symbolic boundaries lead to changes of social boundaries. Processes of ethno-national mobilization against state-perpetrated injustice politicize primary inequality along cultural lines. However, as inequality becomes a central element of the ethnicization process, issues of gender justice often enter the protest agenda of ethno-national movements. Hence, these social mobilization processes lead to the salience and change of both ethnic and gender boundaries.

Boundaries are products of the separation of the world into "us" and "others." The analysis of boundaries and mechanisms of boundary change provides a possibility to explore the relationality of different identity categories and to reveal ways in which changes in ethnic and gender identity categories intersect (Lamont & Molnar, 2002; Pachucki, Pendergrass & Lamont, 2007). Looking at identity categories as subsets of a wider boundary approach enables us to better understand symbolic processes of identity formation and change, particularly the way in which they are connected to social change and to shifts in social positioning (Lamont & Molnar, 2002, p. 172).

Since the 1960s, scholars have contributed to the understanding of convergence of symbolic structures and differing forms of power and inequality (Bourdieu, 1977; Lamont, 2000). Bourdieu's "logic of distinction" reveals internalized power hierarchies and provides a principle for the organization of all social life, which links power, social positioning, and symbolic processes (Bourdieu, 1984). Different to Bourdieu, I am more interested in processes of social transformation than in social reproduction. Bourdieu's habitus allows us to identify conditions for change in identity categories. However, it fails to provide a framework to explain the way in which collective identity is formed and changed, the direction of change, and why change takes place in one way rather than in another (Todd, 2005, p. 433). The differentiation between symbolic and social boundaries (Lamont & Molnar, 2002) provides an opportunity to make the different dimensions of the complex process of identity formation and change visible.

Symbolic boundary processes highlight the intersubjective level of identity formation and change, which I call "perception," the way female activists perceive themselves as woman, as member of their ethno-national group, of their class, and so on. Symbolic boundaries have to be widely agreed upon in order to determine social interaction.

Social boundaries are objectified forms of social differences and institutionalized patterns of gender, class, ethnic, or racial segregation, manifested in unequal access to, and unequal distribution of resources (material and nonmaterial), and social opportunities (Lamont & Molnar, 2002, pp. 168–69). Symbolic boundaries shape the way in which certain practices, roles, and power dynamics feel not only acceptable, but also normal. Social boundaries are visible in the social "positioning" of individuals in society; they translate power inequalities into real life conditions.

The translation of symbolic boundaries into social boundaries is visible, for example, in situations where individuals face stigmatization and punishment for not performing according to community norm and tradition. Gender boundaries at the symbolic level provide meaning to power hierarchies, embodied in gendered institutions that structure society. Institutions such as state militaries, governments, or churches, constitute the social practices, which in interaction with symbolic gender boundaries produce and reproduce hierarchical gendered power relations (Cohn, 2013, p. 15). However, as gender identity is fluid and changing, institutions like the military, must constantly reproduce ideas about appropriate masculinities and femininities (Enloe, 2000). This shows that social structures and symbolic processes are interrelated.

On the one hand, symbolic boundaries can serve to enforce, maintain, and normalize social boundaries (Bourdieu, 1984), but on the other hand, they can also contest or reframe the meaning of social boundaries (Lamont & Molnar, 2002, p. 186); for instance, when the change of symbolic gender boundaries leads to greater gender equality. The way in which symbolic boundaries are linked to social boundaries varies depending on the cultural, political, and social structure they are embedded in (Lamont & Molnar, 2002, p. 169).

Collective identity narratives bring to light how perceptions or symbolic resources are impacting on social positioning, and by doing so provide important insights into boundary work at the micro level of society. Processes of formation and change of identity categories form a subset of boundary work in episodes of social mobilization and of demobilization or conflict settlement.

The way people identify as members of one group in distinction to those of another, or the making of boundaries, plays a central role in social mobilizations. Exploring mechanisms of social mobilization allows to examine more in-depth the fluid, strategic, and interactive operation of social actors, collective identity categories, and forms of collective action. During episodes of contention, boundaries of division between two or more groups become highlighted, a process that allows for the formation of new alliances. (McAdam et al., 2001)

Avoiding "groupist" language, I critically interrogate the development of "group solidarity" and that way distinguish "categories of analysis" from "categories of practice" (Brubaker & Cooper, 2004, p. 7). Doing so, I explore how people begin to feel part of a collective, what meaning they attribute to this collective, and how this meaning changes.

The formation of alliances in social mobilization processes impacts on both symbolic and social boundary processes; it opens independent spaces in which boundaries can converge and leads to shifts in individual perceptions and in social positioning. Alliance formation, or "brokerage," is an important mechanism for social mobilization, as it allows for coordinated action. Within ethnonational mobilizations, ethnic entrepreneurs use brokerage by framing actions as ethnic; they draw on the distinction between us and them. Mechanisms like brokerage impact on the activation, crossing, or dissolution of social boundaries, which in turn leads to a shift of symbolic boundaries. (McAdam et al., 2001, p. 85ff; Tilly, 1998)

Exploring mechanisms of mobilizations is useful to identify conditions for the different directions boundary change can take, and to compare different peace and conflict processes; such an analysis allows me to reveal ways in which social boundaries become activated. In order to reveal how social mobilization produces a feeling of "sameness" and leads to the crystallization and intersection of boundaries, I map the directions, sequences, and trajectories of identity shifts.

The different meanings of identity categories become visible in individual perceptions. Shifts in the meaning of identity categories can, on the one hand, be a key variable in the explanation of change in social behavior. On the other hand, change in identity categories is itself provoked by, and responsive to, changes in institutional structure and social practice. The recognition of the complex and varying meanings of identity categories enables us to see interactions between change, generated within one category of identification, and its knock-on effects on another within a broader context.

Building on scholarly work on directions of identity change (Todd, 2005, 2010), my research looks at the possible outcomes of boundary change. Todd illustrates which conditions are necessary for the convergence and change of different boundaries; her typology allows the analysis of macro, meso, and micro level boundary shifts. For instance, it enables us to reveal that although changes in gender identity during conflict might be invisible at the macro level of demobilization processes, they are still determining the individual's perceptions at the micro level of society. Todd's model provides a possibility for tracing trajectories of change in which initial choices can develop into others.

Bringing together the directions of change in the different identity categories allows me to explore in detail how individuals draw boundaries and interrelate gender and ethnicity. Looking at boundary change (Lamont & Molnar, 2002; Lamont, 2012) from an intersectionality perspective (Crenshaw, 1991; Hill Collins, 1990; Yuval-Davis, 2006) reveals how changes in different identity categories are interconnected.

In this comparative analysis of boundary processes, I demonstrate how the way in which symbolic processes are translated into objectified social changes varies depending on the cultural, social, and political structure they are embedded in. I do so by first exploring female activists' positioning toward the macro (state), the meso (community), and at the micro level (family and intimate partnerships) of society during different episodes of peace and conflict. Second, I examine how within social mobilization and demobilization processes independent spaces open, which change ethnic and gender boundaries. The dimensions of this analysis are determined by "perceptions," which reveal processes at the intersubjective level of the symbolic boundaries, and "positioning," which highlights the objectified forms of social differences (the positioning of women within the existing social structures), within those processes.

Conclusion

My research highlights the need to address complexity of experiences and perceptions of peace and conflict. It asks questions about gendered silences during peace and conflict; more concrete, it asks if gender and ethnic identity have changed, if so, how are changes in these identity categories related, and finally what can we learn from the differences between the two case studies of Chiapas and Northern Ireland. The concept of intersectionality provides a research approach that allows addressing complexity and the feminist critique of essentialist notions of ethnicity and gender. Following the intersectionality approach, gendered and ethnicized identity change has to be analyzed as distinctive, but at the same time as processes that are intersecting. I explore this by examining how collective identity narratives interrelate gender and ethnic identity categories. The concept of "boundaries" allows me to make visible the dynamic between symbolic and social boundaries, which enables me to interrelate social change to the shift in collective identity. Exploring mechanisms of mobilization and directions of identity change brings to light the process and outcome of identity change during ethno-national conflict and conflict settlement processes.

The active participation of women in ethnic or class mobilization can be identified as an incentive for changes in gender identity and in gendered power structures. To understand these changes and their implications for conflict analysis and peace building, I explore how dialogues across different layers of difference have evolved. Within this context, I analyze the positioning of activists toward different levels of society, the sphere of the state, the community, and the private realm. This multilayered and multilevel approach reveals interesting findings of peace and conflict processes and brings to light not only existing gaps in peace-building processes, but also shows the implications these gaps have at different levels of societies in the aftermath of armed conflict.

Chapter 2 introduces the methodological framework for the analysis of female activists' collective identity narratives of their different involvements in social movements during conflict and conflict settlement processes in the two regions.

2

Addressing Complexity and Difference in Research Methodology

A Feminist Participatory Research Approach

In my inductive, comparative study, I address the following set of questions:

a. Has identity change within gender and ethnic categories actually taken place within the ethno-national mobilization and demobilization processes in Chiapas and Northern Ireland?
b. If so, how do these processes of change interrelate? and finally,
c. What are the differences between the two case studies?

Peter A. Hall and Michele Lamont (2013) have reminded us recently of the old adage that the most innovative insights are discovered at the boundaries of disciplines. By incorporating richer conceptions of social relations into analyses of comparative conflict and peace processes through more intensive dialogue with sociology, my research follows the pathways of political scientists studying social movements or ethnic politics (Horowitz, 1985; McAdam, Tilly, & Tarrow, 2001; Todd, 2010) who work on these boundaries.

The analysis of the intersectionality of different boundaries during peace and conflict requires a methodological framework that allows for the explanation of processes and patterns of change and possible differences occurring between the case studies. Further, taking into account that different backgrounds might shape interests of women differently, the complexity of the context of a woman's life and its interaction with the dominant culture should be omnipresent in academic analysis (Leigh, 2009, p. 78). In order to address the complexity of intersecting identity categories in episodes of peace and conflict, I move "beyond descriptive statistical measures, towards an in-depth understanding of historical processes and individual motivation" (della Porta, 2008, p. 202). A qualitative research design that centers on field studies provides a suitable framework for tracing the process of identity formation and change in peace and conflict situations in an in-depth, multi-faceted analysis.

In my research, I am using a two-case comparative-historical study, examining the intersection of formation and change in gender and ethnic identity during different episodes of mobilization and demobilization processes in Chiapas and in Northern Ireland. I have chosen these cases for a variety of reasons. First, they allow me to achieve a maximum variance along relevant dimensions (gender and ethnic identity) and different ways of relating these dimensions. Further, my research question evolved during my work as practitioner in Chiapas and was reenergized in discussions with practitioners from Northern Ireland. While the latter group shared some of the experiences of the activists from Chiapas, they were positioned in very different spaces and had consequently different experiences. My objective is to analyze how different contexts affect similar processes in Chiapas and Northern Ireland in order to develop a framework for comparative research and policymaking.

In this section, I will begin with a reflection on my own positioning toward and within my work. This part will be followed by looking at the reason for, and the way of, using the comparison of two cases of conflict and post-conflict processes. Following from here, I introduce my qualitative, active-participative research strategy and interpretative approach, which allows to actively listening to the voices or the "objects" of my research and to understanding their experiences. I conclude this part by introducing the voices that have not only informed, but are at the heart of this research project.

My Standpoint within my Research

Following the feminist standpoint theory,[1] I recognize the existence of many differences between women relating to, for instance, their class, ethnicity, age, sexual orientation, disability, and so on, and the impossibility to claim one single or universal "woman's experience." Within this context, my own positioning toward and within my research is of importance, as it frames the way I am relating to and interpreting the voices and experiences of the people who inform this research project.

I am identifying myself as a female white Western academic with an activist background in and with a strong value for social justice and human rights, in particular women's rights. Based on my awareness of my own background, I acknowledge my otherness regards my ethno-national identity, my class, my age, my sexual orientation, my experiences, and so on in comparison to the female activists from Chiapas and from Northern Ireland, which form part of this research. Many of the female activists who took part in this research I met while working on peace, human rights, and social justice projects in Chiapas and in Northern Ireland.

My research is motivated by preliminary work with indigenous and mestiza[2] women in Chiapas, by vivid discussions about their perceptions of "being indigenous," of "being a woman," of their experiences of peace and conflict in the region, and about ways to include female voices in ethno-national mobilization. My work in a project for the peaceful transformation of conflict in Chiapas (from July until December 2002 and from October 2004 until June 2005) enabled me to actively participate in these discussions. This work was based on creating spaces for a dialogue between the government in Chiapas and civil society groups, particularly those in resistance against the state. My interest in working about, with, and for women in Northern Ireland developed as part of my work on human rights, peace, and social justice issues on the Island of Ireland (2005–ongoing). These experiences as practitioner and researcher in Chiapas and in Northern Ireland provided the opportunity to create a network of civil society activists, policy makers and other key actors in the two conflict regions. These contacts guaranteed my access to the field, an essential part of this research. Furthermore, my activism and research work in various peace, social justice, and human rights projects draw my attention to my own positioning as a white, Western woman and to the ethno-national and class boundaries between me and the men and women I was working with. The awareness I developed on my own positioning while working as a practitioner in the field has informed the way I am relating to the female activists who participated in this project and my analysis and interpretation of their narratives.

I am aware that the ways in which I physically and psychologically relate to the world, as someone with a strong commitment to social justice and human rights, particularly women's rights, and as a woman who has been working as volunteer and in paid positions on social justice and human rights issues, as a female academic from a white, Western background affects what and how I know. More concrete, my social location, defined through my ascribed social identity contents (female, white, heterosexual) and my social roles (human and women's rights activist, feminist, academic) affects what and how I know. This awareness informs not only the topic of my study, but also my research methodology, the way I am relating to the female activists, and my choice for a co-labor research approach (Leyva Solano, 2010, Leyva Solano & Speed, 2008), which centers on working about, with, and for the participants of this research project, with whom I share a feminist political compromise.

I have learned in working with female activists in Chiapas and in Northern Ireland that working as academic-activist includes the active participation of research participants in the research process, for instance, in the search for solutions to challenges in the research process (language barrier, ethno-national boundaries, and etc.). This cooperation breaks down existing power hierarchies, opens new doors in the research process, and leads to improving research results (Hale, 2006; Leyva Solano & Speed, 2008; Speed, 2006). An emphasis on listening to and learning from the experiences, perceptions, and perspectives of the female activists helped me to maintain the awareness of my own positioning. It further deepened my understanding of the way in which dynamics and mechanisms intersect in different sequences of the conflict and peace processes and what meaning women attribute to them.

Comparing Chiapas and Northern Ireland

How can comparing episodes of contention and peace in Chiapas and Northern Ireland reveal significant endogenous and exogenous mechanisms that impact on intersectional processes of identity formation and change in contentious politics? While my access to the field has been an essential part for this research, I will now outline my case study framework.

Analyzing the intersection of identity change during mobilization and demobilization processes with a variation of outcomes requires a case selection, which allows for capturing the full complexity of and the full range of variation within boundary processes. Following McAdam et al. (2001), my research design looks at different episodes of contentious politics and conflict settlement processes in order to identify in what way similar mechanisms might drive boundary changes in different directions. More precisely, I am looking at ways in which female activists engage in boundary work and ask how boundaries form, converge, and change during episodes of peace and conflict. While these activists come from different geographical and cultural contexts (Chiapas and Northern Ireland), they share similar experiences of being actively involved in contentious politics and peace processes. Comparing Chiapas and Northern Ireland is appropriate as it allows for the selection of cases with various pathways, which follow similar mechanisms, but lead to different outcomes. The objective is to analyze how different contexts affect mechanisms of social mobilization during conflict and conflict settlement processes.

Many contextual differences are evident in Chiapas and Northern Ireland. The Northern Ireland conflict has had a longer duration of violent confrontation and suffered a greater number of casualties, over 3,500 deaths since the start of the Troubles in 1969 (Melaugh, 2013). In comparison, the Chiapas conflict began on January 1, 1994, with 12 days of intensive fighting between government forces and the armed group, Zapatista Army of National Liberation (EZLN). This episode of violent contention has led to between 145 (official government statistic) and 1,000 deaths[3] (according to the Zapatistas). It was followed by a "low-intensity war" after the failed settlement between Zapatistas and the government post-1997, with the Acteal massacre[4] of 45 civilians (December 22, 1997) as its climax. Although paramilitary organizations developed in Chiapas and Northern Ireland, we can distinguish the two cases by the size, tactic, and aims of the organizations. In both cases, armed resistance against state-perpetrated injustice (the EZLN in Chiapas and republican mobilizations post-1969 in Northern Ireland) arose out of previous episodes of contention with a social justice focus (land rights in Chiapas and civil rights in Northern Ireland), and parallel to women's rights activisms. However, the ways in which these mobilization processes intersect differs. In terms of conflict settlement, Northern Ireland has been successful in implementing a negotiated agreement, while the settlement in Chiapas was only partially implemented and left central conflicting issues unsolved. Although mediation and negotiation processes took place in both cases, the terms of the agreements differ: while the recognition of indigenous autonomy requiring the revision of neoliberal socioeconomic processes are at the center of the peace negotiations in Chiapas, Northern Ireland aimed for the establishment of a power-sharing government. Furthermore, the different geographical location of the two cases leads to a distinct engagement and impact of the regional and international sphere. However, both cases share a history of colonization and the development of a settler society, although Chiapas and Northern Ireland vary significantly with regards to ethno-national cleavages, levels of marginalization, or culture.

I am interested in tracing how women have mobilized in relation to both their ethnic and their gender category and how those two categories intersect and change. In Chiapas and Northern Ireland, different feminist approaches have evolved despite, and as alternative to, ethno-national cleavages and have led to changes in both the ethnic and the gender identity category. However, the way changes in symbolic resources interrelate with objectified social practices varies in the two cases. Hence, despite different patterns of postcolonial socioeconomic, political, and cultural development, both cases share similar social mobilization mechanisms in which ethnic claims evolve out of protests for social justice. Therefore, Chiapas and Northern Ireland provide a good basis for comparison.

My analysis is primarily concerned with understanding, meaning, and providing detailed description in order to lend more authority to the voice of the research participants (Thomas, 1993, p. 46), which is not possible in a multicase study. On the other side, exploring only one context rather than comparing two cases overemphasizes its uniqueness and limits the lessons to be learned from women's mobilizations within ethno-national conflicts. Looking at two, rather than one or a larger number of cases allows to map shifting patterns of participation in a micro-level analysis; this will further the understanding of shifting structures and identity categories during episodes of contention (McAdam et al., 2001, p. 317).

The study of two cases allows me to identify similar patterns in boundary processes during the mobilization of women at different levels of contentious politics and peace processes. It provides a framework to shine light on the way female activists shift toward promoting strategic gender interests and the meaning of this for other, namely, ethno-national mobilization processes. My research does not attempt to provide a representative sample for contemporary peace and conflict processes, but aims to expand feminist and ethno-national theories to reach an "analytical," rather than a "statistical generalization" (Yin, 1984, p. 21). Even though Chiapas and Northern Ireland are not representative cases, we can draw interesting lessons learned from the way women engage in similar mechanisms, but in different contexts.

Listening to Women's Voices: A Qualitative Research Strategy and Interpretative Approach

I began my research pathway by asking questions about the gendered silences in international relation (IR) studies of ethno-national conflict and settlement processes. What is traditionally lacking in elite-driven and state-centered IR research is an engagement with insights of individuals positioned at the margins of societies in situations of armed conflict or its aftermath. My research methodology places the voices of research subjects at the center. It draws on ideas and tools from feminist ethnography that determines the nature of the research process and requires the researcher's commitment to ensure that her work is informed by feminist ethics of care. My aim is to obtain knowledge in ways that can be used by research participants to change the exploitative conditions of their society (Skeggs, 1994). That way, embarking on field research involves a redefinition of the subject matter, of the relationship between researcher and those being researched, the meaning of the data, and the presentation of the research findings (Jacobi, 2006, p. 156).

Situated within the wider feminist decolonization framework,[5] my research is based on working *with* people and on the need for, not only understanding and empathizing with the "subjects" of our study, but also for sharing with the "objects" of the research a political compromise (Leyva Solano & Speed, 2008). That way we are able to create what Xochitl Leyva Solano (2010) calls an "other kind of knowledge" (*el conocimiento otro*).

Guided by the idea of co-labor (Leyva Solano & Speed, 2008), my research design evolves out of my own feminist and activist background and is not only based on the academic aim to reveal changing self-perceptions and positioning of women in peace and conflict processes through the meanings they attribute to those processes, but is also centered on a feminist compromise to actively engage in providing a space for women in peace and conflict processes to making their voices heard.

My field research is based on a bottom-up approach and sets out to listen and learn from the research participants. It aims at working *with* women, in order to give the objects of my study ownership on the research project. In order to find solutions to the questions raised within this research project, it is essential to actively listen to the voices of women and to engage them in an active-participative way into the research process. Further, my objective is to work *for* the benefit of the female research participants and their communities. As part of this objective, I created new, and supported existing, spaces for female activists to exchange experiences and to develop an intercultural dialogue. More concretely, as part of my field research, I collaborated with practitioners and activists in the organization of workshops and facilitated women's participation in consultations. My position in this process was: academic researcher, activist, moderator, and facilitator of this dialogue. As a result of this active-participative research approach, I have been able to understand and to value the social and political agency in the way women make and change boundaries in conflict and post (peace) agreement[6] situations.

Designing a research project that is based on the social compromise to not only work toward an understanding of the research participants, but also toward the improvement of their situation requires the researcher to give up his/her presumed neutrality. However, while I was clear in my commitment for women's rights and gender justice, I felt and expressed compassion, but abstained from taking a position within the ethnic struggle for any armed party.

I conducted seventeen in-depth, semi-structured interviews with female activists in Northern Ireland and sixteen such interviews in Chiapas. My field research in Chiapas further included two focus groups, one consisting of fifteen, the other of five participants. I obtained a maximum variety through open-ended questions on the ways in which women became involved in social movements and on the meaning of this involvement for them. Their collective identity narratives (Ashmore, Deaux, & McLaughlin-Volpe, 2004) reveal the way in which different identity categories become relevant for female activists and how they interrelate one category with other categories, with values and so on. The length of the interviews and focus groups, all of which I conducted, transcribed, and translated, varies from one hour to a focus-group discussion organized as a two-day workshop. I conducted all interviews in English and Spanish and translated them. In the focus groups, indigenous translators were used to interpret from the respective indigenous languages into Spanish. Additionally, informal talks and field observation of practices and participants formed an important element of research in each case. This was necessary to obtain qualitative evidence of self-reported identity and identity shift.

Due to my previous work in the conflict regions, I had initial contacts in the field; I used the snowball method to enlarge the sample. Following ethical guidelines,[7] I contacted all interview participants personally. However, to address logistical challenges, some participants of workshops were contacted via the organizations that collaborated with me in the organization of the events. Before the interviews and workshops, I informed all participants about my study and its aims, and obtained their written or recorded oral informed consent. I was the only person who extracted themes from the data.

The different circumstances in Chiapas and in Northern Ireland required different field research approaches. My field research in Northern Ireland (December 2009–February 2010 and in November and December 2010) focused on field observation and individual interviews. I further participated in relevant events and in the organization of workshops on women's experience of peace and conflict in Ireland North and South.[8] These workshops took place in Derry and Dublin as part of the consultation for Ireland's National Action Plan to implement United Nation

Security Council Resolution (UNSCR) 1325.[9] Being respectful of people's busy schedules and following the advice of my collaborators, I did not organize additional workshops in Northern Ireland. In Chiapas, I conducted sixteen interviews and two focus groups, which were organized with and for female indigenous human rights, peace, and women's rights activists in the form of active-participative workshops. I also participated actively in other relevant events as part of my field research.[10]

My field research in Chiapas (May–August 2010) happened to take place during a period of increased political tension due to the regional elections that took place in July 2010; this resulted in limitations in the access to indigenous communities, particularly to autonomous communities that form part of the Zapatista Movement. Due to the security situation, many female activists preferred to meet me in San Cristóbal de las Casas for the interviews, as I would draw attention to them if I visited them in their communities. Together with my contacts, we organized and paid for the journey of indigenous women from the Altos (mountain) and Selva (rain forest) areas to San Cristóbal de las Casas. The interviews were conducted in safe spaces in the town. As a result of the political situation, I encountered significant time limitations, as due to restricted financial resources, my time in Chiapas was limited to three months; these limitations required flexibility in research methodology.

The first workshop with female activists from Chiapas was rather informal and lasted five hours; it took place in a rural village in the Selva (rain forest) region of Chiapas. Following the requests of the workshop participants, the name of the village will remain undisclosed due to security concerns. The second workshop was a two-day event and took place in the town of Ocosingo. It was organized in collaboration with the peace organization SERAPAZ, the human rights center Centro de Derechos Humanos Fray Pedro Lorenzo de la Nada, and with the support of the women's rights center Centro de los Derechos de la Mujer de Chiapas. SERAPAZ kindly provided the space for the event, which enabled women from Zapatista communities to participate in the research without jeopardizing their own safety and the safety of their communities.

Challenges in organizing these events were a) the high illiteracy levels among indigenous female participants and b) the practical and methodological problem choosing a common language for the workshop. The first language of thirteen of the fifteen participants was Tseltal; some did not speak or did not want to speak Spanish; they felt this would reproduce existing ethnic power hierarchies. In order to find an appropriate solution for these problems and to give participants ownership on the project, we included them in the organization process of the workshop. Following the advice of the participants, we addressed the "language problem" by using both Tseltal and Spanish as working languages for the event. In the design of the event we ensured that both languages were given the same space; we further used indigenous interpreters to enhance the flow of communication during the event. This process provided an opportunity for addressing and breaking down existing ethnic power hierarchies.

In order to avoid the written word within the workshop, we focused on visual and oral didactical methods, such as artwork and the theater of the oppressed (Boal, 1979). The artwork, which we produced in workshops, consisted of a mapping of their communities before the conflict and in their current stage. The maps revealed visually the intersection of individual experiences of womanhood with the experiences of being a part of a socioeconomic and culturally marginalized group. It encouraged the participants to bring the embodied self into the presence (O'Neill, 2005), and to enter a phase, of transformative learning (Dirkx, 2000).

Both the artwork and the development of theater plays were based on facilitated story-telling sessions, which were followed by discussions of both process and outcome of the event activities. The workshop provided a space that enabled the participants to express themselves visually, through producing visual maps and theater plays, and orally by sharing their own collective identity narratives. Also by interpreting their artwork, workshop participants could explore their perception of and positioning toward their family, community, and the state before, during, and post-mobilization. The data that we produced during the workshop was compiled in an audiovisual resource (video) and shared with the participants; the posters (visual maps) produced remained accessible to all participants and their communities within the local organizations. This means that the participants are able to share the information gathered through the workshop with their communities.

During the workshop, a space was dedicated to the planning of follow-up activities for the newly created female activism network, which has led to the organization of a series of workshops in indigenous communities. Using the methodology and reflections developed in our event, the participants aimed in their workshops to educate about and discuss the Revolutionary Women's Law[11] with men and women of their communities. Second, the participants created during our workshop a network and developed a plan for coordinated activities.[12] Synergy effects (continuing work in communities and coordinated action of participants) and positive feedback I received after the event provide evidence that the workshop has been of benefit for the participants and for their communities.

Following Wolcott (1994), description, analysis, and interpretation structured the organization of my qualitative research data after returning from the field. The descriptive approach allows the women's voices to speak for themselves and the women to actively engage in producing meaning for the roles and positions they occupy (Skeggs, 1994, p. 2). In the second stage—the data analysis—I identified common themes in the narratives of women and organized them in order to understand the data and go beyond the words. My research identifies inductively the principles of classification and identification, which inform the different ways in which the research participants make sense of themselves and of their environment, both as women and as members of their ethno-national communities. To identify the markers of female activists' ethnic and gender identity and the ways in which gendered and ethnic boundaries intersect, it is essential to pay attention to the language women use and to their particular life situation. By looking at how they ascribe value and meaning to the different social identity categories, I explore how women concretely draw the boundaries between "us" and "the other" through the analysis of both content and interrelation of boundary processes. The collective identity narratives illustrate the level of importance of certain collective identity categories as well as changes in salience, content, and intersection of ethnic and gender boundary processes over time.

Motivations for activism are intrinsically linked to the perception of "normality" and play a significant role in the way women form and change their ethnic and gender boundaries in conflict and conflict-resolution processes. In my analysis, I examine the way metaphors are used within women's individual narratives as members of a particular social category to identify and describe the intersection of ethnic and gendered boundary processes.

In order to take into consideration the ontological differences between the ethnic and the gender identity content, I separate the different levels of analysis and look at the way social divisions are expressed in specific organizational settings. I ask in this research who women define as the principal "other" when positioning themselves toward family, community, and the state. The category "gender" is in their identifications interconnected to "ethnicity" and the way these intersecting boundary processes change, produces real effects on women's life situation.

The Voices That Inform This Research

My research includes the voices of fifty-five women from Chiapas and Northern Ireland who have been actively involved in mobilization processes against state-perpetrated injustice and inequality in the two conflict regions. The classification of the participants of my research is based on their organizational affiliation and takes into account the way they identified themselves.

My research in Chiapas is informed by female activists from various peasants' organizations,[13] women's organizations,[14] and peace and human rights organizations.[15] Although it was not possible to conduct interviews in autonomous Zapatista communities due to the political tensions at the time, twenty female activists who participated in this research identified themselves as "Zapatistas." While some of those have directly participated in the armed struggle and are still part of the autonomous Zapatista structure, others perceive themselves as part of the wider Zapatista Movement, what Karen Kampwirth calls the "revolutionary coalition" (Kampwirth, 2004) and Xochitl Leyva Solano refers to as "neozapatismo" (Leyva Solano, 2005) or the "New Zapatista Movement" (Leyva Solano, 1998). In Northern Ireland, the sample included members of the civil rights movement (1967–68), the Republican Movement (from 1969), and various women's rights initiatives (post-1968–69).

In Chiapas, I conducted sixteen individual interviews, two of these being conducted with two people at the time, and two focus groups, one with five and one with fifteen participants. Of the sixteen women who participated in the individual interview process, five identified themselves primarily as members of *campesino* or farmers' organizations, seven as part of women's organizations, ten as Zapatista supporters and two as former activists of the EZLN. Many women have been or are active in two or more organizations; their memberships intersect with their self-identification. The first focus group was organized as an active participative discussion with five indigenous women from a rural community;[16] the five women identified themselves as active members of the Zapatista Movement. Of the fifteen participants of the second workshop, thirteen were members of peace and human rights organizations and came from indigenous Tseltal communities in the Selva region of Chiapas. One mestiza women's rights activist from San Cristóbal de las Casas and one mestiza peace activist from Ocosingo participated in the event. Some identified themselves as members, but most identified as supporters of the Zapatista Movement.

Of the seventeen women I interviewed in Northern Ireland, eleven identified themselves primarily as "member of the Republican Movement," ten of those come from a working-class background and seven have experienced imprisonment for their activities. Seven interview participants perceive themselves primarily as members of women's organizations; three of those also identified as being Republican, but do not support violent forms of protest. Active participation in the civil rights movement was the beginning of the activism pathway of five of those who primarily identify as members of women's organizations. Of those female activists identifying themselves primarily as being Republican, one actively participated in the civil rights movement; she identified as coming from a more affluent background.

Due to access constraints, all participants from Northern Ireland came from an urban background, while in Chiapas the sample includes ten mestiza (mixed race) women from a mainly urban background and twenty-seven female indigenous activists from rural communities. Interviews with seventeen female activists from Northern Ireland were conducted in Belfast and Derry in February and March 2010. In Chiapas, ten interviews took place in San Cristóbal de las Casas, four interviews and one focus group were organized in Ocosingo in the Altos (mountain) region, and another focus group in a small village in the Selva region from June to August 2010.

In order to facilitate comparison, the research includes only narratives of women who have been actively involved in social mobilization processes against unequal power structures. However, women's experiences of conflict and peace cannot be seen in isolation from men's experiences and, indeed of other women not actively involved in mobilization processes. The choice was informed by time and resource constraints and guided by the research question, which asked about changes in social positioning and perceptions of women during social mobilization processes and in the period following the peace negotiations.

Conclusion

Being aware of my own standpoint provides a basis for both the subject matter explored in this monograph and the way I am conducting my research. Qualitative, active-participatory research tools enable me to active listening to and learning from the participants of this research project. My methodology provides a suitable framework for engaging with insights of individuals at the margin of peace and conflict processes. It allows me to better understand the different experiences, perceptions, and positioning of female members of different social movements during episodes of peace and conflict. It provides a space in my research to let those activists speak for themselves.

In the following chapters I present findings from the analysis of female activists' collective identity narratives of their different involvements in social movements during conflict and conflict settlement processes in the two regions. As part of this, I will show how different identities are politicized and perceived by female members of different ethnic groups in their process of boundary formation and change in peace and conflict situations.

II

The Voices

3

FROM THE MARGIN TO THE CENTER: FEMALE NARRATIVES OF ETHNO-NATIONAL MOBILIZATION

INTRODUCTION

What can we learn about identity processes in ethno-national mobilizations by listening to women's voices? How are social and symbolic boundaries bridged during conflict? And in what way do different identity processes intersect?

In order to understand the gender dimension of ethnic conflicts, it is important to make visible processes that obscure and deny its existence by bringing underlying and interacting dynamics to light. Listening to and learning from female activists' voices from Chiapas and Northern Ireland and examining themes emerging from women's collective identity narratives, this chapter illustrates how female activists express thoughts, feelings, and images about their family, their community/network, and the state; doing so the narratives of female activists from Chiapas and Northern Ireland show how the activists draw and change their ethnic, gender, and other boundaries during ethno-national conflict. This in turn allows us to understand the patterns of transformative gender and ethnic identity processes.

The chapter illustrates how during the conflict in Chiapas and in Northern Ireland, the external community struggle becomes connected to the "internal" women's struggle; it further shows in what way alliance formation on women's strategic gender interests across community borders distinguishes the two cases. Going beyond shared dispositions, consciousness, and collective actions, I examine the different ways in which feelings of belonging evolving from different mobilizations are felt, questioned, and changed. Furthermore, the narratives reveal changes in the degree of the "connectedness" (Brubaker & Cooper, 2004, p. 19), the understanding of it, and the meaning female activists attribute to it at different moments of interconnected social mobilization processes.

The mechanism of alliance building has been a central element of episodes of contention in both Chiapas and in Northern Ireland. However, significant contextual distinctions determine how women mobilize, their positioning within the process, and the impact of mobilizations on the way they identify as "woman," and as "ethnic." Differences in women's identification provide a way to understand the potential of ethno-national conflicts to create incentives and spaces for shifting both ethnic and gender boundaries. By bringing together ethno-national mobilizations with processes of solidarity formation on shared gender interests, female activists redefine what both their gender and their ethnicity mean to them. This part of the research provides interesting insights in the connection between individual identity processes and the development of women's networks within and across boundaries. Women's perception of and positioning in relation to the state impacts on the way in which ethnic differences between female activists are either bridged or reaffirmed, and perceived as an obstacle for feminist activism.

This chapter focuses on women's voices of conflict and connects women's stories to a broader analysis of the identity and social mobilization processes during ethno-national conflict. It retraces the different motivations for, and spaces of, women's activism in Chiapas and in Northern Ireland. The subchapters are organized according to time sequences of the mobilization process, the positioning of activists toward the state, the community, and the private sphere, and the meaning attributed to these. Each subchapter begins with a story highlighting some central issues that repeatedly occurred in the collective identity narratives of female activists from Northern Ireland and from Chiapas. In order to comply with research ethics and protect the identity of the participants, these stories are compiled from different narratives and names appearing with direct quotes have been altered.

COLLECTIVE IDENTITY NARRATIVES FROM CHIAPAS: PERCEPTIONS AND PATHWAYS OF ACTIVISM

Explaining figure 3.1, Tori, an indigenous human and women's rights activist from the Selva region outlines the many conflicts of

Figure 3.1 Map of our community conflict.

Note: The map was produced during the workshop "Women and the conflict in Chiapas," Ocosingo (Chiapas) on July 13 and July 14, 2010.

women in indigenous communities in Chiapas; she particularly emphasizes "violence in the home" and persistent inequality, visible in the many duties of indigenous women inside and outside the house. Women are the first people to get up in the morning and the last person to go to bed at night time. While most men rest on a Sunday and in the evenings, a woman is called lazy and receives bad treatment if she takes a rest. She criticizes that although women work so hard, traditionally only men can have posts of responsibility and honor in the community. Sandra, an indigenous women's rights activist adds that the Mexican state pursues a policy that attempts to systematically destroy her culture and implements a neoliberal system that excludes her as indigenous, as poor, and as woman. She perceives the Mexican State as her state, but its structures are those of "the other" mestizo state that disrespects her norms and traditions and does not permit her to live a life in dignity as indigenous, as poor, and as women. The finca system represents for her the "manifestation of oppression and disrespect for human beings." However, she believes that life has changed for many indigenous women through the mobilization processes.[1]

In Chiapas, oppressive colonial policies became embedded into the society structure and formed a part of the nation-building after the Mexican War of Independence (1810–21).[2] The conquest of Chiapas and the later creation of the settler society introduced a pattern of clientelistic control (Stasilius & Yuval-Davis, 1995), which became institutionalized after the Mexican Revolution (1910–17). The marginalization of indigenous culture in the mestizo state became evident, for example, in the denial of land rights or discriminatory employment practices, particularly forced labor, a common practice on large coffee plantations (Tello Diaz, 1995). Ideologically, the formation of Mexican society after independence has been focused on the mestizo founding myth, which is based on the assumption that all Mexicans of common descent go back to the miscegenation of male Spanish conquerors and indigenous native females.[3] This cultural structure provides historical meaning and social cohesion to modern Mexico (Gutierrez, 2001, p. 3), which has an ethnic and gender narrative that positions both indigenous people and women at the margin of society. The historical pattern of marginalization of indigenous people was an underlying current in the modernization policies of the 1980s and continue in the neoliberal trend of Mexican politics in the 1990s.

The uprising of the Zapatista National Liberation Army (EZLN)[4] in Chiapas on January 1, 1994, brought to light a new definition of "being indigenous" in Mexico, by questioning the homogenizing incentive of the "mestizo (mixed race) founding myth" and revealing deeply entrenched intersectional inequalities. Indigenous ethnic identity has undergone a significant transformation, which did not start in 1994, but is a result of a long history of mobilization.[5] During the 1970s, both indigenous and nonindigenous peasants and farmers organized in their struggle for land and freedom with the support of liberation theologists and other advisors with university education and a compassion for social justice. The various peasant groups became part of three national organizations: the Emiliano Zapata Peasant Organization (Organización Campesina "Emiliano Zapata" OCEZ), the Plan de Ayala National Council (Coordinadora Nacional de Plan de Ayala, CNPA) and the Independent Confederation of Agricultural Workers and Peasants (Central Independiente de Obreros Agrícolas y Campesinos, CIOAC). Women were part of these movements and began to further form their own organizations, such as artisan cooperatives or Christian women's groups (Millán Moncayo, 2008, p. 77). These mobilizations were the basis for the formation of the Zapatista Movement and its protest for indigenous autonomy and against neoliberalism.

Different interrelated social mobilization processes in Chiapas brought together the land question with indigenous cultural rights and women's rights. Indigenous women have influenced and have been influenced by these mobilization processes (Milán Moncayo, 2002b; Toledo Tello & Garza Caligaris, 2006). The collective identity narratives of indigenous and nonindigenous female activists from Chiapas on their perceptions of the family, the community, and the state, reveal the way in which these agents reproduce different discourses of symbolic inequalities and violence. In the following section, I retrace how women from different backgrounds became actively involved in drawing ethnic and gender boundaries during the different phases of mobilization: farmer's movements (1960s–early 1970s), the Zapatista Movement (1983–95), and various mobilizations for women's rights (1970s-1995). Chapter 4 continues this discussion with narratives on the demobilization process (1995–2010).

Experiencing Intersectional Inequality: Indigenous Women in Chiapas

Carmen, a women's rights and Zapatista activist from a marginalized indigenous community in the Altos—the highlands of Chiapas, feels anger and frustration when reflecting on her life before becoming actively involved in the Zapatista Movement and in a women's group. All her life she has only known work, getting up early in the morning and working until late at night. As a young girl she was not allowed to go to school and was sold into marriage without her consent at a very young age; she was as a woman not allowed to leave the house and regularly experienced physical violence by her husband. Before learning about women's rights she believed that men were beating their wives as a sign of love; today (2010), she labels this act as domestic violence.

> How I lived before [being an activist]? Well, I was sold into marriage as a very young girl. What does that tell you about my life? Well, a lot of sadness and not much joy... My life was less worth than that of an animal.[6]

Indigenous female activists criticize that at a very young age, girls are sold into marriage and considered to be the property of their husbands and the community rules that oblige women to obey and to accept this arrangement. They describe themselves as being defined culturally not as human beings, but as assets or property in their indigenous communities. Hard labor and lack of freedom, education, and self-determination feature as common concerns in all narratives of indigenous women. However, the women's stories reveal not only the different workloads of men and women, but also the different positioning they have in the communal decision-making structure. Women struggle not only with their workload, but also with having their voices heard and more generally with living a life in dignity as "indigenous women."

The relationship between family and community is interdependent and the collective or the community has priority over the family and is therefore considered as more important than the individual. Within the collective, men and women have different positions, responsibilities, and duties, which are determined by a set of norms and traditions. The organization of indigenous communities is focused on those traditions, which define land as the physical basis of community (Ronfeld, Arquilla, Fuller, & Fuller, 1998). Traditionally, in most indigenous communities, landownership is impossible for women, as in these communities only male children can inherit land.

> It's often been said that only men work the fields and women stay in the house, but we can see here that men and women are working equally beside each other. But women are not allowed to own or inherit the land. That's a huge problem especially when men emigrate and leave women and children behind.[7]

However, on the other side, all participants of this workshop (15 of 15) supported the collective cultivation of land, institutionalized in Mexico in the "ejido" system (Tello Diaz, 1995; Villafuerte Solis, 2002), as a good indigenous tradition. Within this context, many respondents (11 of 15) criticize the change of article 27 of the Mexican Constitution[8] in 1992, which has led to a reprivatization of indigenous land and is a central aspect of the Zapatista protest agenda. In the Mayan Cosmovisión, land not only has economic meaning; it also links the indigenous communities to their ancestors and is regarded as "sacred," particularly for women who link their existence to "mother earth" (Marcos, 2005, p. 88–89). In this way, indigenous communities distinguish themselves from the mestizo structure that determines the social, economic, and political system in Mexico (Gutiérrez Chong, 1999).

References to violence are a central element in all narratives of indigenous female activists, emphasizing the physical domestic violence and the inequalities they experience as indigenous, as poor, and as woman. This includes, rights-based violations such as racial discrimination and marginalization, lack of freedom, health care, education, and the like.

Some activists' reflections on violence (7 of 35) referred to the finca system, which was both an economic system of land cultivation and a system of domination; it led to the colonization of mostly indigenous peasants in the period after the independence of Mexico from Spain in 1823 (Leyva Solano & Ascencio Franco, 1996, p. 58). The finca system was supported by the state and created a structure of "obedience, fear, and oppression"[9] in Chiapas; this structure reveals the positioning of indigenous people at the lowest strata of society, visible in the "slave-like" working conditions. Women were particularly affected by the finca system (Garza 1999, 2000; Toledo Tello, 1996). Female activists (8 of 35) emphasize that indigenous women were obliged to have sexual intercourse with the owners of the fincas the night before their wedding, a rule that formed part of the marriage ritual and was practiced until the 1970s; they were further exposed to sexual abuse working in the kitchens of the finca and also suffered domestic violence in the home as a result of unequal community structures and their husbands' alcohol abuse; many indigenous men turned to alcohol in order to find an outlet for their despair.

Silvia, a mestiza liberation theologian and women's rights activist, describes the fincas in Chiapas as "a feudal system, as conditions of agrarian slavery."[10] She remembers feeling outraged witnessing the finqueros (owners of the fincas) using their right to sexually abuse all women working on their plantations. Supporting the indigenous farmers in their protest against this inhuman system she perceived as her moral obligation as human being.

In the light of the existing inequalities, indigenous women's image of the state is predominantly determined by feelings of absence, ignorance, and violence. The state is perceived as being responsible for the poverty of indigenous people and as oppressing indigenous people either directly or indirectly by supporting other oppressors, for instance, the finqueros in the 1970s or the transnational companies in the 1990s. The rebellion against the finca system and against state-perpetrated injustice in the 1970s focused on a claim to "land and freedom" that indigenous farmers perceive as their entitlement, a result of the Mexican Revolution and further institutionalized by President Lázaro Cárdenas[11] (Tello Diaz, 1995; Villafuerte Solis, 2002). In the 1980s, the modernization process of the Mexican state encouraged a shift from a leftist socialist agenda to an opening for neoliberal development. Neoliberal state policies promoting private land ownership have undermined the strength and culture of indigenous communities, in particular, the traditional cooperative land ownership structure, namely the ejido system (Villafuerte Solis, 2002).

Many female activists (16 of 24) criticize the government's land privatization programs and its neoliberal agenda, which open a space for multinationals to take over indigenous land and increase their marginalization. Further, indigenous women experience the state mostly as "absent" by referring to the lack of infrastructure (health, education, poverty, and marginalization) and as repressive and criminal when it comes to activities such as public security, defense, the development of paramilitaries, organ theft, forced birth control, and so on.

Fear, despair, anger, and the feeling of being restricted are emotions indigenous women express when referring to their life before mobilization. In their reflections on the meaning of conflict,[12] they interrelate their experience of state-perpetrated injustice they experience as members of their indigenous community with oppressive traditional community structures they suffer as women. This layered experience of insecurity and conflict causes indigenous women to distinguish their experiences from those of male members of their communities and from mestiza women within Chiapas and Mexico.

The mobilization process changes women's perception of the state from mainly absent to mainly oppressive and violent. However, indigenous women feel Mexican and as part of the Mexican state they demand reforms of the Mexican concept of citizenship; these reforms need to include different ways of "being Mexican," in particular allowing for the indigenous identity to gain equal importance to that of the mestizo or mixed-race population. During the mobilization process, women started reflecting on their situation within a local, regional, national, and international context.

Building Alliances during the Farmer's Protests

The formation of alliances between mestiza and indigenous women were part of the farmer's mobilizations for "land and liberty." This traditional claim of Mexican farmers symbolizes a relationship that highlights the interconnection between culture and land. In the 1970s, this claim was embedded and impacted on by ideas of social justice, particularly liberation theology. Further, during the farmers' mobilizations in Chiapas it became closely connected to indigenous ideology based on the Mayan founding myth.[13]

Las Mestizas (Mixed-Race Women)

Elena, a mestiza women's rights and farmers' activist, originally from Mexico city, came to Chiapas in the 1970s to support the farmers' mobilizations. She began to work with indigenous women because "although they were physically present at meetings, they mainly remained silent."[14] Elena organized together with other mestiza collaborators programs for indigenous women in which they taught Spanish and other skills. These workshops became for her spaces of reflection and connection and were supported by the male indigenous leadership of the respective communities. The workshops were symbolic for her as they allowed women to leave their homes and demonstrated that women can do the same work that men do. Elena was motivated by the enthusiasm and excitement of indigenous women organizing their work in craft cooperatives. She highlights that the indigenous women wanted to discuss politics; their discussions first focused on the state politics in Chiapas and Mexico, and then moved on to gender politics in their own communities.

Many mestiza women initially became involved in urban mobilization processes. Particularly in the 1960s, Mexican society embraced a wide political spectrum with a range of outspoken activists, including members of leftist political parties and the student movement, who believed that the PRI (Institutional Revolutionary Party) government had abandoned the ideals of the Mexican Revolution (Bartolomé, 1995). Activism within student or farmers' movements not only raised awareness about the repressive nature of PRI politics,[15] but was also a catalyst for raising awareness on the discrimination of indigenous people in Mexico. Many female mestizo activists joined leftist groups during or in the aftermath of the movements of the 1960s. During the 1970s, their activism led them to Chiapas, where some got involved as liberation theologists and others in advisory roles to the farmers' organizations and later to the Zapatista Movement; some mestiza activists started working on women's issues.

During the 1970s farmers' protests, which led to the end of the finca system and the creation of the new ejidos, references to indigenous autonomy and culture already came into play in the symbolic destruction of the monument of the conqueror of Chiapas, Diego Mazariegos, in San Cristóbal de las Casas. Reflecting on this event, Elena highlights that "the farmers' movement in Chiapas was on the way to re-creating itself... around the notion of indigenous people's rights that became a central element of the indigenous farmers' rebellion. It's the fight for land, it's the fight for democracy, but it also became increasingly a positioning toward the rights of indigenous people. This is before [the Zapatista uprising of] 1994."[16] The Zapatista mobilization of the 1980s, the struggle for land was linked much more closely to the liberation and cultural representation of the indigenous people in Chiapas.

The work of liberation theologists under the leadership of the bishop of San Cristóbal Don Samuel Ruiz and mestizo farmer's supporters diffused ideas of social justice, an interpretation of Christian faith through the poor's suffering, Marxism, and feminism (Eber, 1999). Events to highlight the oppression of indigenous people, organized in 1975 around the commemoration of the 500th anniversary of the Spanish conquest of Mexico, politicized indigenous people; this politicization is evident in violent escalations of marches organized by the farmers' organizations. In the 1970s, the land question was at the center of the violent protests of the indigenous farmers against the finqueros and against the state as a protector of the repressive finca system (Tello Diaz 1995; Villafuerte Solis 2002).

The farmers protests opened a space for alliance building across ethnic differences. In supporting "the poor and the oppressed by educating and mobilizing them politically,"[17] liberation theologists and other mestizo supporters increased the self-confidence of indigenous people and created agency for indigenous people's concerns. These processes provided an entry point for female mestizas to begin working with indigenous women.

While indigenous women provided essential support to the 1970s mobilization through food and shelter, they were not yet "making their voices heard within the struggle,"[18] a fact that changed with the Zapatista organization process in the 1980s. However, the 1970s mobilizations already opened a space for alliance building between mestiza and indigenous women (Kampwirth, 2004, p. 8ff; Millán Moncayo, 2006, p. 77–78).

Indigenous Women

Antonia, an indigenous women's rights and Zapatista activist, remembers that she was a young teenager when the fight for land began. Her father was involved in a farmers' organization in the 1970s and the Zapatista Movement from the early 1980s. Together with her mother and her sisters, she had been one of the many indigenous women who supported the mobilizations of indigenous farmers in the 1970s. Her participation initially involved providing food and shelter for the male fighters, both indigenous and mestizos. Antonia emphasizes that women played a very important role, albeit on the practical level, from the very beginning of the mobilizations. Through this involvement, she was listening and learning about politics and injustice, which increased her political awareness and led to self-reflections on her situation as a woman in an oppressed indigenous community. These processes provided a space for her to connect with mestiza women who supported the farmers' movements. While preparing food in the kitchen, they began to talk to her about their lives in their families and communities. While these initial exchanges were challenged by the language barrier, they opened for Antonia a "space to reflect on her life and to create herself."[19]

Indigenous women began to organize in the farmers' mobilization of the 1970s when a space opened for them to reflect on their life as women at different levels of society (family, community, state). These reflections led to a deeper understanding of their social positioning and had an empowering function.

Indigenous women claim that their eyes were opened by the mobilization process. Having become politicized on social justice and human rights issues, their level of acceptance of community traditions like arranged marriages decreased. Indigenous women began to wonder why they led a life that was so different to that of men within their communities. This "wondering why" was for most indigenous women the first step toward their active involvement in an organization process against community and state-perpetrated injustice.

The social mobilizations of indigenous landless peasants and farmers in the 1970s were a stepping stone for alliance building between indigenous and mestiza women, for the politicization of indigenous women and for their organization against oppression from inside and outside the community. It changed the way in which indigenous women perceived being a woman and being indigenous and with that their gender relations. Furthermore, female indigenous activists claim that perceptions of men have changed through the mobilizations as well and that some indigenous men involved in the struggles against violent and unequal power structures were supportive of the fight against the oppression of women.

> [During the farmers protest] my father began to understand the problem with selling young girls into marriage without their consent; he had changed the way he saw things. I remember when they came to ask for my older sister he told them "I don't have the intention to sell my daughters to [potential] husbands anymore. She has to decide and will get married when she likes and to whom she likes."[20]

As result of the father's involvement in the farmers protest, he broke with indigenous norms and traditions and gave his daughters the freedom to decide their future. Although some indigenous women highlighted this change in some men (4 of 24), others emphasized that they joined the Zapatista Movement to escape those traditions (7 of 24).

The Zapatista Mobilization (1983–1990s): From Awareness to Strategic Political Action

Antonia, a female indigenous women's rights and Zapatista activist, had the feeling that things were not right for women before she joined the Zapatista Movement, but she accepted the tradition back then as just how things were. By joining the EZLN, she entered into a process of internal change, of transformation, which increased her pride in being indigenous and in being a woman. Antonia pushed in the movement for the inclusion of women's voices; she promoted the creation of networks of support to get more women involved through a consultation process, which identified some traditions as barriers for women's participation. Antonia is proud of having "women who are now represented in different roles and at different levels of the organization; although not quite in the same numbers as men."[21] She describes the way toward gender justice as challenging, but for Antonia getting women involved was not only a matter of justice, but also a matter of survival for the Zapatista Movement. Antonia is pleased that indigenous women's demands arising from the consultation now feature prominently in the EZLN-protest agenda. She considers this as one of the main successes of the movement.

The involvement of indigenous women in the farmer's movements in the 1970s began as a response to a necessity: providing food and shelter. However as Antonia's narrative reveals, once indigenous women became politicized and mobilized, their pragmatic participation changed to a multifaceted activism that linked the fight for land and for indigenous rights to the fight for women's rights and dignity. Female activists describe their participation in the Zapatista Movement as a natural progression to their activism pathway (13 of 16).

The Zapatista Movement went further in its demands than the farmers' movements, which was mainly focused on the struggle for land. The Zapatistas positioned themselves against the Mexican government and criticized the government's decision to move its focus away from national issues toward a neoliberal modernization of the state, which included Mexico's integration in international free trade agreements (Mattiace, 2003). In "comunicados" (communications), the Zapatistas particularly highlighted their opposition against the change of Article 27[22] of the Mexican Constitution in the context of the creation of the North Atlantic Free Trade Zone. The "anti-neoliberalism" protest of the Zapatista Movement provided possibilities for creating networks linking the local to the international dimension of their protest (Olesen, 2005). From the beginning, women were represented at different levels of the Zapatista Movement.

Many female indigenous activists like Antonia joined the Zapatista Movement in the 1980s to escape violent community traditions and/or to fight for indigenous peoples' rights, for instance, to collectively own and cultivate the land. However, all Zapatista activists (16 of 16) remark that their fight for land and for indigenous rights was connected to their demand for a voice for women, to end traditions that justify violence against women and the imbalance of men's and women's voices, roles and responsibilities in the community, in the organization, and in the home.

Zapatista women's motivations to join the armed struggle show similar patterns, but are also distinct, having been determined by the individual context. Some mestiza activists, often from more affluent and urban backgrounds with higher education degrees feel morally bound to support the Zapatistas by their commitment to social justice, equality, and human rights. Mestiza farmers from a lower social strata share with the Zapatista Movement demands for instance concerning land ownership, which affects them directly. For many indigenous women (14 of 16) their activism in the Zapatista Movement has become a question of survival; not only of their community but also of them as women within their community. Some of those indigenous women (6 of 14) decided to join the Zapatista Movement to avoid being exposed to violent community traditions like a forced marriage; leaving their communities to become part of the armed struggle allowed them to regain control over their lives.

The experience of domestic violence within their home is a common pattern among female indigenous and nonindigenous activists and features prominently in their narratives. However, the meaning of domestic violence distinguishes women from indigenous and nonindigenous background. Unlike mestiza women, indigenous women interconnect their experience of domestic violence with other experiences of violence against indigenous people.

For most indigenous women, the desire to live a life without fear of violence in the home and the end of violent community traditions is a central motivation for becoming actively involved in various organizations (15 of 25). For some indigenous women who became involved as fighters in the EZLN (6 of 14), the fear to be forced into a marriage, "to be locked into a prison of life,"[23] is replaced by the fear to die as fighter in the armed struggle; these activists prefer the fear to die "for the liberation of indigenous men and women."[24] The experience of domestic violence is connected to the feeling of being "less worth than an animal,"[25] whereas fighting for the liberation of indigenous people and women in the

Zapatista Movement is connected to an increased sense of "self-worth and of dignity as a human being."[26]

Mestiza activists[27] highlight the absence of indigenous women from the farmers' mobilizations in the 1970s in comparison to their vocal and visible presence in the Zapatista Movement. Although many mestiza activists support the indigenous struggle, their positioning and experiences are, as part of the dominant ethnic group, different. Reflecting on the hierarchy of voices during meetings in women's groups, some indigenous (5 of 25) and nonindigenous (4 of 10) women note that indigenous women generally speak less in mixed groups than in groups that include only indigenous people. However, Elena emphasizes that indigenous women who were or are involved in the Zapatista Movement are more outspoken than women who were not.[28]

Within the Zapatista discourse, images of oppression direct the gaze of the society on the indigenous people as "the invisible other" and highlight their need to become visible. Female indigenous activists transformed this discourse by translating it into their experience of being oppressed and invisible on the basis of their gender and of their ethnic category. This reveals a change in the ways in which inequalities are politicized in Chiapas has changed over time.

Margarita, a mestiza women's rights activist, feels that indigenous women with military roles demonstrated their pride of being a woman and of being indigenous through their appearance in the Zapatista uprising on January 1, 1994.

> What was very different about the female Zapatista fighters was that although they were wearing military uniforms, they have never hidden their identity. You can identify the Zinacatecas, the women that come from the Selva region; their personal markers, their cultural symbols formed a part of their uniform, for example, the way the Zinacatecas wear their hair is very different from the Chenalho women's hairstyle. They preserved the identities of every indigenous group in their appearance as female fighters in the EZLN; you always knew exactly what indigenous community they were from. In their uniforms, they protected both their feminine identity and the traditions of their communities.[29]

Indigenous women resisting soldiers and attacking them by using their bodies as a weapon became a famous image of the Zapatista revolt (Huffschmid, 2004). The image of female Zapatista activists places emphasis on their dark eyes and their traditional ornaments, for example, their blouses or hair ribbons. The increasing visibility of indigenous women was an important aspect of the uprising of 1994 and enabled female Zapatista activists to liberate themselves through mobilization and organization. Mestizo women's rights activists, like Margarita, highlight the way in which indigenous Zapatista fighters express their feeling of pride of being indigenous and of being a woman in their appearance as a particular feature of the mobilization of indigenous women. While male indigenous fighters' identities disappear behind their military uniforms, female military activists highlight their ethnic and gender identity in their appearance. By doing this, female fighters transformed the image of indigenous women as passive and silent victims of oppression into the image of self-conscious and self-confident activists with a voice.

A Revolution within the Revolution: Female Symbols of Protest

For Antonia, a women's rights defender and female leader in the EZLN, "the Revolutionary Women's Law was the first uprising of the EZLN, but internally."[30] *Highlighting the uniqueness of the Revolutionary Women's Law, Antonia emphasizes that "it was the first time indigenous women were expressing in public what they want and what they don't want. That the woman is also free, that she has the right to not be beaten, that she has the right to know things and be part of the political decision-making process in their own community."*[31] *For Antonia "traditions are important; they make us, who we are, but it's the bad norms and traditions that place women in an unequal position, that make us sad." She underlines that "the law should only protect the customs and traditions that the women, communities, and organizations deem as good. The customs that we have should not cause harm to anyone."*[32]

Indigenous women became symbols of the Zapatista mobilization process. In some academic literature they have been portrayed as an image of the "oppressed Indian" (Huffschmid, 2004); however, indigenous women's narratives reveal proactive self-identifications of activists, who perceive themselves as an image for women's transformation and resistance. However, the appearance of female indigenous leaders on public platforms and the Revolutionary Women's Law[33] have an important symbolic meaning for indigenous women: it challenges the image of the "oppressed Indian woman" by creating agency and space for voicing indigenous women's gender specific interests.

For many mestiza and indigenous female activists, female Zapatista commanders, in particular Commander Ramona, embody the symbol of the rebellious indigenous woman, which is central to the indigenous women's movement. Female indigenous activists describe Ramona as "a physically tiny woman, but a great indigenous leader with a powerful voice."[34] They see Ramona as a role model; she embodies the possibility of overcoming the traditional image of "the oppressed" by emphasizing female, indigenous spiritual leadership, dignity, and responsibility. For indigenous activists "spiritual leadership" entails the ability "to move the heart to motivate other women"; [35] this leadership "comes from within" and is rooted in "bringing other women with you."[36] For indigenous women (20 of 25) the meaning of leadership is not "having the power over people,"[37] leadership should rather be understood and practiced as "responsibility to empower others."[38] Within this context, the symbol of Ramona embodies simultaneously strength and softness.

Nonindigenous activists also highlight the importance of female indigenous leaders. Elena sees Ramona as "this tiny indigenous woman who rises up with her people, takes up arms, but also emanates a sense of dignity and a sense of responsibility."[39] Reflecting on her experience in working with indigenous women she emphasizes that "many indigenous women feel that if she [Ramona] as an indigenous woman can be a commander, then all women can claim their rights."[40]

The participation of indigenous women in the Zapatista Movement has created symbols of female participation that has impacted on the life of indigenous and nonindigenous women. Female indigenous commanders have changed not only the image of the indigenous woman but also indigenous discourses and internal structures of indigenous communities connected to the Zapatista Movement and beyond. A central step in their activism pathway was the creation of the Revolutionary Women's Law.

Evolving out of a consultation process with indigenous women, which female Zapatista leaders organized in the 1980s with women in the movement, the Revolutionary Women's Law has institutionalized the transformation of gendered images into social practice within the Zapatista Movement (Speed, 2006). The Revolutionary Women's Law of 1993 consists of ten demands of revolutionary women; in 1996 these were extended to thirty-one, and forms an essential part of the Zapatista protest agenda. It contains rules for internal gender relationships in the Zapatista movement and formally connects the struggle for the recognition of ethnic identity and indigenous rights in Mexico to the struggle for more gender equality and women's rights within the indigenous communities in the Zapatista protest agenda.

The distinction Zapatista women make between "good" and "bad" norms and traditions becomes institutionalized in the Revolutionary Women's Law and reveals a shift in indigenous women's self-understanding as both a woman and as an indigenous person. This legal framework of the Zapatista movement represents the different levels of the normative rights of women: the right to political participation and the inclusion of women in positions of political decision making within the movement (point one and nine) and within their communities (point four), the right to work, education, and health (point two, five, and six), the right to physical integrity (point eight), and the right to decide over their own body (point three and seven). Point ten emphasizes that this law gives women both rights and responsibilities regarding the implementation of the regulations (Millán Moncayo, 2002a, p. 204).

The Revolutionary Women's Law is an important framework for understanding indigenous feminist activism and the way female indigenous activists changed their way of being indigenous and of being a woman. By distinguishing good from bad traditions, indigenous women transformed one of the central elements of the indigenous ethnic identity. The Women's Law highlights the tension between the gender equality discourse of the movement and indigenous norms and traditions. Tensions between the collective demands of the indigenous collective and of women within this setting required a shift of certain norms and traditions in order to ensure a life in dignity for both indigenous men and women. Indigenous women's demands demonstrate a shift in emphasis from ethnic to the gender boundary; this highlights the impact indigenous women have had on discourses and practices within the Zapatista movement. The Women's Law provides not only evidence for a change in indigenous women's perceptions but also in their positioning within the Zapatista movement and subsequently in their communities. Hence, it connects shifts in gender and ethnic identity to structural changes.

While based on female activists' demands, the Revolutionary Women's Law also highlights that change can only be achieved if "men and women work together";[41] an emphasis that stems from the complementarity between "the male" and "the female," which forms an important part of the founding myth of the indigenous Maya peoples, the Mayan Cosmovision;[42] (Marcos, 2005). By highlighting "that a better life for indigenous men and women can only be achieved if men and women work together,"[43] indigenous female activists distinguish their activism for gender justice from that of nonindigenous women's rights activists.

Crossing of Activist Pathways: Spaces of Contentions and Convergence between Feminisms

Elena acknowledges the different spaces that mestiza and indigenous women occupy. She believes that ethnic differences play a significant role, for instance, in meetings between indigenous and mestiza women.

> *Many nonindigenous activists come from an urban background and have an academic perspective, which distinguishes their gaze from that of indigenous women. Although some mestizas might be poor, their participation is different than that of indigenous activists. There is definitely a cultural hierarchy we need to be aware of.*[44]

* * *

Carmen, an indigenous women's rights and Zapatista activist, was invited by a religious mestiza woman to participate in a women's group of the CODIMUJ—Diocesan Council of Women (Coordinadora Diocesana de Mujeres).[45] *This involvement provided a way for her to leave the house, which she had experienced as "a prison"*[46] *since she was a child. Every Monday, Carmen participated in bible meetings to reflect on the "word of god with the mind, the eyes and the heart of women,"*[47] *allowing her to gradually better understand her own situation as an indigenous woman, by situating herself within the context of the struggle against violent and unequal structures: as an indigenous person against the state, as also a women against some traditions of her indigenous community. These meetings increased not only her knowledge but also her self-confidence and pride in being an indigenous woman. Once a part of the women's group, Carmen took on a role of responsibility and began to lift other women out of their misery, to organize them, and to give them the possibility to reflect on their lives. While being grateful for the support she received from nonindigenous women in the CODIMUJ, Carmen criticizes that many mestiza feminists direct their discourses against men, portraying men as evil. She emphasizes that the only way forward is "for men and women walking together and talking to men, engaging them in our struggle."*[48] *She distinguishes herself from the nonindigenous activists by emphasizing the "duality of men and women" in her indigenous feminist discourse, which has its roots in the Mayan founding myth.*

> Women have [in the Mayan founding myth] a more prominent position, as mother earth, as the source of life. But men and women have to be in balance, one cannot dominate the other. The Spanish conquest has brought imbalance in our relationship with men. It is bad to be imbalanced, so we need to work together to get back to the balance.[49]

Most female activists I interviewed and met at events during my field studies organized on the community level of the Zapatista movement and in organizations that were supporting this mobilization process.[50] As is evident in Carmen's story, for many women (21 of 35) memberships in different groups and organizations were intersecting. Many female activists (19 of 35) were members of farmers' organizations and supported as such the Zapatista movement; some (7 of 35) became involved in the CODIMUJ in the 1980s parallel to their involvement in the Zapatista mobilization process.

With the support of Bishop Don Samuel Ruiz, a group of nuns and lay religious activists began to promote from the 1980s a Women's Doctrine. The doctrine called for the appreciation of women's role in their families and communities and for the struggle against the oppression of women; it connected its interpretation of the situation in Chiapas, in particular of that of indigenous women with activists who came to Chiapas with a commitment to social transformation. This initial work resulted in the creation of the CODIMUJ in 1994. The CODIMUJ combined the promotion of gender consciousness and women's empowerment with the exchange of practical skills in women's collectives, including gardening, bread-making, or chicken farming (Toledo Tello & Garza Caligaris, 2006, p. 100–101). Similar to the CODIMUJ, some feminist nongovernmental organizations focused their work on women from rural areas, "combining their support for indigenous women's economic participation with the promotion of gender consciousness" (Hernández Castillo, 2006, p. 60).

Reflecting on their collaboration with nonindigenous or mestiza activists, many indigenous activists (8 of 25) perceive those spaces as dominated by the experiences and perspectives of urban mestiza activists, often with academic education, which informs their interpretation of women's shared gender interests and the realization of those in Mexican and Chiapanecan society. Although they appreciate the support of nonindigenous activists, these indigenous women feel that they need to be aware of the dominating-subordinated dynamic that underlies current encounters of indigenous and mestiza activists. By highlighting the hierarchical dynamics in their interaction with mestiza feminists, they emphasize on the salience of the ethnic boundary in shared spaces that places mestizas in a dominating position and indigenous women in a subordinated position, thus leading to distinctive standpoints and different feminisms. Carmen emphasizes that "even if mestizas are from a poor family, they are not as oppressed as we are as they have still more access to resources and a better education,"[51] which shows that the ethnic and class boundaries largely converge in the distinction of indigenous and mestiza or nonindigenous women.

The gender boundary is salient in the promotion of women's shared gender interests of both indigenous and nonindigenous women. However, the meaning attributed to this boundary distinguishes female activists from indigenous and nonindigenous background. For the indigenous activists, the cooperation with men is important as women share with their male counterpart a common fight for social justice. On the other side, nonindigenous women's rights activists highlight the distinction between male and female and the need to protect women from violence perpetrated by men.

Carmen emphasizes that the Spanish conquest brought "imbalance" into the male-female relationship. "Balancing the relationship between men and women" needs to be a central element of indigenous feminism, which can be distinguished from the "mestiza feminists' 'struggle for women's rights' against men." Many narratives of indigenous activists (5 of 25) trace the existing gender inequality back to the Spanish conquest. Within the history of Mexican nationalism, the role of women is often connected to the binominal Malinche-Guadalupe image (Ramírez Barreto, 2007, p. 113), "our original besmirched mother" (Glantz, 2001, p. 16), and the Holy Virgin. The image of Malinche as the indigenous woman who betrayed her community by having a sexual relationship with the Spanish conqueror Hernán Cortez appears frequently as a historical and cultural justification for the discrimination of women in Mexico (Gutiérrez Chong, 2007).

During the mobilization process, indigenous women's activism changed to a strategic struggle for women's gender interests with the support of alliances with nonindigenous feminists. However, the Revolutionary Women's Law brings to light the intersection of the gendered and the ethnic element of the struggle, distinguishing indigenous women's protest agenda from that of mestiza women even though their social mobilization processes are intertwined. Indigenous women link the process of mobilization to learning skills such as reading and writing and understanding "politics"; the attainment of these skills are perceived as positive results of the alliance with mestiza women. However, mestizas and indigenous women occupy different spaces of participation and differ in their understanding of who they are and what their struggle is about. Many mestiza women became mobilized because of women's issues, while for most indigenous women the socioeconomic and cultural rights of their community are initially the focal point of their activism; the latter remains important and becomes connected to the struggle for women's rights in indigenous feminist activisms. The distinction between indigenous and mestiza activists reveals the multidimensional nature of unequal power structures in Mexico, which are entangled with the question of ethnic, class, and gendered identity.

The different ethnic power hierarchies become visible in the use of the Spanish language as a basis of communication between indigenous and mestiza women. This places indigenous women, who do not speak the Spanish language or do not speak it well, in a subordinated position. However, through their participation in different social mobilizations, the self-confidence and pride of indigenous women in "being indigenous" and in "being a woman" has increased. As a result of this increased self-confidence and pride, indigenous women's perceptions of their use of indigenous languages have transformed from "feeling of shame" to a "feeling of pride."[52] Some indigenous women even claim that they feel "better than the mestizas"[53] and are proud to be able to communicate in one or more different indigenous languages as well as Spanish, while the mestizas "speak only Spanish."[54]

Alliance building between indigenous and nonindigenous women opened spaces for indigenous women to reflect on their positioning and on their life as women within their indigenous communities and within the Mexican state. For most female activists (25 of 35), both indigenous and mestiza, their activism for shared gender interests is an important lesson learned in which they experience the need to provide support for and receive support from other women. Despite their differences, the creation of alliances between indigenous women from different ethnic groups within the Zapatista movement, and between indigenous and nonindigenous activists in women's groups and organizations, was central to women's active participation in the different mobilization processes.

COLLECTIVE IDENTITY NARRATIVES FROM NORTHERN IRELAND: PERCEPTIONS AND PATHWAYS OF ACTIVISM

Northern Ireland has a long history of ethno-national conflict, which dates back to the sixteenth and seventeenth century. First colonization, then the Union, followed by partition, and finally direct rule were all stepping stones in the historical development of contentious "systems of relationships," which produced "a set of differences, a structure of dominance, dependence and inequality and a tendency toward communal division" (Ruane & Todd, 1996, pp. 144–45). As a result of this, inequality is deep and historically entrenched on a multiplicity of dimensions that have only begun to diminish since the 1990s. Traditionally, the position of women in Northern Ireland is entangled with both religious and national identity. Conservative ethno-nationalist discourses have characterized women's identity as "apolitical, more orientated to peace, physically fragile and naturally suited to the private sphere" (Ashe, 2006, p. 162). However, the conflict has often spilled over into the private sphere or the "female territory," in particular, in situations where the welfare of the family and the home were under threat (Aretxaga, 1997). The uncertainty and insecurity experienced through events within and around their communities have mobilized marginalized Catholic women into action. Prior to this process, women with egalitarian values, often from more advantaged backgrounds and mostly outside subaltern republican communities, have mobilized for civil rights. The different experiences of women explored in this chapter result in the formation of women's solidarity on shared gender interests in parallel universes: within and outside the republican community boundary.

The sequences of contentious politics relevant for my analysis begin with the civil rights marches in Northern Ireland during 1968–69 followed by Protestant counterdemonstrations, violent confrontations with security forces, and a series of violent attacks on life and property. Over 3,500 people lost their lives between the start of the conflict in 1969 and 2008 (Melaugh 2008); while the intensity of violence diminished, violent attacks continued into the 1990s.[55]

The civil rights marches set into motion new sequences of contentious politics, which included different processes of mobilization against unequal power structures and state-perpetrated injustice. My analysis in this chapter focuses on the time sequence starting in 1968 with the civil rights marches and ending with the start of the peace process in the early 1990s.

In the following part, I trace how women from different backgrounds become mobilized into activism and draw ethnic and gender boundaries during the following episodes of contention: civil rights movement (1960s–early 1970s), the Republican Movement (1969–1990s), the women's rights movement (1970s–1990s); chapter 4 continues with narratives on the demobilization process (1990s–2010).

Mobilizing for Civil Rights and "Feeling" Inequality (1968–69)

Radicalized in the 1960s, Aine, a civil and women's rights activist joined different social justice groups and campaigns before becoming actively involved in the Northern Ireland Civil Rights Association (NICRA). She highlights that "feminism was not really part of [her] politics at that time. Despite the struggle for equal rights and justice, the rights of women were absent from the agenda [of NICRA]."[56] Aine recalls that "they chanted 'one man, one vote' without a thought about women. [Those protesting against the civil rights marchers], on hearing the 'one man, one vote,' chant, would shout back, 'one pill and no pope.'"[57]

Many female civil rights activists became politicized before the civil rights campaign through their involvement in different egalitarian initiatives in the 1960s, for instance, in the umbrella group Campaign for Social Justice in 1964. For all respondents who shared this experience (7 of 17), it was, in Aine's words, "just a natural thing to join the civil rights movement"[58] as it complied with their moral values and ideologies. Female activists assumed prominent positions in the NICRA, formed in 1967 (Shannon, 2002). However, a feminist agenda was largely absent from the civil rights campaign. Women's issues were "secondary (and) less important, [because] when people being in prison, people being shot dead...campaigning for women's rights didn't seem necessarily *that* [emphasis by interviewee] important."[59] Hence, among civil rights activists, there was no consciousness yet about feminism; the gender boundary remained largely silent.

* * *

Aoife, a republican women's right activist and member of the PIRA during the war[60] *in the North of Ireland comes from a Catholic, working-class family; she emphasizes that during job interviews the question "what school did you go to?...determined usually whether you got the job or not."*[61] *However, this was all part of normality for her. Before 1969, she recalls being against violence as part of her Catholic values. Some of her family members fought in the British army, while others were imprisoned during the "war" in Northern Ireland for their membership in the Republican Movement. Aoife describes herself as not very political before the civil rights marches. But by listening to people talking about the civil rights demonstrations in 1967–68, she learned "that things weren't quite right here."*[62] *However, until 1969, she "just accepted things how they were."*[63]

Aoife's story reveals that before the civil rights movement, existing inequalities, specified by some activists (5 of 17) as "institutionalized discrimination against Catholics," were perceived as "normal"; women from marginalized Catholic communities had adapted to the prevailing situation, which they accepted without questioning and indeed often without even being aware of it (10 of 10).

Inequality was deeply entrenched in the society in Northern Ireland, evident in references to names and schools as markers of identity. These markers of identity have been highlighted by female activists (9 of 17) as central to the way inequality was experienced. The segregated school system enabled employers to identify, without asking directly, their prospective employee's ethno-national identity. Being identified as "Catholic" was often disadvantageous as Catholics were believed to be disloyal to the British state (Bardon, 1992). Some women from Catholic working-class background (4 of 10) reflect in their narratives on sectarian attacks, which they occasionally experienced at their workplace; they describe these attacks as humiliating, confusing, and frustrating.

Before the civil rights mobilization the underlying feeling of fear of being exposed as different, as Catholic as opposed to Protestant, formed a part of everyday life for the women from republican working-class areas I interviewed. It determined their behavior not only in the workplace, but also at other everyday activities, for instance doing the shopping.

> When I was younger, my mother would take us up the Shankill[64] [to do the shopping] and she would have said "now, I'm not going to call you by your names, don't mention your names, don't be saying your names out loud" and we didn't understand at the time. But many years later, mummy explained to us that you could be run out of the Shankill or Sandy Row[65] or they just would refuse to serve you.[66]

Tension between Catholics and Protestants arose every year during the traditional marching season in the month of July[67]; most respondents from Catholic working-class areas report that their Protestant neighbors would stop speaking to them and Protestant children would not play with them (8 of 10). "Keeping your distance from Protestant people during the marching season" was, for Aoife, a "sort of an instinctive thing, you just did it."[68] Aoife's "instinctive" behavior reveals a learned experience of "us" and "otherness," which is deeply rooted in her self-perception. It is expressed in certain behavioral patterns that she does not interrogate but just reflects upon as "normal" in certain circumstances; it is a part of her way of "being Catholic" and of experiencing difference. While their ethno-national distinction from those identifying as Protestant was triggered at certain times, Catholic women generally wanted to fit in and just get on with their lives. Although events such as isolated sectarian attacks at the workplace or the annual marching season brought ethnic differences to the fore, they did not raise a permanent consciousness of the ethnic boundary.

For Catholic working-class women, before the civil rights demonstrations, the image of the state was connected to a feeling of powerlessness and to the perception that you had to accept things as they were. Many respondents (7 of 17) link this acceptance to a lack of understanding about the broader context of their political, economic, and social situation.

The civil rights campaign highlighted not only political, but also socioeconomic, inequality along cultural lines. It created a deeper understanding of existing inequalities amongst marginalized Catholic women. Like Aoife, most female activists from Catholic working-class backgrounds (8 of 10) express their transformation from perceiving and accepting inequalities as normal to feeling that things have to change. However, the transformations in perceptions did not motivate many Catholic women from working-class areas to take action. Until the sectarian riots in 1969 and the following politicization in the Republican Movement, the claims of the civil rights movement remained somehow abstract for many (9 of 10).

However, regardless of whether female activists from a republican working-class background participated actively in the civil rights movement or supported the mobilization process passively, they reported an increase in self-confidence and a more positive self-image of "being Catholic" as a result of the first mobilization process. However, it was not so much a feeling of communality or communal solidarity; it was rather the belief in having the right to be treated equally as a Catholic and an Irish citizen of the Northern Irish state that was highlighted during the civil rights protest, than their connection to people in the south or their Irishness. Further, reflecting on expectations for change before 1969, most women from Catholic working-class areas (8 of 10) highlight that they felt that the state has to respond to their needs and create a more equal society.

In 1968, all female activists I interviewed shared the belief in the possibility of reforming the Northern Irish state through peaceful protest. Motivations for supporting these claims varied depending on the way the discrimination they protested against affected the women directly. Civil rights activists came from different community backgrounds and bridged the Protestant-Catholic distinction in their compassion for social justice.

The gender boundary remained silent for female activists during this first phase of protest. However, the content and salience of the ethnic and gender boundary differed between activists and changed during their mobilization; these changes were determined by shifting perceptions of the family, the community, and the state. The perception of the state as absent, as not responding to their needs, increased among women from republican working-class communities with the civil rights mobilization in 1967–68. From 1969 onward, this feeling particularly increased among women who reported that the Northern Irish and British state actively supported the sectarian attacks of what republican working-class women identify as the other part of the society.

Mobilizing the Ethno-National Boundary (1969–70s)

Eilish grew up in a Catholic, republican family in a mixed area in Belfast. Before 1969, her local parish encapsulated her understanding of "community." However, with the start of what she describes as "the war that was thrown at you" in 1969, the Republican Movement became her community. After 1969, life for Eilish became a permanent state of emergency, her normality determined by enduring intimidations and violence carried out by the state's security forces. Everybody in Eilish's neighborhood, was helping people affected by organizing places for them to sleep, food, and so on. The way people helped each other created for Eilish a spirit that connected people; she began to feel part of "a common thing in the center,"[69] which formed the basis for her political education and awareness. Her community began to organize and develop a collective voice. Through this process, Eilish began to feel that she needed to change the inequality she experienced as part of a Catholic working-class community. This understanding motivated her to get involved in the Republican Movement, an involvement that meant to her that she "wasn't sitting idly by, ... wasn't letting things happen."[70] *"Not being worried about what was happening on your street, to your neighbor" shows for her a "total lack of humanity."*[71]

While she first believed that the British security forces would protect her, she quickly experienced that "they were on the other side, that of the Protestants." Subsequently the state—both the Ulster and the British state—became her main enemy. Eilish's family had been affected significantly by violence carried out by the British army. From 1969 onward, her life became determined by a "war" that became a part of her normality. She recalls one Christmas morning when British army soldiers kicked her door in. She decided to give them her key and asked them to use it next time as it was far too expensive to get the door repaired always. Eilish felt that as member of her republican community she was perceived by the state as criminal anyway, no matter what she did.

> *You were trying to live a normal life, but after a while you didn't know what that was meant to be anymore. You felt like those in the cuckoos' nest film, you didn't know who the crazy was anymore. Was it us or were it them. I have a track record ... for [supporting] the IRA (Irish Republican Army) ... but who cared? It didn't matter.*[72]

The narratives of most republican activists (11 of 17) reveal that before 1969 their everyday life was centered on their family, neighbors, and on their local parish that organized their social life and informed the way they felt as a woman and as Catholic. References to Catholic values and community changed when the conflict spilled into the private sphere. For most respondents (7 of 11), before 1969, the perception of community was connected to a geographical location, to the place where they lived, often connected to their parish. From 1969 onward, the meaning of community changed; now "Irishness" became highlighted, rather than "being Catholic," and the imagined republican community became central to women's identification.

With the sectarian riots, being an Irish Catholic became a question of life and death. Having experienced and been directly affected by the sectarian violence of 1969,[73] the Falls Road Curfew in 1970,[74] Internment in 1971,[75] and Bloody Sunday in 1972,[76] "normality" for all respondents from a Catholic working-class background changed radically. The feeling of powerlessness to defend their homes, the intimidation of the security forces, and the image of army tanks in the streets became central to everyday life; regular house raids were perceived as part of the new normality. Women identifying as members of the republican community (11 of 17) shared feelings of fear and powerlessness, which they related to experiences of losing their homes, family members, close friends, and of being very close to death during the sectarian riots, often referred to as "pogrom" (5 of 11). The use of the symbolic notion of pogrom reveals a process of politicization on the "national question," linking present experiences to historical narratives of oppression (plantation, British colonization of Ireland, etc.) and a traditional northern Catholic communalism (Burton, 1978, p. 80; Todd, 1990, p. 35) by drawing a boundary between "us" and the Protestants, and identifying the state and its security forces as "the other." Hence, women's sense of place and of community post-1969 became "at once material and symbolic" (Aretxaga, 1997, p. 24).

From 1969 until the 1980s, two parallel and intrinsically linked developments changed women's perception of "community": first, the feeling of being let down and attacked by the British army whom they had hoped would protect them against the sectarian violence. Second, the organization amongst Catholic working-class people resulting from the need to survive, which started a process of building alternative community structures to the existing state structures.

Solidarity among women developed in the need for survival, particularly during events such as the Falls Road Curfew in 1970, which tied women to their communities (Aretxaga, 1997, p. 56; Coulter, 1993, p. 54). Strong feelings of belonging to their ethno-national community, connected to a "pride of place" (Kenney, 1991, p. 41), did not leave much space for the development of shared gender interests until the 1970s. The organization of women based on daily survival was situated within the politicization process of the Republican Movement, which created a political community, often referred to as "the republican family" (8 of 11).

From the 1970s, an independent space opened within the Republican Movement for the convergence of ethno-national and gender interests. Increasing politicization of women on women's issues led to a redefinition of what being Irish meant to them. However, republican women drew the boundary between themselves and women organizing solely on women's rights by positioning the women's rights activists "within" and themselves "outside" the Northern Irish state. The mobilization of republican women on women's rights issues evolved out of the community-building process. In emphasizing the gender boundary, women changed the ethnic boundary through reframing the traditional republican notion of care, the image of women within republicanism, and community traditions, which institutionalized gender violence.

Care, Commitment, Comradeship: Women's (Re-)Inventions of Republicanism

Different boundary processes intersected within the social mobilization of marginalized Catholic women, highlighting an external divide between republican feminists and women's rights activists outside the republican community boundary and an internal male-female distinction within the Republican Movement. Furthermore, an internal boundary distinguished experiences and perceptions of activists who cared for the community and supported "the war" without getting directly involved in violent activities of the IRA and those who as members of the IRA actively engaged in violence. Respondents distinguish the two categories with references to their role and their level of commitment to the community struggle.

Care and Commitment: From Family Making to Community Making

After 1969, Eilish, a Republican community activist, was like many women pushed into activism through the experience of attacks on her family and on her home. Self-defense as only way of survival marked the beginning of her activism, which was first practical and focused on the caring for the community through, for instance, looking for food supplies. However, as part of her community activism, she began, from the mid-1970s, to support particularly women and their interest in her community with the protest against the sexist community culture.

> We started changing the social fabric we women did... There were our little victories, they were not big victories demonstrating all the women's strength, but there were practical victories and they made

> *women who hadn't been involved previously think "OK, we can do that."*[77] *Women's issues need to be looked at from a women's perspective by women. We weren't just looking after nationalists, it was women. It was women and we were quite open to work with women from the [Protestant] Shankill [area of Belfast], because their needs were just as great as the women's needs here... It shows that the Republican Movement was much wider than the IRA.*[78]

Regaining control over their lives, republican women's increasing awareness of being a woman in their community and of the feeling of being able to change its "social fabric" shaped women's perception of social relations. Moving from family support and homemaking in the private realm to political confrontation and community making in the public sphere changed the positioning of women within their community. Women's voices and perspectives began to determine the community-building process, as men were largely absent (imprisoned or on the run/ in hiding) due to the introduction of internment in 1971. Becoming the backbones of the republican community, women's way of seeing themselves as Irish and as women started changing. New female perspectives and notions of gender equality in the community-building process led to changes in the republican historical narrative: the reinterpretation of "equality and justice" and "community care and commitment" from a female perspective.

Community or "caring for others," "justice," and the "nation" are concepts associated traditionally with Irish nationalism (Todd, 1990). Caring for your own people as republican is intrinsically linked to the national question, more so than to Catholic social thinking or Catholic communalism. The republican community is perceived as a leading part of the wider nation, which forms the national identity in Northern Ireland (Todd, 1990, p. 36). As part of their republican community, female republican activists often refer to "caring for the people in the community," as a "natural thing" (6 of 11), and as a form of being spiritually connected to the ethnic identity content, to their way of being Irish. However, while female republican activists perceived their ethnic identity as tied into the process of reconstructing republicanism in the 1970s, they brought their own female experiences and perspectives to this same process. Female civil activists distinguished their way of "caring for the community" from traditional male leadership approaches in the Republican Movement by linking their way of caring to their experiences in the home.

Republican women's activism interconnects different dimensions: the political struggle for a United Ireland, the caring for their community, and the organization of everyday practical needs in the private realm, for instance, assuring daily food supplies. This connection led to a different political women's activism as it brought private concerns into the political sphere. From 1969 until the early 1970s, female republican community activists contributed a practical activism based on caring for, cooperation within, and commitment to the struggle of, the Republican Movement. By doing so, they distinguished themselves from the activism of their male counterparts, which one female republican activist describes as focused on "power and competition."[79] Female notions of community activism focus on soft skills such as teamwork, supporting each other, and finding the grey instead of painting situations in black and white.

> I would love to open up a discussion about an alternative to that black and white of male structures, bringing in that softer edge that is needed in society, [realizing] that there is other than a right or a wrong; women can always find a grey. They see things, they identify gaps and instead of having a meeting about it they *do* (emphasis by respondent) something to fill that gap.[80]

The distinction between male and female notions of community activism highlights the gender boundary. In this early phase of women's practical activism, notions of community are rooted in women's experiences of the home and the altruistic values, "cooperation and nurturing" (Elshtain, 1981), as parts of a female "ethic of care" (Gilligan, 1983). However, republican women's activism changed in the 1970s from a more practical approach to a strategic promotion of women's strategic gender interests.

The formation of Women against Imperialism in 1978, a feminist group within the Republican Movement as well as the "dirty protest" of female republican prisoners and the "antistrip-searching" campaign in Armagh jail in the early 1980s are examples of women's "internal" feminist activism and reveal an evolving convergence of ideas of women's rights and gender equality with republicanism. Despite internal opposition and contention, gender equality concerns became part of the official program of the Republican Movement; in 1980, Sinn Fein adopted its first policy document on women and created a Department on Women's Affairs, in 1982 the Falls Women's Centre opened.

> The Women's Centre was so important because there wasn't really anything, if you were suffering domestic violence, there wasn't really anything, an outside organization you could go to for support when you separated from your husband or divorced him...[There] was quite a lot of challenge in that. A lot of men sort of thought "it's just a lot of women japing" [and questioned] the need to have a Women's Centre. But [women] fought the fight and they got what they needed.

The struggle against domestic violence and sexist community traditions shows a change toward an understanding of equality from women's gendered perspective from the late 1970s. By standing up for women and against men in their community, female activists transformed the image of women from the passive ideal of the Catholic mother (Beale, 1986; Ward and McGivern, 1980) to the active community leader.

A stepping stone for the promotion of women's strategic gender interests within the Republican Movement was the organization of local women's groups in republican working-class communities, particularly the creation of the Falls Women's Centre, which was set up to address "the need to have a place for women only...a space for themselves, where they could feel safe and discuss what was important to them" (Falls Women's Centre: 6). Eilish highlights that "women's issues need to be looked at from a women's perspective"[81] and the need for women's solidarity across borders; she further criticizes male comrades' reaction to the organization of the Women's Centre. By doing so, she reveals a shift from practical activism to a strategic promotion of women's concerns, from the emphasis on the ethnic to highlighting the gender boundary. The recognition that the Republican Movement was wider than the IRA shows a change in the content of the ethnic boundary, a change that is manifested through addressing the male and sexist structure of the Republican Movement (Hackett, 2004, p. 161) for instance, the sexist pub culture.

> We marched into a pub and demanded to be served on a Sunday. And it went further than that, every time we did find out that men were

beating their wives we went into all the pubs and clubs and handed their names in and demanded "don't serve them, because every time you serve them a pint, she is getting a punch"... Although it was small progress you were aware that you made changes, and we actually did make significant changes in the system.[82]

Eilish's narratives on addressing domestic violence by asking publicans not to serve perpetrators reveals how women used and changed the content of available social networks from the end of the 1970s. Discovering that they have the power to "make significant changes in the system,"[83] republican women became more outspoken, openly criticizing the sexist attitudes of many men in their communities. Women's internal activism changed both the gendered perspective of "Irishness" and the ethicized perception of "womanhood." It has led to an increase in self-confidence and gender consciousness, evident in the feeling of pride in "being Irish" and "being a woman."

A change in the perception of appropriateness in the behavior for men, for example, domestic violence or excluding women from pubs, reveals a transformation in gender relations. This change was supported through policy initiatives such as Sinn Fein's policy on women and the setup of its Women's Department in the 1980s, which promoted women and their strategic gender interests within the Republican Movement. However, in turn Sinn Fein's gender discourse required loyalty and commitment of republican women to the movement. Therefore, republican feminist activism remained within the borders of the Republican Movement. Although some limited spaces opened for the collaboration with grassroots activists from across the ethno-national divide and feminists from the women's movement outside the republican community, the close connection between ethno-national and gendered policies within the movement reaffirmed the opposition of women's activism within to that happening outside the Republican Movement. This was visible in rejections of "feminism" as a general label, or its reinterpretation as "republican feminism" in some responses (4 of 11). Republican women's notions of feminism often make the connection between socialism, Irish nationalism, and feminism.

> I would also describe myself as a feminist. The pursuing of a feminist agenda or the pursuing of women's rights rather than a feminist agenda must be central, the positioning of women must be critical to any peace-building initiative that we undertake, both

internally and that we can affect externally. You know that's the old thing [James] Connolly said about the flag, if the status of women remains the same, lower paid jobs, insufficient child care, no provision of care facilities then we will have failed.[84]

Comradeship and Commitment: "The Girls" in the IRA

Aoife became involved in the IRA during what she calls 'the war', because it was important for her that her "voice was being heard in whatever way, physically and verbally."[85] *When she felt that words were not being responded to, the only way left for her was the use of physical violence; it began for her with throwing stones and then what she describes as "military activity [as part of her] active membership in the IRA."*[86] *For Aoife,*

> violence is a terrible thing and it's a terrible thing to commit and to come to terms with. Violence was really, to most people I know, it was alienated. It is this strange thing we were now part of. So, that part wasn't easy. It's not easy to lift a stone and if you lift a stone the reason is to be aggressive and to hurt, you know, and that is not easy to come to terms with.[87]

However, once she committed to the struggle, Aoife became "part and parcel of the organization."[88] *Aoife did not feel discriminated against in the IRA, it was the "best person for the job that got the job [in the armed struggle], and it didn't matter if you were a man or a woman."*[89] *She believes that she was a feminist before she even knew what the word meant. However, her central criticism on what she calls "radical feminism"*[90] *is that it is geared often toward a "women only" approach. For Aoife, "there was never any desire to eat men or to be a man,"*[91] *she believes that men and women have to work together. Her "comradeship in prison," particularly the solidarity amongst women in the Armagh protest are central elements of her republican and feminist activism. This solidarity is not only of political nature, but forms part of her everyday life.*

> Friends and acquaintances come when you tell them that you have trouble and you call them, comrades are people who just come, they just turn up, you don't have to tell them, they are there.[92]

The internal distinction between community (or civil) and military activists becomes visible in the different spheres and levels of commitment female activists attribute to the community struggle. While republican community activists emphasize on caring and community building in their activism, for military activists their commitment is "to defend and die for the community."[93]

These different experiences and perspectives led to a distinct perception of gendered discrimination within the movement and a distinction in feminist consciousness: while republican community activists began to consciously challenge gender discrimination and sexist community traditions, female IRA activists like Aoife highlight the absence of gender discrimination within the organization. However, gendered distinctions within the IRA are evident in the distinct language used for addressing male and female detainees, in male-female distinctions made in perceptions of violence, and in the symbolism of the dirty protest in Armagh prison in 1980. Many republican activists (9 of 11) use the term the "girls in Armagh" when referring to the female republican prisoners interned in Armagh prison, but the "men in the Kesh" when addressing the male detainees in Long Kesh prison. In some cases they show awareness of making this distinction and some activists justify it by emphasizing the young age of the women (4 of 11). However, male detainees are always referred to as "men" regardless of their age.

The justification of engaging in violent activities marks a further male-female distinction. Some female activists distinguish themselves from the men in the movement by positioning their "reluctance to carry out violent activities [against] a man's more natural engagement in violence."[94] However, rather than essentializing these distinctions as "male-female nature," Aoife, a former IRA-activist, links them to different socialization processes; she believes that "men are more geared toward aggression from playing cowboys and Indians [in their childhood]."[95]

Membership of the IRA provided female activists a space in a new world outside their private sphere. Some female former IRA members (7 of 11) reported a greater closeness to their male comrades in comparison to other women in the movement. Notions of "fear" reveal distinctions between civil and military activism; while most civil activists refer to a constant fear of intimidations and house raids as part of their community activism (10 of 11), some military activists (4 of 7) claim that they lost all their fear through their IRA activism.

The experience of imprisonment shifted the image of normality for female activists and reveals male-female distinctions in IRA activism. Aoife highlights that in contrast to the male volunteers in "the Kesh," the women in Armagh prison were "forced" into the dirty protest on February 7, 1980, as a result of being denied access to toilets during a cell searching action that same day.[96] Images of the female prisoners' protest "having your own excrement, including menstruation blood on the wall"[97] were seen as different (Aretxaga, 1997, p. 144–45) and caused more outrage than the men's dirty protest (Coogan, 1980, p. 114). While the "blanket men" and the hunger strikers in Long Kesh tell a narrative of endurance, the dirty protest of the "Armagh girls" transgresses traditional codes of femininity (Corcoran, 2006, p. 179), breaking with the chaste, pure, and desexualized ideal image of womanhood (Inglis, 1987; McWilliams, 1993). The prison protests of the men and women share a dynamic of violence and the use of the body as a weapon of resistance (O'Keefe, 2006); however, the women's protest also brings notions of gendered difference into the equation.

The gender boundary also became highlighted during the hunger strike of 1980 when some female republican detainees of Armagh prison decided to participate in the hunger strike, although "the men didn't want the women to go on it...but it was not in any way them being sexist, but them caring for us."[98]

While the male-female distinction is highlighted in narratives of female activists, they demonstrate in their narratives their reluctance to problematize gendered distinctions within the IRA (5 of 7). Both civil and military republican activists emphasize their commitment to the community struggle. However, while female community activists highlight the "difference" in male and female life experiences, former IRA activists' narratives often entail a persistent claim of "sameness" in the experiences of male and female volunteers (5 of 7).

Republican women define their republican feminism as developing from and based in grassroots activism, connecting gender inequality to experiences of socioeconomic and cultural discrimination. They position their feminist activism in opposition to the feminism outside the Republican Movement and criticize that the 'the other feminism' leaves no space for their community struggle. For all female activists from republican working-class communities

(11 of 11), a feminist activism solely focused on women's rights issues presents an incomplete picture of women's lives by only highlighting gender issues and not including all dimensions of inequality.

Becoming "Feminist": From "One Man One Vote" to "Women's Rights" (1969–1990s)

Coming from a middle class Catholic background, Bairbre, a civil rights and women's rights activist, has not experienced hardship herself, but feels a compassion for social justice, encouraged by her parents who were known in the community for helping people. In university, she became involved in student and civil rights activism. In 1969, outraged at seeing the sectarian violence in parts of Belfast, Bairbre put a lot of energy into supporting people who had been burned out of their homes. However, she kept her religion and nationality separate from her political work. A fluent Irish speaker, Bairbre identifies as Irish and holds two passports. She believes that her people in the nine counties of Ulster, not only in Northern Ireland, are shaped by different influences than those in the south of Ireland, particularly historically with settlers coming to Northern Ireland from England and Scotland. However, for Bairbre "Northern Ireland is too small a society in itself."[99] She believes that a reunited Ireland would not only comply with "realigning the people in the North, but also with the need to create a new kind of politics in the South." However, she is not interested "in putting [her] main energy there."[100]

> It's not that I would ever say I'm not Irish, but I hate people who are only about those agendas... my identity is made up of a belief in equality and in human rights, I'm a woman, I'm a partner, I'm a mother... and all those things matter to me.[101]

Bairbre began to work on women's rights issues after her involvement in the civil rights campaign. She set out to create a feminist solidarity across ethnic and class boundaries with fellow feminist activists. However, the alliance with working-class republican women was difficult. "We went to some of these meetings in Sinn Fein's headquarter, but (those meetings) were not autonomous." She felt that women could not freely express themselves as it was "men who were overseeing [the meetings]." Bairbre felt that the women in West Belfast were "much more anti-imperialists and that was the (emphasized by interviewee) struggle." She distinguishes herself from "their struggle" by emphasizing that "we were more about bringing in other issues like abortion or law reform." She remembers the split in the Northern Ireland women's rights movement as a "dreadful" event, after which she continued working on "women-only issues." While Bairbre would have been "kind of sympathetic to anti-imperialist women...in the beginning she became less sympathetic" as she felt that the Republican Movement was "very controlling" and that it was "very difficult for women to find a voice, any kind of autonomous voice to raise other issues."[102]

Some female activists, who actively participated in the civil rights movement, progressed afterward to a feminist activism focused on women's rights; they often share an "academic, professional [or] trade union background" (McCoy, 2000, p. 13). Although cultural identifications differ ("Irish," "Irish nationalists," "Catholic," "Unionist," "Protestant"), the gender boundary was more salient than the ethno-national boundary in their activism; these women do not report an intensive feeling of belonging to an ethno-national community. Instead they perceive their protest agenda as wider than the ethno-national dimension. While the experiences of discrimination of women's rights activists vary, depending on ethnic and class background, a common pattern in their narratives is the compassion for social justice and human rights issues.

After the civil rights campaign, many female activists found it difficult to place themselves, particularly if they identified as "nonsectarian," "nonviolent," and resisted taking sides in the ethno-national community struggle. Most women's rights activists (4 of 6) might have felt some closeness to ethno-national issues, for instance, a United Ireland, but if so, it was perceived as less significant than women's rights concerns. Feeling a distance to a republican, single-axed agenda and its prioritizing of "being republican" before "being a woman," many female activists perceived their progression from civil rights to women's rights as "natural." The development of feminist solidarity was centered on a shared closeness to generalist universalist claims, in spite of the fact that family tradition and ideology of women's rights activists vary. Within the women's movement, members were asked to keep their positioning toward the constitutional question to themselves. By abstaining from taking a stand in the ethno-national conflict and by agreeing that opinions about the politics of nationalism or unionism should be a private matter, the women's movement reverses the radical feminist slogan "the personal is political" (Roulston, 1997a).

Influenced by the women's movement in Britain and in the United States, women began organizing for women's rights in the 1970s. The women's movement brought together women from different community backgrounds, in groups such as the Northern Ireland Women's Rights Movement (1975) or the Socialist Women's Group (1975), which later split into the Belfast Women's Collective (from 1977) and Women against Imperialism (from 1978). The split of the Socialist Women's Group reveals the general pattern of "division" within the Northern Ireland women's movement. It brings to light the limitations for creating a united women's solidarity for shared gender interests across ethnic and class boundaries. The many splits and regroupings occurred as a consequence of an attempt to deny and suppress difference (Roulston, 1997b).

Bairbre's narrative reveals how the different positioning of women in Northern Ireland determined and limited the development of alliances on women's shared gender interests. A broad alliance of republican left-wing organizations campaigning against internment brought feminist activists from the Belfast Women's Collective and Women against Imperialism together in single-issue campaigns at different times. However, initial open solidarity with the struggle of working-class Catholic women in West Belfast decreased by the end of the 1970s, as many feminist activists became alienated by the "patriarchal structure and dynamics" of the Republican Movement and rejected the idea of a women's activism "controlled by men" on the other hand. Most women from Catholic working-class communities based their activism on the intersection of horizontal inequalities they experienced connected to their alienated relationship with the state and the defense of their community (Sales, 1997). A feminist activism dimension developed in the light of the "pub protest" in the 1970s, the dirty protest of 1980s and the antistrip-searching campaign in 1984 (Corcoran, 2006, p. 52ff.), which was determined on the level of commitment to the community struggle.

Women's positioning toward the state determined the way in which they responded to "structural injustices and violence" and their priority setting: while independent women's rights activists emphasized on reform of the state, republican women's activism was geared toward "the end of British rule" and a "United Ireland."

Women's positioning on the national question was a significant motivator for drawing the boundary between "us" and "the others." This led to the development of women's feminist solidarity in "parallel universes" (Galligan & Wilford, 1999, p. 168): within and outside the Republican Movement. While both universes shared an opposition to unequal state structures, feminist activists referred to themselves as 'independent activists' to distinguish themselves from those who identify as women's rights and republican activists. First, independent feminists emphasized on working on social and economic reforms within the state structure, which for republican feminists was "tantamount to accepting British rule" (Ward, 2004, p. 191). Second, they addressed gender inequality not only in state policies, but also within the "patriarchal structure of ethno-national communities."[103]

For most independent feminists being Irish and Catholic did not become a question of survival after 1969; they did not experience and perceive the state as absent and violent in the same way as women in republican communities in Belfast. For the latter, sectarian attacks and the repression and intimidation of security forces became a part of their normality post-1969. Shared altruism and a set of common values are at the center of mobilization of female activists, who continued with women's rights activism after civil rights. Collective women's gender interests become the main source of identification and of alliance formation. Feeling "very much woman-identified," independent feminist activists claim that their "lives were totally obsessed by the women's movement" (Women's News, 1987, pp. 24, 40).

Niamh a lesbian women's rights and republican activist finds that there is "always a little bit of space"[104] for being feminist and republican within Northern Ireland's activism landscape, "but not a huge amount." She particularly recalls challenges in the organization of International Women's Day events in Belfast in the early 1980s: "Some of the women who were probably more involved in equal rights campaigns, maybe trade union activities, were saying that the very visible presence of republican and lesbian women would put ordinary women off."[105] Niamh claims that lesbians and republican women were somehow united in the way they were excluded from mainstream women's rights activism. Lesbian activism was positioned at the margin of both republican and feminist activism and found a limited space during the conflict within the different feminist activisms and the larger gay movement in Northern Ireland and Republic of Ireland in the 1970s (Rose, 1994).

Different Spaces and Pathways of Activism

Although women's activisms vary, both independent women's activism and republican feminism developed from an initially pragmatic response to a lack of social justice (civil rights) or to immediate needs for survival (republican), to a strategic struggle for gender interests. However, how women's activism progressed to the strategic promotion of women's gender interests was determined by women's different backgrounds and experiences of the "brutal, bitter, grief-strewn story of conflict in the North of Ireland" (Rooney, 2000, p. 176).

The history of feminism and women's rights activism in Northern Ireland is marked by the "difficulty of finding ways of including women while allowing the differences among women to find expression" (Roulston, 1997a). Difference is central to women's community activism, connected to their experience of political neglect, poverty, and violence (Cockburn, 1998). Members of the independent women's movement are often criticized by community activists for claiming the voice to speak for all women in Northern Ireland and for eliminating difference, while peace activists are criticized for essentializing womanhood. On the other hand, republican activists are perceived by independent feminists as reaffirming patriarchal structures by promoting armed violence and engaging in military structures. These different views reveal the "very contested nature of distinctiveness in Northern Ireland" (Porter, 2000, p. 142), which poses significant challenges for the inclusion and representation of different voices in the women's movement.

Different movements in Northern Ireland have brought women from the private into the public sphere. For many women the conflict was a two-way process. The public sphere has penetrated the private life of women, and has pushed women from a republican working-class background to take on public roles in their community and in the wider society. At the same time the mobilization process has brought private women's issues, including domestic violence and child care into the public domain. However, despite moments of convergence between republicanism and feminism, largely due to work that helped cross ethnic and gender boundaries in the 1980s, divisions between female women's rights activists (feminists, republicans, lesbians, peace activists, etc.) remain an underlying current of women's activism in Northern Ireland.

Mobilization and Identity Formation: Intersection of Ethnic and Gender Boundaries during Protest

Ethnic and gender boundary processes intersect in social mobilizations in both Chiapas and Northern Ireland, though there are significant differences in the way solidarity and collectivity around women's gender interests evolve within the respective dynamics of contention. In both ethno-national mobilization processes, the external community struggle becomes connected to the internal women's struggle for gender justice; however, alliance formation on women's gender interests across community borders varies. The positioning of women in relation to the state impacts on experience and intension of violent episodes and on the way in which ethnic differences are first bridged, then reaffirmed (as in Northern Ireland) or bridged (as in Chiapas).

Contentious episodes (farmers' movements in Chiapas and the civil rights movement in Northern Ireland) unite actors from different backgrounds in the protest against state-perpetrated injustice. The active participation of women from the subordinated part of the society (indigenous women and Catholic working-class women) is limited in that period of protest in both cases. However, this first episode of contention opens in Chiapas a space to build alliances between indigenous and nonindigenous women across the ethnic and class divide; in Northern Ireland, the space to cross ethnic and class boundaries during this first phase of social mobilization was more limited than in Chiapas, as Catholic women from working-class backgrounds were largely absent from the civil rights movement.

In Chiapas, the farmer's movement's protest agenda in the 1970s expanded during the Zapatista mobilization from 1983, connecting the local dimension (land rights, indigenous rights, and indigenous autonomy) to the global fight against neoliberalism (Olesen, 2005) and provided an incentive for solidarity-building across boundaries. In Northern Ireland, active and passive support for the civil rights mobilization in 1967–68 disintegrated during the sectarian violence post-1969, leading to the renewal of traditional republicanism (Ruane & Todd, 1996) and to the division of women's solidarity on "the national question." After the first phase of social mobilization the emphasis of activism shifted in both cases from the macro (state) level to the meso (community) level. This opened a space for the active participation of indigenous women in Chiapas and republican women in Northern Ireland. Women from marginalized backgrounds (indigenous/republican) brought their experience of being predominantly positioned in the private realm into the community process. The increasing numbers and changing form of involvement of indigenous women in the Zapatista movement resulted in the creation of a women's protest agenda; this protest agenda was formalized in the Revolutionary Women's Law, which contributed an internal gender dimension of protest to the Zapatista mobilization process. Similar in Northern Ireland, a gender dimension developed in women's community activism and changed both the structure of the Republican Movement and the image of republican womanhood; this is evident in the creation of new institutions such as the Falls Women's Centre or the Sinn Fein Women's Department. The activism of indigenous and republican women changed from being mainly practical and focused on the caring for their community to being a strategic promotion of women's shared gender interests. This shift resulted in female activists from subaltern communities redefining "community traditions" (indigenous and republican) by reimagining traditional images of womanhood.

Notions of "unity" and "community" are at the center of the mobilization of ethno-national identity in Chiapas and in Northern Ireland. The community dimension connects the external dimension of the protest against the state with the internal organization on women's shared gender interests. For indigenous women, "unity and community" amongst different indigenous peoples evolved, particularly from 1980s onward, in opposition to the Mexican government's neoliberal discourse, which endorsed the individualization of the society and denigrated their community structure. Negative perceptions of the Mexican state and its mestiza concept of citizenship are evident in the image of the "invisible indigenous woman" and her position at the margin of society, affected by intersectional inequalities. The community protest opened a space for women to "leave their houses" and build alliances within and across ethnic boundaries. Republican working-class women, pushed from homemaking in a private realm to community making in the public sphere, were leading the process of building alternative communities "outside" the structures of the "repressive" British state. A "strong feeling of community solidarity" developed among republican women in Northern Ireland post-1969, based on their protest against a British state perceived as "the other." This is evident in references to the "republican family" and an increase in the feeling of being Irish and the aim of belonging to the Irish state, expressed in the republican protest for the "unity of the North and the South of the island."

A distancing of subaltern community activists from the state in Mexico and in Northern Ireland is evident in references of subaltern women, though the perceptions of belonging and state boundaries differ. The state is not only criticized as being dominated by those from the other ethno-national group (mestizos in Mexico and British protestants in Northern Ireland), but also perceived as predominantly determined by men and subsequently male perspectives and experiences. Being removed from this center of male power structures, in both cases, women's "community activism" became situated in alternative community spaces; here largely autonomous community structures developed during protest, which allowed for the power imbalance in both community-state and male-female relationships to be addressed.

These spaces also enabled women from marginalized communities to reshape the image of indigenous/republican womanhood and the structure of their community. The community internal organization process of indigenous women highlighted both distinctions in the way of "being Mexican" between indigenous and mestizas and between men and women in their community. This set into motion a process of consultation in the Zapatista movement, which resulted in the distinction between good and bad indigenous traditions and led to a change in the meaning of being indigenous and of being a woman. In comparison, female republican activists reported a shift in ethnic identification from being Catholic to being Irish as a result of the reaffirmation of the nationalist agenda. However, by changing the traditional image of Irish womanhood through their active participation and leadership in community building, they shifted the meaning of being Irish and of being a woman.

Female symbols of resistance are important drivers of the change in the content of ethnic and gender boundaries and central stepping stones in the development of women's activism in Chiapas and in Northern Ireland. Transformative symbols for women within the mobilization processes in Chiapas are the image of female activists in leadership roles, particularly that of Commander Ramona, and the Revolutionary Women's Law. Ramona, reproducing the paradox of the "power of the powerless" (Huffschmid, 2004, p. 275), penetrates the national image by "taking the word" and by bringing indigenous women's rights and liberation into the national debate. With the Revolutionary Women's Law, female indigenous activists demonstrated that they are not only visible images of the Zapatista mobilization, but also active agents promoting indigenous women's rights. In the ethno-national mobilization process in Northern Ireland, the images of women defending their family homes and their republican community challenges the notion of "passive mother of the (Irish) nation" (Beale, 1986; Edgerton, 1986; Ward & McGivern, 1980). In particular, the use of the body and of menstruation blood as "weapons" during the dirty protest in Armagh jail, had symbolic value for the re-creation of the image of women "beyond the gates of the prison" and led to changes in the traditional image of womanhood in the Republican Movement (Aretxaga, 1997; O'Keefe, 2006). Different feminist activisms evolved within contentious politics in Chiapas and Northern Ireland, revealing ethnic and class differences. In both cases women from different ethnic and class backgrounds engaged in mobilization processes against unequal state structures; however, their positioning within and toward the state as well as motivations and forms of activism varied depending on their particular experience of oppression and on the contexts in which the processes are situated.

Women's different positioning toward the state is connected to the way in which ethnic identity is triggered. Ethno-national mobilization of indigenous identity in Chiapas entails the objective of state reform and places indigenous and nonindigenous women's activisms within the existing state borders; this becomes evident in the display of the Mexican flag at public appearances of the Zapatista movement. In Northern Ireland, the triggering of ethnic boundaries post-1969 led to a "conflict over flags" and national identities, placing republican women's activism outside and in opposition to the existing borders of the British state. On the other hand, women's activism outside republican community boundaries continued to be positioned within the British state and aimed for state reform. The different positioning of women's activisms within or outside and against the British state limited the formation of alliances across ethnic and class boundaries and led to women's activisms taking place in "parallel universes" (Galligan and Wilford 1999; Hoewer, 2014; Porter, 2000; Roulston, 1997a; Ward, 2004). While in Chiapas the mobilization processes of women have been based on alliances between indigenous and mestiza women, in Northern Ireland female activist's pathways were deeply divided after the civil rights movement. Existing boundaries between independent women's rights activists and indigenous/republican activists led to different definitions of feminism. Indigenous and republican feminists distinguish themselves from feminists outside the community boundary through the interrelation of women's gender and community demands. These community or grassroots feminists emphasize the need for including men and women into community processes rather than the exclusion of women from society and the male-female divide. The emphasis lays in grassroots feminist activisms on the inclusivity and bottom-up dynamics of mobilization processes to achieve changes in and with the community. Activists who feel oppressed as members of their indigenous/republican community, as poor, and as women criticize these "other activisms" for prioritizing women's rights, for excluding "other" inequalities for their "top-down approach." In Chiapas, feminist activists outside the indigenous community boundary prioritize the promotion of women's rights and also express support for indigenous demands and are connected to indigenous activists in their aim to reform the Mexican state. On the other hand, in Northern Ireland, women who see themselves principally as promoters of women's rights distanced themselves from activisms that compromises women's rights by prioritizing "other" identities and that are connected to physical violence.

The notion of "indigenous autonomy" (Diaz Pclanco, 1998; Leyva Solano, 2001) in Chiapas is less exclusive than nationalist demands in Northern Ireland and is supported by nonindigenous activists; alliance building between female indigenous and nonindigenous activists the indigenous protest agenda has expanded to an "umbrella demand, encompassing a host of cultural, political, economic and social grievances" (Mattiace, 2003, p. 20) in the 1990s. This facilitated alliance formation amongst female activists from different ethnic and class backgrounds.

A highlighting of the gender boundary through a temporary detriggering of the ethnic boundary does not lead to a disappearance of ethnic distinctions, but to their transformation. Mobilization processes in Chiapas and in Northern Ireland have resulted in changes on the community level through the integration of women at different levels of the mobilization process and through changing traditions. Further, the shift in traditional images of womanhood is connected to an increasing pride of being indigenous/Irish and of being a woman. This illustrates changes at both the ethnic and the gender boundary. On the micro level, these changes have been felt as shifts in the perceptions and positioning of women within their family. How do shifting positioning and perceptions of women during conflict impact the negotiation of peace agreements and post-peace agreement processes? In the following chapter, I address this question and look at the way in which these symbolic and social boundary changes are translated into the transition from armed conflict to peace.

4

The Meaning of Contentious Peace: A Multilayered Approach to Conflict Settlement

Introduction

Why is a multilayered approach to conflict settlement essential for the development of a sustainable peace? What do we miss if we only focus on the official peace processes at the macro level of political decision making? Where do identity changes manifest, and what meaning does this have for peace processes?

Listening to the stories of women from Chiapas and Northern Ireland in Chapter 3, I have outlined the way women became involved in the respective mobilization processes. Women's activism pathways differ based on the intersectional inequalities they have experienced, but intersect at different moments of social mobilizations against state-perpetrated injustice. The way women have engaged in processes of boundary formation and change in social mobilizations has been determined by women's positioning toward the state, the community, and the family; this is visible in women's changing perceptions of "normality." In episodes of contention in both cases, subaltern women's activisms shifted from mobilizing for practical everyday needs for the survival of the community to strategically promoting women's shared gender interests. This shift in women's activisms reveals a change in emphasis from ethnic to gender concerns and for both indigenous and working class republican activists this also entails a shift from an external (state) to an internal (movement) perspective.

Alliance formation between women is central to this change, particularly if feminist solidarity evolves across ethnic and class boundaries. In the previous chapter, I have outlined how cleavages between women from different backgrounds are deeper entrenched and multifaceted in Northern Ireland than in Chiapas. However, even where space for alliance building is limited (Northern Ireland), shifts in women's perceptions and positioning reveal the contestability and instability of the identity categories "ethnicity" and "gender."

This chapter examines how changes during conflict are translated into peace processes by focusing on women's positioning toward and perceptions of the public and private domain after peace agreements have been signed in Chiapas and in Northern Ireland.[1] Tracing positioning and perceptions of women in post-agreement processes, this chapter brings to light how the reengagement with the existing state structure in these processes shifts dynamics, positioning, and perceptions of dissident[2] women in Chiapas and in Northern Ireland. It connects changes in women's positioning toward the state, their community, and their family with shifts in their perception of normality.

In this chapter, I identify spaces for changing ethnic and gender identities, which enforce a change in unequal gender structures. I particularly highlight challenges in finding acknowledgment for shifts in ethnic and gendered perceptions and positioning evolving during conflict and in conflict settlement processes. These findings are fundamental in understanding what happens to women and to women's activisms in the aftermath of armed conflict. The chapter illustrates how identity and social processes either create contentious or constructive dialogues on women's shared gender interests across the gender, ethnic, class, and other boundaries. It further highlights the need for adapting changed gender images and more equal gender structures into the rebuilding of society post-peace agreement and the consequences if those needs are excluded from official peace processes. In a multidimensional analysis, the chapter highlights problems arising when changed female self-perceptions collate with remaining traditional male gender concepts, affirming gender inequality in Chiapas and in Northern Ireland.

Providing a deeper understanding of the potential for post-peace agreement contention between men and women or between individuals of the same gender, this chapter explores the centrality of dynamics, identity, and policymaking in the public sphere on the private realm. By doing so, it reveals opportunities and challenges resistance, focused on the core of indigenous organization "the collective" (Lenkersdorf, 1996), and the protest against the continuing neoliberal privatization discourse of the national government. The resisting Zapatistas highlighted in their protest against neoliberal Mexican government policies their connection to global dynamics, as evident in Mexico's cooperation with its northern neighbors, the United States and Canada in the North Atlantic Free Trade Zone and further free trade agreements.

The international dimension of the Zapatista protest, namely the resistance against neoliberal policies at the international, national, and local level, provided a space for alliance building beyond the borders of the core indigenous dimension and communities of the Zapatista Movement (DeVos, 2002, p. 399; Speed & Reyes 2002, 2005). Three events, the peace negotiations (1994–96), the "massacre of Acteal in 1997,"[9] and the "march for indigenous dignity" in 2001 marked key moments in the alliance-building process between the Zapatistas and a national and international support base. This support base includes civil society organizations, left-wing media,[10] prominent journalists,[11] and academics. Women's concerns, in particular those of indigenous women, featured prominently in the negotiation process, and in the post-agreement phase.

The focus on building autonomous indigenous community structure, the "caracoles,"[12] constituted the key element of the post-agreement process at the local level, which was significantly influenced by the development of a stronger international dimension: the alliance between the Zapatistas and civil society organizations through "the Other Campaign."[13] At the national level, important developments in the post-agreement period were informed by the Zapatista mobilization process. First, the end of the 70 years of PRI (Institutional Revolutionary Party) dictatorship in Mexico in 2000 and second, the reduction of military bases in Chiapas under the PAN (Party of National Action) government of President Vicente Fox (2000–2006). However, contemporary political, socioeconomic, and cultural developments in Mexico and Chiapas are marked by a return of a PRI-led national and regional government after the 2013 elections and a continuation of neoliberal government policies, evident in an emphasis on privatization and free trade agreements.

Reengaging with the State and Crossing Boundaries in the Public Sphere

As an indigenous woman, Blanca encountered many barriers to participating actively in society and being able to organize her private life the way she wanted to. As part of a farmers' organization, she supported the Zapatista uprising in 1994 and has shifted the focus of her activism from demands for farmers' and indigenous rights to the struggle for indigenous women's rights after the uprising. The peace talks were a powerful experience for her and opened a space to bring indigenous women's voices into government politics; from 2000 she lobbied with the support of mestiza feminists candidates of political parties running in local, regional, and national elections. She believes that using this strategy she can break down the dominance of male and mestiza women's voices and increase the visibility of indigenous women at government level. Together with other indigenous women she also presented their demands to international organizations, such as the United Nations, the European Union, and the like.

Though Blanca supports the Zapatistas, she believes that their resistance is "not enough to change the system. You need to engage with the government to create change, but it is important to remain critical and independent and not to get sucked into politics. I can talk to members of the Mexican parliament, I can negotiate a compromise, I can build alliances, I can achieve many things, I can be there and stand as a woman... and the men in the communities respect me for this."[14]

* * *

Maria, an indigenous Zapatista and women's rights activist, lives in an autonomous Zapatista community. The way indigenous women claim leadership functions in the movement was, for Maria, a fundamental aspect of her own progress; she highlights in particular the visibility of indigenous women in the peace talks in 1996 and Commander Esther speaking on behalf of the Zapatista Movement in the Mexican national assembly in 2001.

> Commander Esther has moved my heart when she spoke in the deputy chamber in parliament. She did not only speak for herself, she spoke for all of us; she expressed exactly what I wanted to say, it was what all of

us indigenous women wanted to say.[15] *Today [2010], I feel good, I feel confident and I feel supported by my fellow women: they share with me their voice and I share with them mine. There is a great solidarity amongst us women and a respect for everyone, no matter what ethnic group or organization we come from, no matter what education we have. There are sometimes barriers between women, but we know we can and have to overcome them. I am continuing on my way and I am walking every day a step more, I am constantly progressing. And that's my story.*[16]

A reengagement with the state in the peace negotiations (1994–96) and in the dialogue with the PAN government of President Vicente Fox in 2001 has strengthened women's belief in the peaceful transformation of unequal power structures. Indigenous women are proud about their active engagement in the peace process and feel encouraged in their activism for women's gender interests by both male and female comrades. Like Maria, many indigenous women (20 of 27) feel that the new forms of women's participation are stepping-stones on the way to greater gender equality.

The active participation of women in the public sphere during and after the peace talks has shifted the image of the "indigenous women" from a silent victim to an active agent of change. This is evident in particular in the symbolism of Commander Ramona displaying the Mexican flag at the peace talks in February 1994 and of Commander Esther speaking as representative of the Zapatistas in the Mexican parliament in 2001.

The march of the Zapatistas from their autonomous zones in Chiapas to Mexico City during February–March 2001, following the political change in the governments of both Chiapas and Mexico in 2000, was particularly important for revealing the way in which an opening of the movement has led to a shift in gender and ethnic boundaries. As part of the event, Commander Esther, an indigenous woman dressed in traditional clothes of her community in Huixtán, led a Zapatista delegation into the Mexican parliament and addressed the congress. In her speech, she condemned the racism of Mexican society against indigenous people and addressed oppression and violence against indigenous women in everyday life by "bad norms and traditions."

Not only their physical presence, but in particular their voices, representing the "voices of the voiceless" are of significant symbolic meaning for indigenous women's perceptions and positioning in post-agreement Chiapas. When Commander Esther, a small indigenous woman, raises her voice in the Mexican national assembly and speaks out not only for indigenous people, but in particular for indigenous women, she transforms the national image of indigenous women.

While individuals like Commander Ramona or Commander Esther became symbols of indigenous women's potential to transform their public images and positioning in society, they are not perceived as individuals, but as a voice of a collective of indigenous women. Instead of representing individual empowerment, they reveal a wider trend toward indigenous feminists' collective political action (Rovira, 1997; Stephen, 2002).

The boundary between women within and outside the Zapatista community is visible in the positioning of activists toward the state. While Zapatistas engaged as a group with the government in different episodes of conflict settlement (1994–96 and 2001), indigenous and mestiza activists positioned outside the movement boundary created different spaces of individual engagement with the government in Chiapas and Mexico; the peace talks opened opportunities for creating those spaces.

Blanca's story reveals how her participation in the peace negotiations (1994–96) has influenced her activism pathway in the post-agreement phase. Her belief in the possibility of changing unequal power structures is visible in her dual activism approach, consisting of first empowering indigenous women with the support of mestizas in independent grassroots activism and second in lobbying government and international agencies at the macro level. Through this engagement, her relationship to indigenous men has changed; men respect her and listen to her. In post-agreement Chiapas, the gender boundary is priority for her, evident in her decision to engage with the government to promote indigenous women's rights, rather than complying with the Zapatista approach of "nonengagement" and "silent resistance."

From 2000 onward, many women from the grassroots movements, particularly from farmers' organizations, became involved in the government of change in Chiapas, led by Governor Pablo Salazar Mendiguchía; some attaining leadership positions. This expanded the perspective of women from the grassroots to that of official state politics. Like Blanca, some female activists (8 of 36) talk about their engagement in a double dynamic: at the community level they support the Zapatistas in resistance, and at the state level they engage with government structures to create change. They highlight the opportunities and challenges occurring when working "en dos blusas"[17] (in two shirts); the central difficulty is to "work in an independent space and not becoming a part of official government structures [she] would like to change."[18] This is visible in the decision some activists (7 of 8) made to end their engagement with the government in Chiapas whenever they felt that "changes could be better made from the outside."[19]

Indigenous activists (8 of 8) feel that through their engagement with official government structures in Chiapas they have learned different skills in communication, negotiation, administration, building alliances, and so on. This has resulted in an increased self-confidence and respect shown to them by male members of their communities.

Identifying themselves as agents for women's issues, all female activists who participated in this project revealed the continuing priority of the gender boundary for them in the demobilization phase. Some indigenous women's (9 of 26) objectives of activism expanded from changing internal community structures to changing the politics of the state in Chiapas by bringing indigenous women to the fore. The freedom of choice to participate at different levels, including government agencies, shows an alteration in the social positioning of women. Their participation in government has reenforced Blanca's motivation to challenge unequal power structures rather than being absorbed by them. From their participation in government, female activists have learned that it is not just people but the whole system that has to change toward more "democracia de la base" (basic democracy).

While the positioning toward the state distinguishes activists (Millán Moncayo, 2006, p. 82), what unites them is the belief (22 of 36), that a bottom-up approach of democracy is required to institutionalize indigenous communities' autonomy and changes in its gendered structure toward more equality. Further, female activists are united across borders first, in their critique on the top-down approach of government, second, in their demand for radical change of the system, and third, in criticizing the negative impact of continuing neoliberal government discourses on their lives. Within this context, indigenous female activists living in Zapatista communities and indigenous and mestiza activists outside these boundaries (31 of 36) highlight the attempt of the government to divide women with welfare programs such as "Oportunidades."[20]

> Those programs are designed in a way that they incorporate female activists into the system and take away so much time from their daily schedule that it leaves without any space for activism... Despite being disempowering, they divide the Zapatista communities. If you are part of Zapatista communities in resistance you cannot join programs of the Mexican government; if you do, you need to leave those resistance communities.[21]

Another negative impact of government policies, highlighted in female activists' narratives (28 of 36), is the continued attempt to privatize indigenous community land; land pressure has been identified as a central reason for migration. Once they join the land-privatization program PROCEDE[22] program of the government, indigenous farmers who acquire land titles and take their piece of land out of the collective scheme are often obliged to sell their land due to financial pressures. This leads to an increase in migration of men to the north of Mexico or the United States, while women and children are usually left behind (Olivera, 2008). This migration is connected to the privatization of community land and affects both mestiza and indigenous women. However, the problem of male migration impacts differently on indigenous women's lives.

> In traditional indigenous communities women have to fulfill both their own duties in the home and their absent husbands' duties in the community to keep the position of the family within the collective landownership scheme, the ejido; this increases their workload.[23]

In autonomous Zapatista communities, traditional landownership and community leadership rules have changed to increase gender equality and women's participation; this has shifted women's positioning in the community. However, these changes have created additional difficulties for women, namely adapting their public role to their role in the private realm. While the number of men helping in the house has increased, some activists report that this change is happening slowly (8 of 36).

The transformation of indigenous women from "wordless"[24] via "discovering the words" in the mobilization phase to "having/possessing the words" in the post-agreement phase reveals how indigenous women gained self-confidence and dignity and regained control over their life. This process rooted them in their new identity; "knowing their rights" has "opened their eyes and their heart."[25]

This has also increased the self-confidence and the organization potential of indigenous women, which is evident in the growth in numbers of indigenous women protesting against sexist aggression against women from 200 in 1989 to 6,000 in 1996 (Kerkeling, 2003, p. 148). Indigenous women have further strengthened their positioning in their communities, which is visible in changes in landownership and community-leadership rules in the newly created autonomous communities. Third, indigenous women have through their participation in the peace talks and in the 'Alliance for Chiapas' government in 2001 increased their capacities and skills.

Improved educational attainment among indigenous women[26] has led to a better self-consciousness, a feeling of more security, and to a better ability to navigate in the post-conflict society. Their increased social capacity includes a greater outspokenness in their dialogue with mestizas and better access to positions in government agencies. Indigenous women's voices have found a new space to be listened to in the civil society organizations, particularly in the independent women's movement and in government agencies, which are often looking for bilingual speakers for development programs in indigenous communities. Many indigenous women have found employment that way, particularly in the Department for Indigenous People in Chiapas (SEPI). Recent research from this department provides evidence of the impact of indigenous voices within its work, for instance, the development of new indicators for collecting census data (SEPI, 2006).

A reengagement of the EZLN with the Mexican state in the peace negotiations (1994–96) and in the dialogue with the PAN government of President Vicente Fox in 2001 has led to a national dialogue on indigenous peoples' autonomy and has increased women's belief in the peaceful transformation of unequal power structures. The shift from violent to peaceful protest is also linked to an increased potential for wider alliance building with national and international civil society organizations during the peace negotiations, which it is felt has more potential for creating pressure for change in state structures through bottom-up approach than armed violence.

Female Zapatistas' aim to change Mexican citizenship or the "orientation of the nation" (Esteva, 2001, p. 249) has not been fully translated into political practice post agreement; however, indigenous women express the feeling that their voices are being heard and that progress has been made. For female indigenous activists, changes are particularly felt and are visible in private male-female relationships and in their dialogue and collaboration with mestiza women. In 2010, female grassroots activists, both indigenous and mestiza, continued their protest against both neoliberal and exclusive state policies and against unequal gender structures in their communities. Within this context, concerns about personal security interconnect in women's narratives on three different levels: the family (domestic violence, education, freedom of choice as regards marriage and children), the community (gender equality in land ownership schemes and community leadership), and the state (concept of citizenship as manifested in the constitution, militarization of the region, or attempts to divide the "activism community" through government programs). This has led to a multilevel approach in their activism.

Both indigenous and mestiza female activists feel that counterinsurgency policies of the Mexican government have changed from being openly repressive and violent in the immediate aftermath of the uprising of 1994 to being subversively destructive in post conflict. The low-intensity warfare of the state includes development programs that have had a negative impact on indigenous communities, such as the PROCEDE[27] or the antipoverty program Oportunidades. These political processes on the macro level are intertwined with the evolvement of new community structures (indigenous autonomy) at the community level and with women's lives in the private realm. Changes in the post-agreement episodes of contentious politics in Chiapas have led to shifts in the salience and in the content of women's ethnic, gender, and class boundaries.

Alternative Space for Building New Community Structures and Alliances

Tori, a human rights and women's rights activist from Tseltal community, describes the community of dreams map (fig. 4.1) she had drawn together with other indigenous women as follows:

This community map shows some ideas about how we would imagine our ideal community to be. We have painted a big house to

Figure 4.1 Map of the community of dreams.

Note: The map was produced during the workshop "Women and the conflict in Chiapas," Ocosingo (Chiapas), July 13 and 14, 2010.

symbolize the unity of our community. It is a house for women, where they can organize workshops or courses to make women stronger and to exchange our ideas with the men, this is a dream we would like to have realized in three years or so. We called it "the house of women" (snaj ansetic). We can see two compañeras facilitating a workshop for women. And outside the school boys and girls are playing together. We need to support the right of girls to go to school; equal access to education for girls and boys is a dream we have for the future. Everything is united under the Mexican flag, which we see at the bottom of the picture. We would like peace and social justice for all communities, not only for our communities, but for all communities. This is symbolized by the "palomas" (doves).[28]

Tori's narrative highlights a continuity of importance of the gender boundary in the phase after the peace talks, which is evident in the meaning she attributes to "community." The "unity of [her] community" refers to the indigenous women she cooperates with in the promotion of their shared gendered interests. While her emphasis is on the work with and for women in her own community, she further emphasizes the significance in integrating men into this work and in expanding her activism aims beyond her indigenous community. Tori's story connects the internal dimension of community building with the need to build alliances with those positioned outside her own community boundaries. As visible on the extended meaning of community beyond the indigenous community and that of women within those boundaries shows the changing dynamics in social movements in the aftermath of the armed confrontation between the EZLN and Mexican security forces.

In this phase, community building was influenced by the engagement with a wider national and international civil society and by changed gender dynamics; this is visible in the institutionalization of indigenous autonomy in the Zapatista Movement and in the development of farmer's organizations in the post-agreement episode (from 1996).

Zapatista Communities

For Antonia, her participation in the Zapatista Movement is an important part of her life; she was a fighter in the EZLN, but returned to live in a Zapatista community when she and her husband decided to have children. Antonia participated in the peace negotiations of 1996; it was for her a phase when many dynamics in the movement changed. Antonia feels that the vision of the Zapatista Movement began to change during the peace talks; when the movement moved closer to the civil society, the way of seeing things has changed as a result.

> *You see the very same situation you are in through another prism. Well I guess the armed conflict was one episode of the struggle and now we have entered another phase. It does not mean that it is the end of the fight, but we fight with other means now. But you do suddenly start to wonder about the origins of the struggle, has it been left behind when we moved into this different phase?... Everything seemed to have happened so quickly that I found it challenging to catch up. The discourse has changed and somehow some people from the base of the struggle felt suddenly a little bit distanced, a bit disconnected.*[29] *I*

don't regret what I have suffered in the struggle, what I have lived; on the contrary I feel that I am someone, it made me a woman, well I feel that now I am a woman.[30]

The failed implementation of the San Andres Peace Agreement has led to the institutionalization of an autonomous government structure (Burguete Cal y Mayor, 2005; Leyva Solano, 2001; Rus, Mattiace & Hernández Castillo, 2002). Although officially tolerated by the government, indigenous people are still at a risk of being attacked by state-sponsored paramilitaries and experience occasional harassment by security forces.[31] Women play an important role in the Zapatista autonomous structure, in particular, by being increasingly represented in community leadership through affirmative action and in this context through changing community rules and traditions (K'inal Antzetik, 1995; Millán Moncayo, 2008). By institutionalizing a quota system in the autonomous government structures, the Zapatista Movement has further increased women's participation in its internal political decision-making process. In particular, the voices of female Zapatista commanders provide evidence for a change in gender roles within both the EZLN and Zapatista communities (Speed, 2006; Stephen, 2002).

The Revolutionary Women's Law,[32] which manifested a women's vision of autonomy in the Zapatista discourse, was extended from 10 articles of Zapatista women's demands declared in 1993 to 31 articles in 1996, amendments that confirm the continuity and reflexive discursive processes of Zapatista women. While the first version of 1993 focuses mainly on gender roles in the Zapatista Movement, on the community level, the 31 demands of 1996 emphasize processes in the private realm: intimate partnerships and in particular the "meaning" and institution of marriage in indigenous traditions. The 1996 version of the Revolutionary Women's Law, for instance, sanctions the "right" of men to have more than one wife and outlaws domestic violence. The Women's Law forms part of the structure of indigenous autonomy in the Zapatista communities (Kerkeling, 2003, p. 151ff). Changes are visible for instance in Antonia's freedom as indigenous woman to choose her partner and to decide if she wants to have children and how many.

Indigenous women outside Zapatista autonomy do not completely reject either Mexican nationalism or autonomous indigenous discourses. Instead they have asserted themselves as simultaneously Mexican and indigenous (Hernández Castillo, 1997, p. 110). This self-identification provides evidence not only of the blurring of the ethnic boundary, but also of the transgression of the content of women's ethnic identity as a result of the Zapatista mobilization process. Developments toward a transnational Zapatista solidarity network dating back to 1995, which became more politicized and began to intersect with other transnational networks from 1996 onward (Olesen, 2005, p. 11), have opened new independent spaces for alliance building between mestiza and indigenous feminists.

Post-1996, the low-intensity warfare has increased the necessity of building a broader national and international alliance to support the objectives of the movement and to guarantee its survival. Consultations with the Mexican public and events such as marches and protests of Zapatistas to raise awareness of and increase support for their demands were stepping-stones in the organization of solidarity "outside" the movement's borders. In 1999, a nationwide consultation process on the San Andres Peace Accords was held, in which three million Mexicans cast ballots in favor of the implementation of the accords. The engagement with a wider civil society beyond the boundaries of the core Zapatista communities has secured the survival of the movement and its impact on Mexican politics and in the global movement against neoliberalism. While generally welcomed by Zapatista activists (15 of 17), some of them (3 of 17) highlight the change in dynamics that came with the increased emphasis on international Zapatismo.

For Antonia, the way of seeing and understanding things has changed; she feels it has changed because cooperation with the outside world became more important. This has shifted dynamics within the movement and has resulted in a feeling of "distance" and of "disconnect" from this new episode of social mobilization. At the same time, the opening to the wider civil society has supported the institutionalization of new, more equal gender structures and transformed gender images, which manifest this social change.

The Zapatista Movement connects different demand agendas (ethnic, national, gender, class) and different dimensions of protest (local, national, global); it therefore needs to be situated in, first, its particular history, second, in relation to the shifting contours of citizenship in Mexico, and third, in the changing relationship between nation-states and global capitalism (Berger, 2001, p. 150). The Zapatistas represent an important effort to renegotiate the relationship within marginalized groups and between those groups, the nation-state, and global capitalism. They address the marginalization of cultural communities and their indigenous traditions in the construction of the Mexican settler society and in the contemporary neoliberal globalization project. However, at the same time, their gender demands call for a transformation of some of those traditions, which are harmful in the way they affect women as part of indigenous communities.

The post-conflict shift in emphasis of the work of the Zapatista Movement from "the military" to "the political" and increased alliance building with local, national, and international civil society organizations reveals a "change in the vision and in the goal" of the movement, from a "marxist leninist" vision toward an awaking of global consciousness, based on a notion of mutual solidarity (Olesen, 2005, p. 111). The former Zapatista leader, Subcomandante Marcos,[33] has justified this change in direction by describing the armed struggle as "inevitably leading into an authoritarian situation and benefitting only a minority of the population" (as cited in, Olesen, 2005, p. 113). He further emphasized the need to cooperate with civil society to create social change; this way the movement begins to provide a platform for the empowerment and politicization of civil society (Bellinghausen, 1999).

The interconnection between the Zapatista Movement and national, regional, and international civil society organizations has intensified post-1996 and broadened through the creation of the "other campaign"[34] in 2005, which was formalized through the Sixth Declaration of the Selva Lacandona (Leyva Solano, 2008). The other campaign has further encouraged the "translocal organization of women" (Blackwell, 2008, p. 121ff), by creating a platform for constructive dialogue on indigenous rights and feminism, which has allowed for different aspects of feminisms and of women's ethnic and class background to be explored.

The change in perceptions and in positioning of indigenous women becomes visible in civil society organizations from 1996. In particular, the increase of indigenous women's voices in the women's movement and their different positioning in the farmers' movement in Chiapas has resulted in the blurring of ethnic and class boundaries between indigenous and mestiza women's rights activists. Development toward a constructive feminist dialogue across boundaries has been positively impacted upon by the shift in the Zapatista Movement from an internal focus on local indigenous communities and armed resistance to an emphasis on political work and on alliance building with civil society organizations, academics, and the like at a national and an international level in the settlement process.

The Farmers' Organizations in Post-Agreement Chiapas: A Space for Convergence of Indigenous Tradition and Feminist Activism

Mariana, an indigenous farmers' activist, highlights the symbolic function, Compañera Vicenta, the first indigenous female coordinator of a farmers' organization in Chiapas, for other indigenous women; it is increasing their participation not only in numbers, but also in changes in the way they participate. Addressing issues of gender equality on a regular basis, Compañera Vicenta encourages male members of the organization to support this agenda. However, Mariana observed that the increase in women's participation and the change of policies toward more gender equality has created a "difficult dialogue with men in the organization. Men don't want things to change. Men have more power and don't want to lose it."[35] For Mariana, the way women participate in the organization is determined by their situation in their home. She describes how the organization has created through workshops an open dialogue with men about their anger and anxieties. Progress is for her visible in the way more and more men in the organization speak up for women.

> "Men are aware that things are going to change if they want it or not. They are not saying anymore that 'it is good to beat a woman'; if they are abusive they are as ashamed about it."[36]

Through its long tradition of organization and mobilization, the farmer's movement has increased the visibility of indigenous women (Millán, 2008, p. 97; Toledo Tello & Garza Caligaris, 2006). From the 1990s onward, indigenous women's presence has increased in farmers' organizations both in women's groups and in leadership roles of organizations. While the voices of mestiza women as advisors have been respected from the 1970s onward, within the movement it was more difficult for indigenous women to make their voices heard. This began to change in the 1990s when the participation of indigenous women shifted from "simply being there" to "promoting each other" and "taking an active part" in the decision-making processes of the organization. In most farmers' organizations, a strong women's sector has developed that increases the active participation of indigenous women through extensive outreach work (Toledo Tello & Garza Caligaris, 2006).

The development of bringing indigenous women into leadership functions is slow and has been supported by affirmative action. However, evidence of the progress of indigenous women within farmers' organizations is the ARIC-Independiente, a farmers' organization which supported the Zapatista Movement and elected its first female president in 2010. The election of a female indigenous leader has increased indigenous women's self-confidence and has changed perceptions of what an indigenous woman can do. The inclusion of gender equality in the organization's agenda has impacted on moral principles in the farmers' movement, which is evident in perceptions of appropriate or acceptable behavior. The independent farmers' movement has provided a space for convergence of indigenous women's activism and the mestiza feminist agenda.

From Where We Stand: Toward a Constructive "Feminist Dialogue" across Borders

"Our plan illustrates a women's assembly to bring women together and to talk about our problems, to organize women we have to go back into our communities, and organize women in workshops like this one. We need to do this with men as well, women cannot change alone. We plan to have an assembly where we discuss women's issues and a march to raise awareness about the still existing gender inequality and violence against women."[37]

Describing the action plan toward change (fig. 4.2), Maria, an indigenous women's rights activist, feels that one day is never equal than the other, because together women make progress every day.

> *The gains that are made remain and occasional setbacks are best addressed by learning from them and by organizing to moving forward.*[38]

Figure 4.2 Action plan toward change.
Note: The map was produced during the workshop "Women and the conflict in Chiapas," Ocosingo (Chiapas), July 13 and 14, 2010.

She feels that while there is still a lack of understanding amongst men, there is also progress and men begin to understand better what is in women's hearts." Reflecting on her work with other women, Maria emphasizes that it is important to her to share the knowledge, ideas, and experiences each of them acquires through their activism. Change is for Maria a process, which can only be achieved if women and men from different backgrounds work together. While she feels that her indigenous feminism distances her more from mestiza feminists than from men in her own community, she is grateful for the support of mestiza activists. Through her increased awareness of women's rights she has begun to work for a women's organization after the armed conflict. "Being indigenous" is in this work of advantage, and not an obstacle. She has different experiences and different skills than the mestiza colleagues. Her mestiza colleagues appreciate her for being indigenous, for her language skills (Spanish and three different indigenous languages) and for the organizational experience she gained through the Zapatista mobilization process. Her collaboration with mestiza women is based on shared gender interests and on "respect for difference."[39]

* * *

In the fight for farmers' and for women's rights, Cristina, a mestiza feminist and community activist, experienced discrepancies between indigenous and mestiza women's rights activists; both the aims and strategies of their struggle were different. However, through her work with female Zapatistas after the uprising, Cristina came to "understand and to respect"[40] *the different experiences of oppression of indigenous women that distinguished her from them. In her view, this understanding and acknowledgment of differences was important for the cooperation between indigenous and mestiza activists.*

Post agreement, the meaning of activism for female indigenous activists is connected to "having learned how to walk"[41] and to being on the right path toward further progress. Indigenous women are proud in leading the way and feel encouraged in their activism for women's gender interests by the support of both male and female mestiza comrades. In order to work together across ethnic, class and other boundaries, female activists feel that they need to acknowledge these distinctions first. "Being aware of where women come from"[42] is important when working with other women.

The participation of indigenous women at the peace table is of symbolic significance, as it provides evidence for changing dynamics and self-perceptions of indigenous women on an internal level in the Zapatista Movement and externally in the relationship between mestiza and indigenous women (Gutiérrez & Palomo, 2000; Rojas, 1994).

The increased consciousness of being indigenous and being a woman harmonizes two processes: first, the creation of solidarity amongst men and women within the Zapatista Movement for gender equality, and second, the development of solidarity amongst women from different ethnic and class backgrounds on shared gender interests. The increase in "pride of being an indigenous woman" has not only resulted in highlighting male-female distinctions, but has also served to bring to the fore ethnic and class differences between female activists. While some mestiza feminists

(2 of 10) criticize the emphasis on ethnicity and class as dividing difference within women's activism, other mestiza and indigenous activists (20 of 36) have spoken about ways they have found to bridge these differences and move from a contentious to a constructive dialogue. Being conscious of their own identity and their own background at the same time as opening a space in their heart to listen and learn from the experiences of the other has led to a transcending of the hierarchies in the head. Engaging in a dialogue on women's gender interests by highlighting equality in difference, has become for many mestiza and indigenous activists the double intervention strategy, which they feel is needed to move forward and to create social change.

By acknowledging gender, ethnic, and class differences, and engaging in a dialogue of change with mestiza women and indigenous men, indigenous women feel that these boundaries have been transcended. This transformation process is based on the formation of "mutual solidarity" (Olesen, 2005, p. 111), which is centered on a reciprocal or two-way relationship between providers and beneficiaries, and blurs the differences between the two, allowing for indigenous and mestiza women and indigenous men and women to meet at the same level. Respect for difference is, as evident from Maria's narrative, seen as a stepping-stone in the development of shared solidarity on women's gender interests amongst mestiza and indigenous women. The impact of the formation of mutual solidarity between mestiza and indigenous women becomes visible in the way in which many indigenous Zapatista women, who have put emphasis on working on women's issues in their activism, have changed the dynamic of the independent women's movement in Chiapas post-1996.

Although ethnic and class boundaries have not gone away, they have been blurred by mestiza women changing their mind-set from "working for women" to "working with women." The initial relationship constructed between mestiza and indigenous activists during the farmers mobilization in the 1970s was based on a form of solidarity, which reaffirmed ethnic and class power structures by creating a relationship of providers (mestizas) and beneficiaries (indigenous), often called substitution solidarity (Watermann, 1998, 1999) or altruistic solidarity (Olesen, 2005). This dynamic began to transform in the 1990s, but it is particularly in the post-agreement process that a relationship between mestizas and indigenous women that acknowledges differences and is also based on the attempt to meet "the other" at the same level has formed.

The increase in the participation of indigenous women in the independent women's movement in Chiapas is evidence of a change in the dynamic between mestiza and indigenous activists toward a constructive dialogue. This demonstrates a changing trend in social activism from a top-down to a bottom-up dynamic; while the first is based on middle-class activists working for indigenous women, the latter focuses on the cooperation of women from different ethnic backgrounds on an equal level (Espinosa Damián, 2005, p. 85, Hernández Castillo, 2006, Lamas, 1986, p. 184

The Private Realm in Transition: From Traditional to Transitional Relationships

Carmen, a Tsotsil women's rights and Zapatista activist, feels that the "pain and rage" her husband expressed at the beginning of her active participation in women's groups has been transformed into "more calmness and understanding,"[43] highlighting a change of the dynamic in her intimate relationship. Her husband now "understands" that Carmen is her own person and not his property. Carmen believes that this change is a result of the Zapatista mobilization and that her continuing work on women's rights helped to manifest this change in her family.

After the armed conflict Carmen initially felt trapped between the old and the new indigenous world, but her work on women's rights provided her with the strength to stand up to her husband and his "macho lifestyle."[44] He was unfaithful and reacted violently when his behaviour was challenged. But his behaviour subsequently changed and their relationship improved.

> The seeds that were sown in the [Zapatista] movement, all that learning about equality between men and women is there and helped us to develop a new relationship. He understands now that his macho behavior is not OK.[45]

Carmen describes that the "heaviness of their relationship lifted once he began to support her and help in the house and with the children when she went to workshops and other events."[46] This transition has not been easy, but working with other women helped her acquire different skills, confidence, and created a space to reflect on her own life, which was for her transformative. Bringing together indigenous and women's rights in her activism is for her like "adding salt to lemon."[47] *She perceives as natural consequence of her activism in the Zapatista Movement becoming a women's rights defender. Today (2010), Carmen describes her relationship with her husband as balanced and based on "understanding."*

> *Life is a constant adjustment and as much as he needs to understand me and my needs, I need to understand the challenges this new balance brings for him. But things around us have changed and it is not OK anymore for men to treat women badly. But change is slower in men than in women... This is visible in the many young girls who decide to remain single; they are more afraid to end up in a violent relationship, than to be a "mujer dejada" (left behind woman). And being a single mother is now a part of the new normality.*[48]

For indigenous women, change in the home is interconnected to change in the public sphere, both at the community and at the state level. A result of the Zapatista mobilization process is that many young women now consciously decide against the tradition of becoming wife and mother (Collier & Lowery Quaratiello, 1999, p. 114ff). They remain single and decide not to have children or raise them as single mothers, expressing the need to take control over their lives. The image of single mothers has changed in indigenous communities from "being inappropriate" to "being acceptable" and a part of the new normality. The former "fear" of remaining unmarried, of being a *mujer dejada*, has been replaced with the desire for more independence, self-respect, and dignity. On the one hand, the new image of the "single mother" as part of the normality illustrates the change that has happened in the lives of indigenous women. However, on the other hand, the rise in the number of single mothers is an indicator of how this change has been slow and in a way asymmetrical as men have more difficulties in adapting to it and women often lack trust in men accepting "that a woman can do whatever she likes to do."[49]

Changes in perceptions and positioning of indigenous women become particularly visible in power shifts in male-female relationships in the private realm; this becomes evident in a better "understanding" amongst men for women's situation and for women's needs as a result of the mobilization process. Many female indigenous activists (9 of 17) refer to a change in men's attitudes toward them from "being violent" to "being supportive," but emphasize that this concerns mainly male Zapatista activists who are more supportive than non-Zapatistas of women in both the public (autonomous government) and the private (family) sphere. However, problems remain in adapting new public gender roles to the private realm. Many indigenous women (11 of 17) feel that transformative processes are confronted with remaining traditions, which are based on gender inequality. Accounts of changes in women's positioning and perceptions often reveal male anxiety, confusion, and lack of self-confidence, but also an increased understanding for the need for changes in male-female relationships. For many female activists, this understanding of men is central for the transformation and reconstruction of male-female relationships. The dialogue on community traditions in the Zapatista Movement provided a space for this understanding to develop as it brought men and women together, debating discrepancies in male and female roles and perceptions. Many activists (9 of 17) feel that this dialogue has helped them to transform the relationships to their husbands in the aftermath of armed conflict.

While men largely accept and support the active participation of women outside the private sphere, "domestic duties and child care are often barriers for complete transformation of gender roles."[50] However, there is evidence of changes in the private sphere, for example, whereas indigenous men carrying their children was considered not normal and inappropriate in the public domain before the social mobilization process, now it forms a part of the new normality post conflict. This is particularly true for Zapatista communities, where men taking care of their offspring while their wives attend public duties have become a part of the "normal" community life.

Peace Patterns of Change: Women's Perceptions and Positioning in the Demobilization Process in Northern Ireland

The Good Friday/Belfast Peace Agreement, signed in Belfast on April 10, 1998 (Good Friday), by the British and Irish governments and endorsed by most Northern Ireland political parties, was a major political development in the Northern Ireland peace process. Women gained a significant profile in the first phase of the peace process, which took shape in the early 1990s, with a marked deescalation of violence from 1994. As rumors of ceasefires and planned peace negotiations began to dominate the political arena from 1993, female activists organized within and outside the Republican Movement to discuss strategies to include their voices and experiences in a meaningful way in the process (Cockburn, 1998; Hackett 1995, 2004; Ward 2004).

Republican women came together in 1992 in a coalition of feminists, the Cumann na d'Teachtaire (League of Women Delegates), and organized a feminist conference, Clár na mBan (Women's Agenda for Peace), in Belfast in March 1994, which was attended by 150 women. Oonagh Marron, one of the conference participants, outlines the purpose of the conference as follows:

> As nationalist women and as feminists, we have very often given our support unconditionally to the overthrow of British colonialism in this country. We have often buried our demands for the sake of a common purpose—Brits out. In the past, that has been a way of censoring our demands. The danger is that once again we will be asked to bury our demands, this time in the common purpose of achieving peace. (Clár na mBan, 1994, p. 9)

These concerns and interests of women were addressed to the political domain of the republican community and beyond its borders. Within and outside the Republican Movement, women perceived the ceasefires of republican and loyalist paramilitary groups in 1994 as a catalyst for change. The ceasefires opened a space for increasing women's political involvement and for promoting women's concerns in a peace agenda (Fearon and McWilliams 2000). In the early 1990s, conferences were organized[51] to address concerns about the exclusion of women from the official peace process. These conferences addressed the problem of the traditional absence of women from macro-level political decision making in Northern Ireland, as often remarked in secondary literature (Bell, 1998, Galligan, Ward, & Wilford, 1999; Miller, Wilford, & Donoghue 1996).

The Northern Ireland Women's Coalition (NIWC), an alliance representing women's concerns at the forum and the multiparty peace talks starting in 1996, emerged as a result of these conferences. Promoting "inclusion, equality, and human rights" and containing both nationalist and unionist women in their ranks, the Women's Coalition brought a social agenda to the peace table that went beyond the major parties' focus on sectarian issues. Many aspects of the peace agreement are linked to the women's participation in the talks, such as the recognition of the victims of the conflict, the civic forum, references to women's rights to full and equal participation in the political process, and so on. Despite this progress, gender equality remains post agreement a central feature in the different dimensions of society in Northern Ireland. Distinctions between female grassroots activists, "community feminists, and independent feminists" have been reaffirmed during the peace talks. Female activists' concerns over "who is representing women's voices" in macro-level political decision making reveals how not acknowledging women's different identities and experiences (Hackett, 1995, p. 115) can limit women's activism.

The episodes I am focusing on in this chapter include a) the beginning of the peace process in the early 1990s leading up to the multiparty peace talks starting in 1996, b) the formal peace negotiations from 1996–98, and c) the following demobilization or conflict settlement process (1998–2010). With communities in resistance moving closer to the state level during the peace process, interconnected dynamics between the state, community, and micro level of society or the private realm are changing. During these times of transition, intersecting boundary processes, in particular at the gender boundary, were determined by the interconnection of changes in relationships and structures at different levels of society.

Reengaging with the State: Women's Activism between Increased Horizons and Limited Structures

Increased Horizons in the Preparation for Peace (Early 1990s–96)

For Bairbre, a feminist women's rights activist, the leading up to the peace talks "was a moment in time where people felt that this might work and it was a feeling about the new millennium, a tiredness of weariness."[52] *Back then, she felt anxious and angry about the possibility that women who kept the communities going with their voluntary activism would be excluded again.* Bairbre believes that "women were actually needed to make peace work properly."[53] She remembers that working for women's inclusion in the political peace process "was a feeling like if you have been at the bottom of a hill and you can see the peak and then once you reached that, you can see that there is a peak behind the peak, and then again a peak behind that and then there is one behind that and so on and so forth."[54]

The peace process in Northern Ireland opened different spaces for women's activism in a changing political environment. Opportunities for women's activism in a first episode of peace (early 1990s–96) are connected to a new normality, in particular, for republican activists whose perceptions shifted from "fighting the war to fighting for peace."[55] Second, most female activists from within and outside republican communities entered this first episode of peace with changed perceptions; these changes were evident in an increased self-confidence and an awareness, as well as an active promotion of women's shared gender interests. Third, new mechanisms were introduced, such as a proportional representation voting system with single transferable votes for peace talks, which favor women's participation in political decision making at the macro level of society.

Republican Women between Alternative and Tradition

For Niamh, a feminist republican community activist, the start of the peace process has opened a space where it was possible for her to "start combining [her] feminism and republicanism more actively." During the conflict she felt sometimes alienated from her republican community, as here "the priority was always the war, the military movement"[56] *and she did not feel part of that military movement. In the lead up to the official peace negotiations, Niamh and other female republican community activists were putting pressure on Sinn Fein to make sure that women's rights are part of what they would have been negotiating for. However, the space for bringing feminist and republican demands together became limited for Niamh, when Sinn Fein was excluded from the talks.*

> *So my campaign then became, to get Sinn Fein at the talks, not even around what they were going to do in the talks, but just even to get them there. So, my demands got really reduced there.*[57]

The beginning of the peace process opened new spaces for creating alliances for republican female activists mainly within the republican community. Concerned that women's voices would be pushed to the margin again and be absent from the formal discussion and debate when negotiating peace, republican women organized around the Women's Agenda for Peace in the hope to achieve peace with justice and guarantees of equality for all the citizens of their country, male and female (Clár na mBan, 1994). Feeling no longer stigmatized as outcasts, female republican activists speak out against an overwhelmingly male composition of traditional political parties. Sinn Fein, having a significant amount of women in its ranks, stands out for them from the traditional political arena; however, Sinn Fein was also the primary target of some female republican community activists (5 of 11), as the women felt that Sinn Fein could not always be trusted to make women's gender interests a priority (Hackett, 2004).

Identifying with anti-imperialist feminism formed the basis for cooperation and coordination of republican grassroots activists in 1992. Female activists report feeling "totally engaged" and "absorbed" by the process and "excited" by the thought that "feminism" and "republicanism" were coming together as opposed to being seen as contrary.

At a republican Women's Day event in 1995, women highlighted the absence of female voices at the peace table and criticized the fact that "men are negotiating with and for men" (An Phoblacht/Republican News, 1995), while women were mainly present "in the background" (Bell, 1998, p. 223). Some female republican activists (4 of 11) felt that the initial exclusion of Sinn Fein from the peace talks reduced the space for their roles and their demands in the political decision making process. (Ashe, 2012, p. 233; Byrne, 2009) The way in which concerns of having their own community represented at the talks (from 1996) became a priority over gendered interests is evidence of the reaffirmation of the ethnic boundary in the second phase of the peace process.

The NIWC as Space for Activism

For Bairbre it is an important step in women's activism in post-agreement Northern Ireland that both grassroots women and what she describes as "independent feminists from more traditional women's groups"[58] *came together and created the NIWC. She remembers* that "*it wasn't easy, because the nontraditional grassroots women's groups were criticized by independent women's groups for their lack of structure. They have no AGMs, constitutions, set procedures, and so on.*"[59] *Bairbre feels that the criticism was justified, but also acknowledges that community women's groups organized in a different way.*

Within the process of organizing the NIWC she begins to notice "*that the difference is not between nationalist-republican, unionist-loyalist in the working class communities, (but) it's actually between the classes.*"[60]

Alliance building between women in the north and the south of the Island of Ireland, in addition to the collaboration between rural grassroots activists and urban feminists, centered on the aim of representing a "strong female voice" in the process from conflict to peace, as expressed at a conference organized in 1995 by the Northern Ireland Women's European Platform (NIWEP) and the National Women's Council in the Republic of Ireland (Fearon and McWilliams, 2000, p. 134). In this context, the consultation process of the Opsahl commission[61] in 1992–93 and experiences in preparing for and attending the Fourth World Conference of Women in Beijing in 1995, both criticize the one-dimensional politics focused on the constitutional position of Northern Ireland and its alienating and disempowering impact on women (Hinds, Hope, & Whitaker, 1997). These processes are often mentioned (7 of 17) in their function to build the groundwork for the NIWC. The Women's Coalition brought a broader social agenda to the table, focusing on "inclusion, equality, and human rights," which expanded the major parties' focus on sectarian issues.

Despite externally criticizing the NIWC for not taking a stand on the constitutional question, which was perceived as an attempt to homogenize women, and failing to acknowledge difference in background and experience, many female republican activists (8 of 11) gave Sinn Fein their first and the NIWC their second preference in the elections for the peace talks. Some grassroots activists (5 of 11) felt that their voices were less represented in the NIWC than those of "middle-class feminists."

> The Women's Coalition wasn't that inclusive itself, it was pretty much based in this middle class kind of level. All the women on the top were academics and when it came close to the elections and they had to look at the grassroots they were just pulling in a few women and that was it.[62]

Feminists (3 of 6) from "traditional women's groups"[63] outside the republican or loyalist community boundaries contest their identification as being "middle class" and, in turn, criticized community activists for a lack of effective organization and for their patriarchal community structures. However, traditional women's rights activists also acknowledge that "it's very easy that more grassroots and working-class women get squashed by more articulate middle class women."[64]

Despite these contentions, the NIWC was a stepping-stone to bringing women into the political peace process and to ensuring "that any talks or any elections for talks should involve more [voices] than those of the traditional political parties."[65] Including the voices of women who identify themselves as unionists and Protestants was a further challenge. While a historical accommodation between republicanism and feminism existed in the links between feminist and ethno-national protest against state perpetrated injustice, the lack of these connections in unionist ideology created a challenge for women from unionist backgrounds to engage in the women's initiative (Rooney, 1995b, p. 45).

The NIWC was successful in its aim of revealing the exclusion of women and women's concerns from the peace process and in the impact it had on the development of unique post-agreement human rights, equality, and justice bodies. However, it was limited in its achievements as the emphasis on power sharing in the Good Friday/Belfast peace agreement reduced the space for the representation of women's issues in post-agreement politics. As a consequence, the process started by the all-women coalition lacked continuity within Northern Irish politics.

While spaces for activisms promoting women's shared gender interests open in the early 1990s, they are limited as result of the increased emphasis on the ethno-national boundary in the formal peace talks (1996–98). The formal peace process from 1996 has detriggered the gender boundary and has retriggered already existing cleavages between female activists, based on their different experiences and perceptions.

Limiting Peace Structures Post-Peace Agreement (1998–2010)

Elizabeth, a civil and women's rights activist, feels that women in Northern Ireland "are not in a good place right now."[66] *She believes that there was a space "earlier on in the peace process"*[67] *to include the experiences and perspectives of women, but that the external pressure required to do so was missing. She criticizes that therefore the issues the NIWC was raising still remain to be addressed, in particular, in terms of women's representation in all of the institutions that have been set up after the peace agreement was signed; "women are still not there in terms of numbers."*[68] *Elizabeth emphasizes that although women's voices have not gone silent, there is not that much space for them, due to the fact that "the political parties are still so male dominated."*[69] *While acknowledging that a lot of parties have more than 50 percent membership of women, she criticizes the lack of women in leadership functions. She further believes that an autonomous women's movement is required to bring women's rights into political decision-making processes and achieve long-term changes.*

* * *

Female activists feel that post agreement, the Northern Irish state remains dominated by conservative male dominated politics, and by the traditional divide between Protestants and Catholics, a distinction, that has been reemphasized through the emphasis on ethno-national identity in the framework of the Good Friday/Belfast peace agreement. The negotiations of a power-sharing model of governance, emphasizing the major ethno-national cleavage, were at the heart of the formal peace process, which led to the signing of the Good Friday/Belfast peace agreement on April 10, 1998,[70] upheld in referendums in Northern Ireland and in the Republic of Ireland. Elections to the new Northern Ireland assembly were held on June 25, 1998, and Westminster formally devolved power to the Northern Ireland assembly and institutionalized the new government institutions.[71]

The presence of the Women's Coalition at the peace table was for many female activists (10 of 17) essential and led to the inclusion of general issues of human rights and equality in the peace agreement, resulting in the implementation of a Human Rights Commission and equality safeguards such as the Equality Commission for Northern Ireland. Further, section 75 of the Northern Ireland Act entails the obligation for all public bodies to "promote equality of opportunity, between persons of different religious belief, political opinion, racial group, age, marital status or sexual orientation; between men and women generally; between persons with a disability and persons without; between persons with dependents and persons without" (Northern Ireland Act, 1998). These mechanisms have led to progressive legislation on same-sex civil unions, employment equity, and social welfare, which shows the positive impact of the NIWC on the peace process.

The limitation for space to address women's shared gender interests in the political decision-making process at state level impacts negatively on alliance building on women's gender interests, particular across the ethnic and class divide. Some female activists (15 of 17) feel that the male-dominated political sphere and the lack of a strong, independent women's voice in Northern Irish politics reenforced conservative structures in the post-agreement period and pushed women and women's shared gender interests back to the margin of political decision making.

> Women do all the work and do all the lifting and men do all the heavy politics and all the heavy talking. And they come up as the male spokesperson when things like that occur. And that comes in waves and sometimes that isn't as bad, but at the minute I think we are in a particularly bad phase... electoral politics actually is a sort of patriarchal environment that promotes men because of the way it is structured.[72]

By triggering the ethnic distinction, the Good Friday/Belfast Agreement has reduced class and gender demands in post-agreement Northern Ireland. This becomes particularly visible in the communal designation of MLAs,[73] which bases the formation of political solidarity on the Catholic-Protestant divide (Wilford & Wilson, 2003) and increases the incentive for voters to support Nationalist and Unionist parties as they have more weight in the assembly than others (Gilland & Farrington, 2006, p. 718–19).

Republican grassroots women (7 of 11) feel their gender interests are deprioritized within Sinn Fein as a result of the negative impact of the conservative nature of male-dominated Northern Irish politics at the macro level on their community. In this context, some women (3 of 7) highlight the support of the republican party Sinn Fein for a motion of the Democratic Unionist Party (DUP) against the extension of the 1967 British Abortion Act in 2007 (Northern Ireland Assembly, 2007; Sinn Fein, 2007).

As community work starts to become professionalized and people are getting paid for their activism, the boundary between activism outside the state structure and the paid job inside this structure gets blurred. This challenges women's struggles for their gender interests by making women's activisms a part of gendered power structures at the macro level of society it sets out to break down. First, the peace money moves social movements closer to the state structure and brings a new dynamic into social mobilization processes, which limit the protest potential of local communities.

> There is less involvement by the actual local people; it's more that the local people are the clients than having the ownership over the projects. It's rather that the community organizations deliver services than being a more local force of mobilization. It is much less spontaneous, for example, to do a picket, which we would have done of the pick of a hat (immediately), that would take today probably three months to organize, you know.[74]

Second, the way community funding is distributed follows the power-sharing model of governance and highlights the ethnonational boundary, which in turn takes the emphasis away from women's demands for the realization of their shared gender interests. Although European funding requirements entail a strong equality dimension, they lock shifts in republican women's gender perceptions between gender equality rhetoric and unequal gender practice. Furthermore, the emphasis on gender equality has reduced the space for women's issues.

> All had to be gender proofed and...we can't really talk about women in this case we need to talk about gender, because there is that 1 percent suffering domestic violence that are men. [This] became a huge issue to Women's Aid back about six years ago, because they had a phone line for women who were sexually abused and they were told that they would lose their funding unless they would open that to men who were sexually abused. Because that was been seen as discrimination against men and that was been seen as an issue under section 75.[75]

Women's narratives on post-agreement Northern Ireland highlight the difficulties involved in breaking down existing unequal gender power structures at the state level of political decision making. Many female activists (7 of 17) feel that the Women's Coalition had potential to create more substantial social change for women, but did not succeed in pushing for the implementation of crucial structural steps like a voting system based on proportional representation with single transferable vote (PRSTV) for assembly elections or a quota for women's political representation. While the first phase of the peace process (early 1990s) provided a space for forming alliances and for including women and women's perspectives into the peace debate, the formal single-axis peace process (1996–98) with its focus on the ethnic divide limited this space. However, "women have not gone away"[76] and changes in gendered perceptions and positioning remain salient to a certain extent at the community level and in the private realm.

Changing Community Borders: Grassroots Activists between Conflict and Peace

During the conflict, Eilish was part of the republican community support network and active in the struggle for gender equality in her community. Reflecting on the transition phase between peace and conflict, she expresses some difficulties she had experienced in moving from mobilization to demobilization in the beginning of the peace process. For Eilish, the ceasefires meant to enter a sphere of insecurity "by giving up the guns that were not only a symbol of power and security, but also of self-determination."[77] She thought the first ceasefire was a bit premature, but recognizes that "it got people to enter in their mind-set that things could change and that they could change drastically."[78] For Eilish the belief that change was possible is central to demobilization. However, she admits that it takes more than giving up guns to have peace; it requires for the "whole social structure to be changed."[79] While she emphasizes that she still feels part of her republican community, she also notes that her commitment to the community is not that strong anymore, "because it does not have to be."[80] Post agreement, she also perceives the people of Northern Ireland, both Protestants and Catholics as "us." Moreover, after 1998, she perceives the people of Northern Ireland as a united political force and a threat for "the politicians in the South [of Ireland who] are more afraid of 'us'... because there would be no way we would take the nonsense that's going on there [in the Republic of Ireland]."81

* * *

During the conflict, Fiona was active in the IRA. Coming to terms with peace was difficult for her.

> I was very emotional, I was very afraid of what would happen here. The big fear, particularly for people who were so active, within the movement, was that we would be going down the road like the SDLP, like some of those other constitutional parties and that was it. We are just going to go in and sit in these bodies and that's it; and then there was the danger of the movement splitting in many fragmented groups."82

However, the growing awareness "that this was more than about a flag, more than was I Irish or was I British [motivated her] to make the transition from an armed struggle to an exclusively political one."83 *From a post-agreement perspective, she believes that the armed struggle was* "never anything more…than a tactic, [but] it became a tactic you become very accustomed to."84 *Fiona felt she was* "morally duty bound"85 *to move out of the mind-set of the war and the military toward the mind-set of peace and the political. Reflecting on her life today (2010) she notes:* "I'm starting to think now about insurance [and] mortgages, all that stuff of normal daily life."86 *Fiona further highlights that* "there are now more options for women…and they feel good about themselves and they feel more confident now."87 *She left school early and often thought that she does not have the education to do what she wants.*

> [But] that mind-set has changed now, you know, people even if they are older are going back to education and they go to different classes to learn whatever it is they would like to try out… I have a friend who is almost 60 and now she is on a course to try and help others. Whilst before the struggle she would have said "I couldn't do that, I wouldn't have the confidence."88

For many women who have been actively involved in the military activity of the Republican Movement (5 of 7), it was difficult to come to terms with the violence of the conflict and particularly the violence they were involved in themselves and which had become "a tactic you become very accustomed to."[89] Republican activists have moved from advocating the use of violence to the belief that a United Ireland can only be achieved by peaceful means. However, some women who were active in the IRA (3 of 7) connect with the ceasefires a fear that the beginning of the peace process would be the end of a United Ireland and of the Republican Movement. The transition from the armed struggle to an exclusively political further becomes possible with the realization that the conflict "was more than about a flag,"[90] more deep-seated than about ethnic identity; that it was also about socioeconomic justice. Fiona highlights that, for her, socioeconomic issues were more salient in the settlement process than the ethno-national divide.

The republican community continues to play an important role for women who are engaged in political activism in the lead up to the peace talks. However, for female activists who identify as "community activists" the commitment to community politics has changed and is not as strong. It "does not have to be,"[91] as the ethnic boundary has ceased to be a question of life and death.

Many republican activists (6 of 11) describe the post-agreement situation as liberating as it enabled them to be open about their Irishness; not having to hide their Irishness anymore detriggered the salience on their ethnic identity, as now they do not have to fight for it anymore. Within this context, for many female republican grassroots activists, the meaning of security has shifted from concerns about the survival of "the community" to highlighting socioeconomic inequality, antisocial behavior, domestic violence, and the struggle for gender equality within and beyond the borders of the community. A shift in perceptions of normality is evident from Fiona's post-agreement concerns about insurance and mortgages.

Eilish's notion of "the people of Northern Ireland" reveals a shift from a one-dimensional "black and white" perspective of activism to a multidimensional perspective, including class and gender perspectives. For female republican activists, a new feeling of communality marked the first episode of the peace process (early 1990s–96) as a "gray zone" in which compromises could be found based on the respect and equal acceptance of individuals from different sides of the ethno-national divide. In order to make peace work, republican women moved out of their comfort zone, from the black and white "us" versus "them" to an "us and them" perception of Northern Irish society. Grassroots activists from republican communities made a transition from the rejection of "the orange state for orange people"[92] to an active engagement with and participation in the Northern Irish state. This shift indicates an increasing acceptance of Northern Ireland as their state. While the republican community remains important, "we people and politicians in the North"[93] in opposition to the politicians in the south becomes a second dimension of female activists' identification. This identification is connected to a feeling of pride in the way the communities in the North have managed to overcome their differences and to move from sectarianism to promoting human rights and social justice. The positive self-identification with the Northern Irish community indicates a change in the ethnic identity category through the extension of the notion of community from republican to Northern Ireland linked to shared values of social justice, experiences of violence, and culture. This allows for changes in the content of gender identity to feature more prominently in republican women's narratives of the early 1990s.

Highlighting the positive changes for women in their communities, female republican activists (8 of 17) highlight that their grassroots activism has widened their horizons and allowed them to attain a higher level education. The engagement in further education has provided for some grassroots activists a space for formalizing their experiences to improve their access to the labor market. Further, having a degree has increased the self-value of working-class women.

However, the role of republican women in community activism changed post agreement; although they stay "involved, they do not always come to the fore."[94] Mainly the voices of those women who adapt to male structures are represented at the macro level of political decision making, while others are silenced again.

While voluntary activism during the armed conflict opened an autonomous space for women to participate and to create new structures and identities by bringing their private issues into the public sphere, paid post-agreement activism has brought back traditional male power structures in the community or grassroots sector.

> Because a lot of men have come back to the local communities after 1999 a lot of the paid jobs have been taken by the men. So women would have done the work on a lower pay or volunteer basis, and they would have been pushed back and men would have come back in.[95]

Women often step down and "let the men get into the jobs,"[96] particularly when as a result of the Good Friday/Belfast Agreement, men detained for IRA activities were released and had to be reintegrated into their communities; as a result the competition for jobs increased. Within this context, some female grassroots activists (6 of 11) criticize the way women's activisms are perceived in public discourses as natural extension from women's homemaking and how as a result of this, women are expected to return again to the private realm.

Many republican activists (5 of 11) note the benefits of the peace money for their communities and their own development; they highlight the way in which their community jobs allow them to be independent, albeit the work in the community and in the home increases their workload. However, some of them (3 of 5) are cautious about the dependency on the peace money and the need for their community to be self-sufficient.

> Well I see all that money coming in now and that's brilliant, but we need also a back-up plan. Yes, the money helps us to develop further, but we need to remain creative...I think that people are more self-sufficient than they think and they are stronger then they think. We need to be careful that that does not go away.[97]

Shifting from war to peace required from grassroots activists a change of mind-set and resulted in a decrease in the strength of their commitment to their community, and in a change in the meaning of community. This shift on the ethno-national boundary becomes visible in the emphasis of republican grassroots activists on "we" meaning the Northern Irish people. As a result of the structural changes evolving from the implementation of the peace agreement, grassroots activists from republican communities are moving closer to the official state structures. This leads to a shift in perceptions of "being Irish" from an outsider to an insider identity in the Northern Irish State. This development limits the alternative space for transforming gender images and structures that opened during the conflict and in the first episode of peace at the community level. The peace agreement leads to the development of new ethno-national structures at the state level, where traditional gender structures remain. These traditional gender power structures place women as wives and mothers in the private realm. The way traditional structures and images that determine the state level penetrate the community sphere reduces feminist agency in republican communities. This becomes visible in the structures, which are created by the peace money and supported by traditional gender images.

From Where We Stand: Toward a Contentious "Feminist Dialogue" across Borders

Post agreement, the way in which different cleavages (ethnicity, nationalism, class, education, generation/age) are triggered limits the space for women to unite across these borders to promote their shared gender interests. For instance, the new dynamic the peace money has brought to Northern Ireland's society diverts the emphasis from the gender boundary.

Grassroots activists (7 of 12) criticize that it is "more likely that middle-class women get the money and jobs, than the working-class grassroots activists, because they are better educated and more structured."[98] Educational attainment plays a significant role in women's activism post-peace agreement, in particular, in connection to access to available financial support for community projects.

Community feminists (8 of 17) highlight that their grassroots activism has widened their horizons and allowed them to engage in further education; this has provided for some grassroots activists a space for formalizing their experiences in order to improve their access to the labor market. Having a degree has increased the self-value of republican working-class women and allowed them to proudly defend their "community feminism," which is based on their experiences of being a woman, being from a working-class background, and being Irish. However, not all grassroots activists have attained higher education degrees as a result of their engagement. The formalization of community work and its restructuring into a professionalized sector has pushed some female activists to the margins of this sector; this includes some women from loyalist working-class backgrounds or from older age cohorts, who have contributed significantly to community-building during conflict, but have not translated this experience into formal education degrees.

> There are a lot of opportunities and training for women to join public bodies, consumer board, but many women do not have the qualifications to run for it, well they have the school of life

qualifications, they have managed to running a house, you are mediator and a negotiator on a daily base...They might not have it in form of an educational certificate, but they do have the skills through their experiences and the challenges.[99]

Generational, class, and ethno-national boundaries are highlighted in reflections on the availability of jobs in the public sector and on the connection between education and paid professional activism in post-agreement Northern Ireland.

Formal education is very good as it helps people to achieve something, to get jobs in the community sector, but there are an awful lot of people sitting here in their 40s or 50s who have been unable to get that formal education, but have an amount of experience which are just, you couldn't buy, you know.[100]

The professionalization of community work has limited the access to the sector for many women from loyalist working-class communities and from older age cohorts. The way funding for activism and community jobs can be accessed triggers the ethno-national, generation, and class boundary. The availability of public funding for community work has changed for some (8 of 17) the meaning of and the dynamic within their activisms. Access to jobs and funding is more easily available for "academic activists,"[101] meaning activists with a third-level education degree. Some female activists (5 of 11) from republican working-class areas also report a perception of their own disadvantage in comparison to "more middle-class activists" who are often better educated and therefore have advantage in applying for financial support for projects. This provides evidence of an increase in the competition between women for the peace money, which contributes to a deepening of the divisions between "academic activists and community activists."[102]

Divisions between grassroots women, deeply rooted within their community, and independent feminist activists "outside the community" highlights the significance not only of ethno-national identification, but also of class solidarity, of age and education. The highlighting of these boundaries has resulted in a detriggering of the gender boundary; this leads to an emphasis on the distinction between academic, often middle-class feminists with a well-structured mode of organization, and rather unstructuralized grassroots activism. This shows how the competition for financial support and jobs has limited the possibility for alliance building among women from different backgrounds in the settlement process.

The Private Realm between Transition and Tradition

As IRA volunteers, both Aoibhin and her husband have served time in prison, but this experience has shaped their lives differently. Aoibhin, a republican community activist, believes that while women outside the prison environment moved on, men who have been interned for many years "come out with a different view and things were different back then... It is very hard for a marriage to survive when someone was in prison, many marriages didn't survive... Some men got out and expected women to fall back into that traditional role. But women are not going back, I certainly wouldn't."[103] *Her husband did not cope well with the changes in their private life; he started drinking after prison. For Aoibhin, her husband's alcohol problem is proof of the "invisible wounds people get through the struggle and the unresolved issue of gender inequality."*[104] *Aoibhin knows that she is not the only woman with this problem, and that it has happened in many other families too. Her activism on women's issues and her active involvement in post-conflict local politics are "as important as breathing"*[105] *for her. She feels "pride of being a woman" and of "being a mother, a homemaker, a fulltime worker, and a political activist."*[106] *Balancing her time between fulltime job, activism, and family is difficult, but has increased her self-confidence and her independence. Providing a "new" female role model for her children is Aoibhin's strategy to "change the social fabric" of society and its mind-set. She feels that the state needs to support this strategy, but fails to do so. In Aoibhin's view, "culture, confidence, cash, and child care remain central barriers for women in Northern Irish society and make it harder for men to adapt to changes."*[107] *"Although more fathers get involved in child care now, it is just not enough happening yet and certainly not encouraged in legal frameworks."*[108]

However, Aoibhin also believes that a big change was the acceptance of a "freer lifestyle in Catholic communities, both morally and socially. "Single mothers would have been judged years ago as, 'she's a tramp she has three kids and so...' But women are making choices now. If they want to have a relationship with the father dead on and if they don't that's dead on too"[109]

During the conflict, the survival of the community was intrinsically linked to the survival of the family; the notions of "caring for home and children" and "caring for the community" merged. In this context, the occupation of roles of responsibility in the public sphere by women detriggered the centrality of motherhood in women's lives. With the deescalation of violence, normality changed for women during the peace process. However, having "created autonomy in their lives through confronting power structures in a variety of ways" (Hackett, 2004, p. 166), female republican activists were not prepared to return to the private sphere.

The salience of the gendered boundary at the beginning of the peace process (early 1990s) is evidence for a shared concern amongst republican women of bringing their voices into the process of reconstructing Northern Irish society to address intersectional inequalities in the positioning of individuals in society. Ethnic, class, gender, age, sexuality, and other dimensions are interconnected in this process. Post agreement, republican women perceive their place both in the community and in the home; having a role and responsibility in society remained important to them.

Child care has become a central concern as the duties of women expanded from the private to the public sphere; this concern addressed the deeply rooted understanding of the function and positioning of women within society. Once women became actively involved at the community level, "there [is] no going back."[110] However, as it became unacceptable anymore for women to concentrate on looking after home and children and to be financially dependent on their husbands, the public as the private sphere had to adapt to the new needs of women.

Reflecting on their role in the post-agreement society, many republican women (8 of 11) express frustration that "culture, confidence, cash, and child care" have remained central barriers for women and emphasize that gender equality requires a change of mind-set of both men and women. The reevaluation of child care in society is an important incentive for adapting changed gender images; the failure to do so has led some women (4 of 17) to decide against having children in order to fit into male power positions. Women are not prepared to return to their homes and give up their jobs and community activity. Therefore, child care has become a bigger issue during peace time than it was during conflict. Bridging the distinction between the private and the public sphere is central to the process of "reconciling motherhood" and building a more gender-equal society in post-conflict Northern Ireland for many activists. Further the emphasis on the acceptance of single mothers highlights a change in the perception of women in republican communities.

Another significant change is support for reproductive rights, particularly of abortion, among many republican grassroots activists (8 of 11). They linked changes in their position on abortion to a "freer lifestyle both morally and socially,"[111] particularly to a change in the meaning of "being Catholic," from "practicing Catholicism" to "belonging to a socioeconomically oppressed group" (Mitchell, 2006), which is an outcome of the mobilization process. This allowed for a change in female republican activists' perspective on reproductive rights. Post agreement, republican women emphasize that abortion has become "a big gray area, [and has moved away from] that black and white view of abortion as murder in the womb."[112] Female activists who mention the topic of abortion (12 of 12) indicate that it is now widely accepted that women are making their own choices when it comes to their life and their body.

As a result of the mobilization process, women's image and positioning in their community has shifted, access to money and to economic power positions is of greater importance for many republican women now than during the conflict, when the focus was on daily survival. Men returning to the community after imprisonment started to compete with women for leadership positions and for the paid community jobs. This competition is one example that illustrates how changed gendered images are rather confronted than adopted in post-agreement Northern Ireland. Some female grassroots activists (7 of 11) felt that their demands for a better accommodation of their dual role in society were blocked by conservative post-agreement politics in the Northern Ireland state, where male voices and images of peace are overly represented. This reduced the space for women's voices and experiences in the peace process, which is evident in the small number of women being represented at the peace table and in politics post-1998.

The discrepancy between conservative politics and traditional gender images at the state level and changes at the community level has resulted in contentious male-female relationships in the private realm; this is evident in an increase in martial breakdowns, domestic violence, alcoholism, and drug abuse.[113] The failure to address changes in gender images in macro-level politics obstructs the reintegration of male prisoners into their families. Republican women (7 of 11) identify attitude and structure at the macro level as barriers for women in grassroots activism post agreement. Empowered during conflict, female activists feel that their space is as much in the public sphere as men's space need to be in the private realm. While women feel an entitlement to be in the public sphere, including in leadership positions, their perceptions clash with the male voices and traditional gender images of peace, confining women to the private realm. Women often refer to traditional gender images when highlighting the division of public-male and private-female sphere, such as, "Women staying at home, making the dinner, and raising the children, while men bring in the salary and make decisions in the community."[114]

As a result women have to cope with coming to terms with their husband's alcoholism or facing a marriage breakdown. For many women, encouraging men to talk and providing a space for men and women to construct a society based on equal gender relations can only happen in a bottom-up approach, as the macro level is not open for these kind of changes.

Intersecting Boundary Processes in Peace Processes

The way in which female activists from both subaltern communities and those outside these communities construct and change boundaries in the aftermath of armed conflict becomes visible in the analysis of the different episodes and dimensions of these processes. A shift in identity processes is evident in the changing positioning of activists toward the state, their community, their family and their intimate relationships; these changes are revealed in the understanding of normality in female activists' collective identity narratives. How changes in perceptions and in social positioning of women are translated from the mobilization during the conflict to the settlement process distinguishes the peace processes in Chiapas and in Northern Ireland. These distinctions impact on the ability for changed gendered and ethnicized perceptions to manifest at all levels of society; differences in the two post-agreement processes are visible in the way new gender perceptions inform state and community structures in the public as well as intimate relationships in the private realm. The availability of space for women to mobilize on shared gender interests and build alliances across borders to pursue their shared interests is central to the manifestation of changes in gender and ethnic identity post agreement. During peace negotiations, resistance groups in both conflict regions are reengaging with the state, which entails for both indigenous and working-class republican activists a shift from an internal (movement) to an external (state) perspective; the way this reengagement takes place determines the space for women's shared gender interests in the public sphere.

The positioning of female activists toward the public sphere reflects a change in the perception of normality of the female activists. In Chiapas, the shift from violent to peaceful protest was linked to the perception that more pressure for change in state structures can be created through a peaceful bottom-up approach and through alliance building, rather than through armed violence. In Northern Ireland, the change from a "mind of war" to a "mind of peace" was connected to the realization that the conflict was about more than ethnic identity; that it was also about socioeconomic justice and peace. Significant changes in the meaning of normality are a result of the move from rejection to a reengagement with the state. When resistant communities have moved more closely to conservative macro-level power structures in Northern Ireland, independent spaces for women's voices had become restricted. In Chiapas, on the other hand, these independent spaces have remained open in the form of available alternatives in indigenous autonomous structures at the community level.

In both cases, a first episode of the peace process detriggered the ethnic and prioritized the gender boundary; this created new opportunities for alliance building among women on shared gender interests. However, the reaffirmation of the ethnic boundary in the official peace negotiations has subjugated women's concerns to the ethno-national political agendas and pushed issues of social justice and of gender inequality to the margin in Northern Ireland, whereas in Chiapas, these issues were at the center of the peace process. While power sharing between the two ethnic groups in conflict dominated the peace negotiations in Northern Ireland, the status and content of indigenous autonomy and the relationship between the center of mestizo power and the indigenous people at the margin of Mexican society were at the heart of the peace talks in Chiapas. By including discussions about the understanding of democracy, intersectional inequalities, and women's rights, the peace agenda in Chiapas was multifaceted, while Northern Ireland's peace process was largely one-dimensional.

Whereas in Chiapas, indigenous and mestiza female activists' images and voices featured prominently at the peace table, in Northern Ireland only few female voices were represented in the official peace negotiations. The independent space for feminist solidarity has been restricted by the agendas and discourses of traditional, male-dominated political parties in Northern Ireland. As a result, women's perception shifted from being "agents of change" to being "mediators" (NIWC) and "supporters" (republican feminists) of ethno-national difference. As a result of the peace process in Chiapas, changes occurred in both the image of the indigenous woman in public discourses in Mexico and indigenous women's social positioning in society; this is evident in the way they began to influence government agencies and international organizations. Post-agreement processes in Chiapas opened spaces for indigenous women to develop a double intervention strategy: transforming their communities internally and bringing about changes at the macro level through their engagement with the Mexican state. In Chiapas, the disengagement discourse of the Zapatista Movement, which continues after the failed implementation of the peace agreement in peaceful resistance against the state, has enabled the further development of indigenous autonomy as an alternative to existing state structures. Changes in gendered perceptions and positioning during the conflict found acknowledgment in the creation of indigenous autonomous communities. This is evident, for instance, in the change of landownership and community leadership rules, such as the introduction of gender quotas and the institutionalization of a revised and more comprehensive Revolutionary Women's Law. In contrast, in Northern Ireland male voices and experiences continue to dominate political decision making post-1998. Traditional gender images excluding women from political leadership impact the positioning of women in republican communities. While women remain active at the community level, their involvement is limited by increasing competition with men over paid community jobs.

Processes of development of women's solidarity on shared gender interests in Chiapas and in Northern Ireland can be distinguished in the way alliance formations on strategic gender interests has been supported or challenged. The development of solidarity on women's gender interests unites feminist voices across boundaries in Chiapas, while reaffirmed ethnic divisions have continued to limit solidarity formation on women's gender interests in Northern Ireland. Distinctions between female activists form an essential element in women's activism in both cases. However, the way distinctions intersect and are highlighted in the peace processes distinguishes the two cases; whereas in Chiapas, female activists have progressed from a contentious to a constructive dialogue on shared gender interests across the ethnic and class divide, in Northern Ireland, remaining community loyalties and class divisions are central obstacles to alliance building for promoting women's rights across boundaries. Strategic gender interests, developed within the mobilization process, have not disappeared in the post-agreement phase; however, the way distinctions between women (ethnic, class) are highlighted (as in Northern Ireland) or bridged (as in Chiapas) has restricted or widened the space for the development of women's solidarity on shared gender interests across ethnic and class boundaries. In Chiapas, the Zapatista Movement has created a greater national and global alliance as part of the Other Campaign, which is based on a stronger emphasis on the global anti-neoliberal perspective of protest; this has increased the space for indigenous and nonindigenous women to work together on reforming the sociopolitical, economic, and cultural structures of the state from below. The shift in emphasis from indigenous rights to transforming neoliberal dynamics nationally and globally has provided a common ground for different feminist activisms to work together with respect for and awareness of the different backgrounds of activists. In Northern Ireland, the reaffirmation of the ethnic boundary in the formal peace process has increased the incentive among feminist activists positioned outside republican or loyalist working-class community borders to focus in their activism only on women's rights without addressing difference in the category "women." This dynamic has alienated female grassroots activists, in particular, from republican community backgrounds who often perceive themselves as discriminated not only as "women" and "Catholic," but also on the basis of their "class" background. While women's post-agreement activism in Northern Ireland reproduces the traditional pattern of division through either emphasizing (republican feminists) or ignoring (traditional feminists) difference, these borders between women are crossed in Chiapas by acknowledging them.

The adaption of changes in women's perceptions and positioning in their private realm is essential for female activists. In their narratives, female activists highlight the way the official peace processes at the macro level of society interplay with new gender images and structures at the community level and how this interplay impacts on women's private lives. The private realm is often neglected in political peace processes at the state level, which increases the suffering of women. The divergence between micro- and macro-level processes is visible in the confrontation of changed female self-perceptions with remaining traditional male gender concepts, which confine women to the private realm. However, we can distinguish Chiapas and Northern Ireland by the way in which new gender images are perceived as an appropriate part of a new normality. The way shifts in gender perceptions and positioning are promoted in the public sphere significantly impacts on dynamics in the private realm, and consequently on male-female intimate relationships. The public peace process in Chiapas has opened spaces for the transformation of traditional, unequal gender relationships. The Zapatista Movement provided at the peace table a space for a dialogue on community traditions and for addressing divergence in male and female roles and perceptions. This dialogue has been a stepping-stone in transforming gender relationships post agreement. However, on the other hand, the rise in the number and the acceptance of single mothers in indigenous communities indicates the slow pace and the asymmetrical dynamic of changes at the micro level of societies. In contrast, in Northern Ireland, women's mobilization in republican communities has been primarily connected to the absence of men through internment. Men with a remaining traditional image of manhood are confronted with a "new women's world" when returning to their families after imprisonment. This often leads to contentious male-female relationships, in many cases to domestic violence and marriage breakdown; these contentions in the private realm can further be a contributing factor to an increase in self-harm, evident in suicides, alcoholism, and drug abuse (Hamber 2007; Hamber et al., 2006). The focus on the regulation of ethnic distinctions in the public peace process does not provide sufficient space to address post-agreement issues like the crisis partnerships, which occurs in the private realm. This leaves female activists halfway between unresolved traditional gender inequalities and unfulfilled future aspirations for changed gender relationships. In both cases, the private realm has revealed challenges in the adaption of changes in women's perceptions of themselves and of their role in society. However, while post-agreement dynamics in the public sphere in Chiapas created a space for dialogue on issues of contention in male-female intimate relationships, the space for addressing micro-level contention was restricted by the one-dimensional peace process in Northern Ireland.

Distinctions between the conflict settlements in Chiapas and in Northern Ireland are visible, in particular in the way macro-level dynamics open (Chiapas) or limit (Northern Ireland) first, the formation of women's solidarity on shared and strategic gender interests across boundaries. The impact of these dynamics on the private realm is central as it reflects opportunities and challenges to the transformation of unequal gender relations and traditional gender images.

III

Connecting Voices: Lessons from Collective Identity Processes

5

Connecting Boundary Processes during Episodes of Mobilization and Demobilization

Introduction

This chapter builds on description, analysis, and interpretation of female activist's collective identity stories in Chapters 3 and 4. It aims to contribute new perspectives on intersectional boundary processes in peace and conflict situations by asking "what can we learn from women's experiences in Chiapas and Northern Ireland?" Reflecting on lessons learned from this comparative study of identity processes during peace and conflict, I set out in this chapter to highlight some general trends and tendencies evolving from my findings. However, I would at the same time remind the reader of the differences in perceptions and positioning within each category.

As part of the analysis of collective identity narratives of female activists from Chiapas and Northern Ireland, I have traced their pathways of activism in episodes of conflict and in conflict settlement processes. Listening to and learning from the voices of female activists from different backgrounds has enabled me to examine, first, if and in what way ethnic and gender boundaries form and change. Second, paying attention in my analysis to the complexity of activists' perceptions, perspectives, and experiences of social mobilizations and demobilizations allowed me to understand how these boundary processes intersect. Third, my analysis reveals not only commonalities, but also significant differences in these processes, which become visible in the way in which the gender boundary is triggered during conflict and in its aftermath in both cases.

Commonalities become evident as to how a first phase of contention (the farmers' mobilizations in Chiapas and the civil rights movement in Northern Ireland) unites actors from different backgrounds in the protest against state-perpetrated injustice. In both cases, the active participation of women from marginalized communities (indigenous women and Catholic working-class women) is limited in that period of protest. In Chiapas and in Northern Ireland, women from disadvantaged ethno-national and class backgrounds became primarily politicized on concerns for the recognition of the rights of their respective communities. Further, in both conflict regions, women's activism on shared gender interests developed as part of the community protest and outside the boundaries of marginalized communities; it transformed the way female activists of the Zapatista and the Republican Movement perceived and positioned themselves as women and as part of their communities. The highlighting of the gender boundary through a temporary detriggering of the ethnic boundary during conflict did not lead to a disappearance of ethnic distinctions but to their transformation. In both cases, a first episode of the peace process sees a continuation of the detriggering of the ethnic and a prioritization of the gender boundary; this created new opportunities for alliance building among women on shared gender interests.

On the other hand, significant differences between the two case studies help to understand challenges in the change of gender and ethnic identity that legitimize the different positioning and perceptions of women and men in society during conflict and in its aftermath. While in both cases, ethno-national conflict provided opportunities to change gender identity and societal gender roles, the availability of spaces for doing so distinguishes the two cases. Unlike in Northern Ireland, in Chiapas, the first phase of protest allows for the development of alliances between women from marginalized indigenous communities and those positioned outside these community boundaries. These distinctions are informed by the way community claims address and are connected to macro-level politics, which differs in the two processes. The way ethno-national, gender, and class boundaries intersect is significantly different in the two cases. Ethno-national and class boundaries intersect with gendered identity processes in both case studies; however, the way boundaries are formed affects the development of women's solidarity on shared gender interests in different ways.

While in both regions spaces open for joint women's rights activism between female activists from different backgrounds, in Northern Ireland, these spaces are limited and in Chiapas, they are expanding. The mechanism of brokerage between women from different ethno-national and class backgrounds became activated at an earlier stage in Chiapas (first phase of protest) than in Northern Ireland (second phase of protest). Further, the space for the development of shared solidarity on gender interests across boundaries is informed by distinctions in the perception of and positioning toward the state. While in Chiapas, the Zapatista mobilization takes place within the state, in Northern Ireland, the Republican Movement positions itself outside the Northern Irish and the British state.

Distinction between reform (Chiapas) and secession (Northern Ireland) as focal points for mobilization and demobilization are visible in the degree and duration of violent protest episodes. In Chiapas, the engagement of women from subaltern (indigenous) communities in the violent protest against the Mexican state was of a shorter duration compared to Northern Ireland. The quick move of the EZLN from "the military" to the "political dimension" in Chiapas after only 12 days of armed confrontation facilitated the creation of feminist solidarity across the borders of the movement. On the other hand, the long duration of the armed conflict in Northern Ireland had increased divisions among women along cultural and class lines, which became further entrenched through the highlighting of ethno-national distinctions in the peace agreement.

The formation of solidarity on women's shared gender interests across boundaries in periods of armed conflict has shifted beliefs, ideas, values, and speech that promote male domination and superiority and female subordination and "secondariness" (Rowbotham, 1983, p. 27) and has challenged male-dominated national discourses on "women's place and role" (Sideris, 2001, p. 145). However, the post-agreement processes in Chiapas and in Northern Ireland differ in the way in which these changes are translated into peace processes, resulting in different outcomes for women in the period after the peace agreement. These distinctions become particularly evident in the intimate male-female relationships, which are largely contentious in Northern Ireland and develop toward constructive dialogues in Chiapas. Two central aspects inform these different outcomes: first, the space provided during the peace talks for including women and addressing gender-based violence or the dimensionality of the peace agenda and second, the proximity of ethno-national resistance movements to the conservative macro level of society, which is traditionally dominated by male hopes, aspirations, and privileges (McClintock 1993).

In the following part, I examine intersectional dynamics of symbolic and social boundary change by connecting the different dimensions of transformation, with an emphasis on how solidarity is formed and the way the formation of solidarity is connected to the transformation of identity.

Connecting Intersubjective and Social Dimensions of Change: Intersecting Spaces in the Formation of Solidarity and the Transformation of Identity

My research enhances the understanding of intersectional perspectives by exploring how social change, collective identity categories, and political values are created and the way in which they interrelate and affect each other in peace and conflict situations. Addressing the relative importance of action and structure in processes of identity change and the opportunities for effective action contributes new insights to contemporary research.[1] It does so by connecting intersecting shifts in identity categories during peace and conflict situations to social change. Contentious politics always involve the social construction of politically relevant categories (McAdam, Tilly Tarrow, 2001, p. 58), such as indigenous peoples, republicans, and feminists. Social change is at the beginning of the social mobilizations in Chiapas and in Northern Ireland, and drives shifts at the intersubjective level of ethnic and gendered identity processes. However, the analysis of the social mobilization and demobilization processes shows that identity shifts also lead to social change visible in the way those shifts become manifest in social structures. The formation of solidarity on gender demands during peace and conflict provides evidence of a change of symbolic boundaries; it shows a shift in awareness, political values, levels of commitment (McAdam, Tilly Tarrow, 2001, p. 26), and spaces of belonging (Fortier, 2000; Yuval-Davis 2011). Symbolic boundaries shape the way in which certain practices, roles, and power dynamics feel not only acceptable, but also normal. Therefore we can see boundary shifts in the way female activists' change perception of normality, political values, their feelings of belonging to a particular community, and their positioning in society. The direction identity change takes is informed by the manifestation of these changes as shifts in symbolic boundaries have to be widely agreed on (Lamont and Molnar 2002). Hence, the translation of changes in symbolic gender and ethnic boundaries occurring during conflict into conflict settlement processes require shifts in unequal access to, and unequal distribution of, resources (material and nonmaterial), and social opportunities (Lamont and Molnar, 2002, p. 168–69); these shifts need to take place at all levels of society. To understand the possible adaptation or rejection of symbolic boundary changes into objectified forms of social differences, we need to look at the way in which institutionalized patterns of gender, class, ethnic, or racial cleavages intersect.

Social mobilization processes in Chiapas and in Northern Ireland changed women's social positioning, albeit in different ways. Ethno-national mobilizations at the community level increased the visibility of women and opened an autonomous space outside unequal gendered and ethicized power structures at the macro level. By bringing their voices and experiences from the private realm into the public process of creating alternative community structures, women changed their positioning in and perceptions of their community.

However, the way in which symbolic boundary changes have been translated into structural changes in the transition from the community conflict to the peace process distinguishes Chiapas from Northern Ireland. In Northern Ireland, the translation of changes in women's social positioning occurring within the mobilization process at the community level into post-agreement structures at the state level has been restricted by the exclusive focus on moderating the ethnic distinctions in the peace negotiations. The political activism of women in the formal peace process (Northern Ireland Women's Coalition—NIWC) significantly impacted on the development of unique post-agreement "human rights," "equality," and "justice" bodies. Yet, these issues remain at the margin of the political process as power-sharing mechanisms, for instance, communal designation of members of the Northern Ireland assembly, position ethno-national concerns at the center of the public sphere. The choice of republican women to identify themselves first with their ethno-national group and only second as "women" demonstrates the salience of the ethnic boundary in the peace process at the macro level. This is visible in the reluctance of many republican women to support the NIWC.

Furthermore, the increased competition between men and women and among female activists for jobs and funding reduces the space for feminist interventions within the community and at the state level. In Northern Ireland, feminist activisms have moved closer to macro-level institutions and processes in which unequal gender structures prevail. Equality discourses lock changes in ethnic and gender perceptions between rhetoric (section 75 GFA[2]) and unequal gender practices (low number of female parliamentarians). This shows how these discourses obscure changes of gender boundaries and remaining gender inequalities and reveals the way in which traditional gender structures still feature in post-agreement Northern Irish politics.

In contrast, the emphasis on diversity and "respect for difference" during and after the peace negotiations in Chiapas has led to a complete embracing of converted gender images and roles in the creation of "indigenous autonomy" at the community level. However, the demobilization process in Chiapas has only led to partial structural changes on the state level, even though "incomplete" constitutional reforms have highlighted the indigenous agenda in the national public debate and have led to an increased recognition of the value of the minority group and in particular of indigenous women. The penetration of macro-level politics by indigenous and women's voices and concerns has broken the "discourse monopoly" of the government in the national debate on Mexican citizenship. This is visible when the female indigenous Zapatista Commander Esther addressed the Mexican parliament by highlighting both her ethnic and her gender identity, and in the way indigenous women in civil service positions have contributed to promoting changes in the definition of "indigenous" in Mexican census data (SEPI 2006).

The formation of solidarity on social justice (farmers' movements/civil rights movement), ethno-national (Zapatista Movement/Republican movement), and shared gender interests is at the start and is at the same time the outcome of the transformation of identity categories.

Solidarity Formation

The examination of alliance building on shared gender interests as mechanism of social mobilization shows that women's activism pathways can be distinguished depending on the oppressions they experience, multicausal in its origin, mediated through different structures and that are changing over time. Intersecting collective identifications play a central role in contentious politics, as they define collective "interactions that center on claim making" (McAdam, Tilly & Tarrow, 2001, p. 137). The way ethno-national claims are highlighted and intersect with gender interests during conflict and in its aftermath either facilitates (Chiapas) or challenges (Northern Ireland) the opening of spaces for crossing boundaries.

The objectives of social mobilization and demobilization processes in Chiapas and in Northern Ireland vary in different episodes of contention and conflict settlement, as do resources of protest and alliance building. Shifts in objectives of protest and conflict settlement are connected to women's positioning toward the state, the community, and the family, to the mobilization resources available to them and to the way in which alliances are formed. Previously unconnected women become connected, feminist "brokerage" (McAdam, Tilly & Tarrow, 2001) evolves, when "independent" spaces open and allow for the bridging of ethnic and/or class differences. Ethnicization processes in Chiapas and in Northern Ireland follow a wider mobilization based on egalitarian social justice issues (civil rights, land rights). While the civil rights (Northern Ireland) and the farmers' movements (Chiapas) were situated within the state at the macro level, the starting point for the ethno-national mobilization process is the community level. A significant aspect of the formation of ethno-national movements are the high levels of commitment to the resistance community created in the ethnicization process; these levels of commitment determine how female members of ethno-national movements support or actively engage in the use of armed violence.

Notions of "unity" and "community" in Chiapas and in Northern Ireland are central in most narratives on the mobilization and demobilization process. For many women from marginalized communities the community level became the central space for activism in the second episode of the mobilization process (Zapatista mobilization in Chiapas and Republican Movement in Northern Ireland). Within the Zapatista and the Republican Movement, the organization around ethno-national issues highlighted the relationship between the community and its male and female members; externally, it revealed the relationship between the community, "us," and the state as the "other." Being removed from the center of male power structures at the macro level, feminist "community activism" evolved in an independent space, allowing women to move from the private into the public sphere; women's positioning changed from "being at the margin" to "being at the heart" of the community.

In Chiapas and in Northern Ireland women from disadvantaged ethno-national and class backgrounds became primarily politicized on concerns for the recognition of the rights of their respective communities. Subsequently, women's activism on shared gender interests developed as part of the community protest; it transformed the way female activists of the republican and the Zapatista Movement perceived and positioned themselves as women and as part of their communities. Mobilization processes that started against the marginalization of subaltern communities and their culture opened spaces for female activists to claim their rights as women and to change community traditions that institutionalized gender inequality. Changes in women's activism are visible in the protest agenda of their community, for instance, in Northern Ireland in the creation of a Sinn Fein policy on women and a Department on Women's Affairs (1980) or in Chiapas in the development of the Revolutionary Women's Law (1992).

The way community claims address and are connected to macro-level politics distinguishes the two processes. The claim for state reform that was at the heart of the civil rights movement shifted in Northern Ireland during the politicization of the republican community to claims for a different state membership for a United Ireland. These separatist tendencies did not exist in the Zapatista mobilizations in Chiapas; here the claim for recognition of indigenous rights was connected to a protest against harmful state policies impacted by neoliberal globalization and free trade agendas; demands for indigenous autonomy remained within the existing state structure.

Resistance of ethno-national communities in Chiapas and in Northern Ireland was connected to military activism, which often has been identified as a space that reproduces unequal gender structures (Yuval-Davis, 1997, p. 114)[3]; however recent scholarship has revealed that military revolutionary struggles based on a social justice agenda often have "organized feminism" as an unintended outcome (Kampwirth, 2004, p. 7). As evident in the Zapatista Movement in Chiapas and the Republican Movement in Northern Ireland, feminist activisms have developed within these military spaces, although the support or rejection of violent means of protest has created divisions among female activists in the two conflict regions.

Many ethno-national conflicts have included women's voices and brought women's concerns from the private into the public realm (Kampwirth 2004, Hoewer 2014). As this research has shown, the roles women take on in these processes are diverse: some women use peaceful, others violent means of protest in their community activism,[4] others again mobilize for peace (Cohn and Jacobson 2013, Ruddick, 1989, p. 176).

The formation of female alliances on shared gender interests is central to making a change in women's positioning. The distinction between women's interests informed by traditional gender roles (practical interests), and interests that challenge gender inequalities (strategic interests) is important. Awareness of these distinctions in solidarity formation on women's shared gender interests reveals the intersectional identity dynamics in women's activisms by challenging the assumption that all women share an identical meaning of feminist activism (Molyneux, 1985). The meaning women attribute to their activism and the way their active engagement impacts on their perceptions and positioning is informed by female activists' different backgrounds (ethnicity, nationality, race class, age, and etc.).

Distinctions on how ethnic, class, and gender boundaries intersect in the ethno-national mobilizations in Chiapas and in Northern Ireland are visible in how women's activisms positioned within and outside ethno-national protest communities are interconnected. In Northern Ireland, feminist solidarity led to the organization of women in local women's groups and to the creation of women's centers, such as the Falls Women's Center, which opened in 1982. Women's community activisms at the local level connected some working-class women across the ethno-national divide. However, the pattern of division determined the development of women's activism in the region, which is visible in the organization of separate events for international Women's Day in the 1980s (republican women's protest in front of Armagh prison and independent women's movement march in Belfast city center) and in different feminist interventions during the peace process (Clar na mBan and

NIWC). In Chiapas, the Zapatista mobilization allowed for the different social positioning of indigenous and nonindigenous, poor and middle-class women to be addressed and for cooperation across differences, the success of which is seen in structural changes in the civil society sector, in particular, in the structure of women's organizations post agreement. Indigenous women, empowered through their activism within the Zapatista Movement, have shaped women's organizations with their indigenous agenda.[5] This is visible in the shift of discourse from top-down feminism of more middle-class professionals (Hernández Castillo, 2006, 61) to a bottom-up popular feminism of rural and urban poor women (Espinosa Damián, 2005, 85, as cited in Hernández Castillo 2006) and of indigenous feminists (Hernández Castillo, 2006).

While in Northern Ireland the phenomenon of "single-issue campaigns" arises out of the difficulty to bring women together across the different divides,[6] in Chiapas, the work on women's concerns is based on the creation of dialogues of difference. The emphasis on intersecting inequalities provides alliance building on shared gender interests in Chiapas with a heterogeneous point of departure. On the other hand, the emphasis on ethno-national power structures in the peace process in Northern Ireland has created homogenous points of departure, which place women's community activism in a different space than that of women outside the boundary of republican and loyalist working class communities. The reaffirmation of the ethno-national divide in post-agreement Northern Ireland decreases the level of feminist solidarity across ethnic and class boundaries.

In the demobilization phase, in both cases, a shift from the military to the political dimension of activism within the protest movements (Zapatista and Republican Movement) led to a stronger emphasis on social justice and a reengagement with the state. Amongst other factors, the two peace processes can be distinguished by the way the feminist perspective is represented. In Chiapas, the ethnic component became embedded in the general social justice framework, which dominated the peace process and connected ethnic and feminist demands to the global "netwar" against neoliberalism. In Northern Ireland, the ethnic protest component first became detriggered in the lead up to the peace talks in the early 1990s and reaffirmed during the peace talks evident in the Good Friday/Belfast peace agreement.[7] In this later episode, women's gender interests were pushed back to the margin again.

Distinctions in the transition from conflict to peace at the macro level are visible in way the San Andres Peace Accords in Chiapas and the Good Friday/Belfast Agreement in Northern Ireland were implemented and in the content of the peace agreements. This has led to different feminist outcomes of settlement processes: a limited potential for transforming unequal gender structures in Northern Ireland and an increase in the possibility to do so in Chiapas. The San Andres Peace Accords granted autonomy and recognition to the indigenous peoples of Mexico and placed emphasis on respect for diversity, a greater participation of marginalized indigenous peoples in political decision making, and demanded the Mexican state's acknowledgment of autonomous indigenous structures. These principles were developed through a national consultation process with men and women from different indigenous communities in Mexico, which was organized by the EZLN. The negotiation process allowed indigenous women to include their "feminist" demands in the concept of indigenous autonomy based on the distinction between "good" and "bad" community traditions in the Revolutionary Women's Law.[8] Both the formal and the informal peace process placed the indigenous question within a wider struggle against the unequal treatment of marginalized groups in Mexican society and included the voices of nonindigenous feminist women. Although the peace agreement has never been fully implemented, there has been no return to armed violence as the Zapatista Movement continued their ceasefire and peaceful protest. A new episode of contention following the peace negotiations manifested in a low-intensity warfare, and a new period of social mobilization on social justice issues from 1996[9] resulted in the end of the PRI (Institutional Revolutionary Party) regime in 2000. The Zapatista Movement played an important role in this process of alliance formation. Further these new networks with national and international civil society organizations strengthened the Zapatista Movement both nationally and internationally. The Zapatista Movement has become one of the main actors in the national and global netwar (Ronfeld, Arquilla, Fuller, & Fuller, 1998) for social justice and against the "dysfunctions of neo-liberalism" (Olesen, 2005). Although the PRI returned to power (in Mexico and Chiapas) after the 2012 elections, the strong civil society continues to impact political processes at the state level; its transformative potential is evident, for instance, in stronger electoral oversight authorities (Flores-Macías, 2013).

A first episode in the transition from conflict to peace in Northern Ireland opened an independent space for addressing general issues of social justice and inequality (Bell and Ní Aoláin, 2005) and for women's activism. Women's gendered agenda prevailed in this episode, which made women's voices visible in the public peace process. It also encouraged a critical dialogue on bringing women's voices into the formal peace negotiations at both community level (Clar na mBan—Women's Agenda for Peace) and the creation of an all-women's political party (NIWC) at the macro level. Although representatives of the NIWC were at the peace table, the emphasis on the ethno-national cleavage during the formal peace process reduced the space for women's voices[10] and for women's gender concerns in the peace negotiations. The structure of the peace process limited the role of women's activists within the public sphere from "agents of change" to "mediators" (NIWC) and "supporters" (republican feminists) of ethno-national difference. However, the input of the NIWC resulted in the development of unique post-conflict human rights, equality, and justice bodies. Despite this success, the Women's Coalition was criticized for representing mainly "middle-class women's agendas" and for not leaving much room for highlighting women's different backgrounds.

With the end of absentionism from the Stormont parliament, Sinn Fein developed from a revolutionary movement to a "new, pragmatic and constitutional republicanism" (Tonge, 2002, p. 73). The shift from a resistance community to an electorate, and from a dissident form of community organization to a publically funded community sector,[11] reduced the revolutionary potential for republican feminist activism. By creating competition for jobs between men and women within the community and competition for funding amongst women, the structure of public financial support, the "peace money," has reaffirmed both the traditional gender divide and existing divisions in women's activism. Furthermore, post- Good Friday/Belfast Agreement, the conservative nature of macro-level politics, which remains dominated by male republican and loyalist voices impacted negatively on republican women's activism. Feminist community activism became limited during the settlement process by two intertwined dynamics: first, by the conservative top-down approach created by the power-sharing mechanism at the macro level, and second, by the residual division of women along religious and class lines.

Unlike Sinn Fein, the political arm of the Zapatista Movement in Chiapas did not become a constitutional political party but continued its resistance against unequal power structures at the state level using peaceful means of protest. Its engagement with the Mexican government during the formal peace negotiations did not lead to its participation in, but to its continued resistance to, the Mexican state's political structure. Its peaceful resistance with the aim of "deconstructing" existing power discourses and structures amplified the "neo-Zapatista networks" beyond the Zapatista Movement and increased opportunities for alliance building (Leyva Solano, 2005, p. 283) between indigenous and nonindigenous feminists. In Chiapas, feminist activisms largely maintain their revolutionary potential by interacting with, but not merging into, the macro-level power structures they set out to change. On the other hand, in Northern Ireland, feminist activisms became largely incorporated through public peace funding requirements into formal structures at the macro level in which conservative, patriarchal discourses prevail, and where the emphasis on ethno-national divisions has limited the space for addressing women's gender interests.

While ethno-national and class boundaries intersect with gendered identity processes in both case studies, the way boundaries are formed affects the development of women's solidarity on shared gender interests in different ways. In Northern Ireland, female activists with shared ethno-national boundaries were divided by class boundaries, a result of a middle class, which had developed within the Catholic community in order to serve their own people (Sales, 1997, p. 18); this was different from Chiapas where ethno-national and class divisions run largely parallel. While in Northern Ireland, female activists became positioned in "parallel universes" after the civil rights movement, in Chiapas, the mobilizations on shared gender interests have brought together indigenous and nonindigenous women. This becomes visible in the support for the Zapatista mobilization in Chiapas beyond the boundaries of indigenous Zapatista communities. In comparison, in Northern Ireland, women principally identifying as promoters of women's gender interests distanced themselves from republican women's protest agendas, which they criticize for compromising women's rights by prioritizing "other" identities, for promoting patriarchal military forms of participation, and for being "controlled by men."

Further the mechanism of brokerage between women from different ethno-national and class backgrounds became activated at a later stage in Northern Ireland (second phase of protest) than in Chiapas (first phase of protest). Finally, the perception of and positioning toward the state have determined the space available for the development of shared solidarity on gender interests between female activists across boundaries; this space was limited in Northern Ireland and increasing in Chiapas.

Identity Transformation

Contentious episodes in Chiapas and in Northern Ireland have transformed ethnic and gender perceptions at both the community and the micro level of society. Collective identity narratives from Northern Ireland and Chiapas demonstrate a change in traditional gender images, which are based on the identification of women as "cultural and biological reproducers of the nation and as transmitters of its values" (Yuval-Davis and Anthias, 1989, p. 287).

Feelings of "fear" and the "need for survival" are connected to the mobilization process of both female indigenous activists in Chiapas and republican women in Northern Ireland. Whereas in Northern Ireland, these feelings evolved out of intra-community violence that triggered the consciousness of "being Catholic and Irish," in Chiapas, "fear" is primarily connected to the violent community culture and to "being a woman." For republican women in Northern Ireland, becoming actively involved is connected to the "survival" of the republican community. For Zapatista women in Chiapas, activism is linked to both the survival of the indigenous communities and the liberation of themselves, as women, within those settings.

The ethnicization process changed the meaning of community from a geographical location (the local parish) to an imagined republican unity in Northern Ireland. Shared experiences of intra-community violence and marginalization formed the basis for the feeling of belonging to a renewed republican community, which led to the commitment of women to the republican struggle. The politicization of religious differences triggered women's consciousness of being Catholic and being marginalized and increased their pride in being Irish. Whereas the centrality of religious affiliation in the ethnicization process has brought traditional notions of Irish womanhood as a symbol for the national culture and tradition[12] into the political project, by participating actively in the community struggle, women have changed the meaning of community. Republican women brought through their activism the private into the public sphere; as their world expanded, this changed the way they perceived themselves as women within their family, their community, and within society. The formation of women's solidarity on shared gender interests within the Republican Movement has led to a transformation in women's self-identification. The shift in women's self-image from a reactive defender of the community to an active agent of change, transforming that same community by targeting patriarchal aspects of its culture, has created a new "identity package," at times referred to as "republican feminist." This new identity package has been based on gender (male-female), ethno-national (Unionist-Nationalists), and class (republican working-class women-"traditional" middle-class feminists) distinctions. The multiple distinctions defining republican feminism impact on its representation in the official peace process, which has remained largely dominated by male gender images, competing with female perceptions and perspectives of peace and conflict, as visible during the peace talks.

In Chiapas, by connecting the land to the indigenous question, the ethnicization process has highlighted indigenous culture and traditions. This process has increased the self-worth of indigenous women and has changed their identification as being indigenous and as being a woman. Whereas the triggering of being indigenous was at the center of the protest, this identity was embedded into a political project, which opened a space for transforming its patriarchal content. The reflexive changes of indigenous women have led to the creation of a new identity package. A newly developed "indigenous feminist" image connects new ways of being a woman to transformed meanings of indigenous culture and traditions, evident in female images and symbols of the Zapatista Movement, such as the visibility of ethnic and gender difference in female EZLN fighters' uniforms, the public image of female commanders, and in the indigenous women's demands manifested in the Revolutionary Women's Law.[13] The change in self-identification evolved out of a dialogue between indigenous women and both, indigenous men and nonindigenous women. This process was based on respect for difference among women from different backgrounds and the search for a new way for indigenous men and women to "caminar parejo" (walk or develop together). While struggling against these parts of indigenous culture, which impact negatively on their lives, indigenous women continue to perceive themselves at the same time as "rooted in their culture" (Marcos, 2005, p. 81).

The Zapatista mobilization in Chiapas created a unity of indigenous people and a Zapatista activist identity, which is broader and has less emphasis on ethnic and class divisions. Whereas in Northern Ireland, symbolic boundaries were drawn between Catholics and Protestants (ethnic), and also between marginalized Catholic women who were affected directly by intra-community violence, and those who were Catholic women, but not primarily identifying as "republican," often labeled as "middle class" by republican women. Compared with Northern Ireland, the ethnicization process in Chiapas provided more favorable conditions for the formation of women's solidarity on shared gender interests across ethnic and class boundaries. This was possible through the evolving of a Zapatista activist identity alongside a transformed indigenous identity during the conflict and the convergence of class and ethnic identity in the indigenous-nonindigenous distinction.

In both Chiapas and Northern Ireland, women were actors in the ideological re-creation of the community and in the transformation of its culture in the second episode of the mobilization process. While the image of "the female activist" was initially a "silent" symbol for the repression and resistance of the subaltern (indigenous, Catholics), this image is transformed into a "vocal agent of change." The reengagement with the state in the settlement process reveals differences in the translation of changes of symbolic gender and ethnic boundaries occurring during mobilization into the peace process. Distinctions between the two cases are visible in the competition between traditional and new gender perceptions at the community level, which is influenced by the conservative nature of macro-level politics in Northern Ireland and the salience of transformed images of "indigenous womanhood" at both the community and the state level in Chiapas and in Mexico. Two intrinsically linked post-conflict developments are connected to the different outcomes of symbolic boundary processes; first, the increased (Northern Ireland) versus the limited (Chiapas) influence of top-down macro-level dynamics on symbolic boundary processes at the community level and second, the reaffirmation (Northern Ireland) versus the detriggering (Chiapas) of the ethnic identity category in the formal peace process.

These different developments impact on symbolic boundary processes in conflict settlement in the two regions and are connected to distinctions in the development of women's solidarity on shared gender interest across different boundaries. In Chiapas, the notion of Zapatista transcended beyond community borders (international Zapatismo) and has opened independent spaces for the acknowledgment of difference in the identity package of indigenous and nonindigenous women. Whereas in Northern Ireland, the highlighting of ethnic identity has confined the independent space for acknowledging "difference" in the independent women's movement post-Good Friday/Belfast Agreement.

The shift in "Zapatista identity," from overlapping with "indigenous identity" to a wider activism boundary allowed for new images of indigenous womanhood to penetrate the public sphere not only at the community, but also at the state level.[14] In turn, the transformation of traditional gender images at the macro level ensures the manifestation of the new image of indigenous womanhood at the community level. Whereas the ability for new ethnic and gender images to penetrate the public sphere was restricted in Northern Ireland, it constrained the manifestation of transformed ethnic and gender images in the region. Transformed images of indigenous womanhood penetrate the public sphere in Chiapas, while in Northern Ireland changed perceptions of Catholic women became locked between the community and the private realm.

(Dis-) Connecting Different Dimensions: The Private Realm between Tradition and Transition

The way in which public gendered and ethnicized images have adapted to shifts in female activist's perceptions at the micro level (Chiapas) or have contradicted new perceptions of "womanhood" in the private realm (Northern Ireland) distinguishes the two cases. In Chiapas, while traditional images have not gone away, community discourses and structures promote new gender and ethnic boundaries, which inform a new normality, and are reflected in the change of societal customs. While being Zapatista makes it "inappropriate" for indigenous men to be unsupportive in the home, being republican is impacted by both traditional gender images at the macro level, connecting womanhood to caring roles in the private and "manhood" to leadership functions in the public sphere, and new gender images in the community and in the private realm. Whereas the contradiction between perceptions that gender inequality is inappropriate and the conservative national discourse that manifest gender inequality has prevented the new symbolic gender boundaries from permeating social norms and practices in Northern Ireland in the same way than in Chiapas. While in both cases transformed ethnic and gender perceptions encounter traditional images, in Northern Ireland, new perceptions are locked between tradition at the macro level and transformation at the community and micro level of society. In contrast, in Chiapas, these new perceptions determine discourses at all levels of society, a fact that is evident in the way in which symbolic boundary changes are translated into social practice.

Feminist literature often highlights an increase in domestic violence during and in the aftermath of armed conflicts as proof for a continuation of unequal gender structures in the aftermath of conflict (Alison, 2009 Turshen, 2001). It is certainly of great importance to highlight a continuation of violence against women from conflict into peace processes. However, the analyses of female activists' narratives from Northern Ireland and Chiapas reveals that it is also important to recognize shifts in beliefs that have occurred during the conflict and which question the legitimacy of unequal gender structures and gender violence. This research suggests that rather than questioning the continuity of violence against women in the private realm, we need to look at how traditional gender images that legitimize this type of violence are constituted and changed.

Women's voices and experiences have shaped the structure of both the Republican Movement in Northern Ireland and the Zapatista Movement in Chiapas in different ways. While the positioning of the movements in resistance to traditional power structures at the state level allow for the re-creation of gendered structures at the community level, the possibility of actually transforming gendered structures is influenced by the political project of the movement. Ethno-national discourses emphasizing traditional nationalist ideas are less open for structural change than those promoting an agenda that emphasize on social justice and liberation (Yuval-Davis, 1997, p. 103).

The change of gender roles as a result of social mobilizations in Chiapas and in Northern Ireland has been a two-way process: the male public sphere has been penetrated by the female private sphere, and vice versa, the increased presence of women in the public sphere has impacted on women's private life. While many women remained actively involved in their community during settlement processes, in both Chiapas and in Northern Ireland, they often struggle to harmonize their public and their private duties. Changes in women's positioning in the public sphere have altered women's social status, at the same time increasing pressure on women in the private realm. The lack of visibility of these changes in public decision-making processes and the failure to address these changes appropriately in post-agreement structures and processes increases the potential for contention in private male-female relationships. What we can see in Chiapas and in Northern Ireland is a trend toward male-female competition and confusion concerning gender roles in the family, leading to a crisis in intimate partnerships in societies in transition. Men returning to their families after years of imprisonment (Northern Ireland) and men being confronted with a changing discourse on norms and traditions (Chiapas) struggle to adapt to gendered identity changes resulting from mobilization processes. While contentious intimate partnerships have been reported in the narratives of female activists from both conflict regions, the degree of contention and mechanisms to address changes in ethnic and gender boundaries distinguish the two cases.

In Chiapas, a dialogue between the genders on indigenous norms and traditions was encouraged by Zapatista leaders during the conflict and contributed to an increased acceptance of gendered changes by indigenous men post agreement. In Northern Ireland, the space for the creation of a dialogue between men and women to address shifts in gendered perception and positioning was restricted, as women's roles in Northern Ireland changed mainly in the absence of men, who often experienced long terms of imprisonment during the conflict. Therefore, a dialogue about gender roles within the republican community only evolved in the first episode of the peace process, but was pushed back to the margin due to the emphasis on the ethno-national agenda in the official peace talks. In Chiapas, indigenous women have found support for renegotiating gender roles in the private realm in the increasing solidarity between indigenous and nonindigenous feminist activists and in the gender equality policy of the Zapatista Movement, which made it inappropriate for men to be unsupportive at home. The Zapatista Movement further encouraged a dialogue on male and female roles as part of the discussion on indigenous autonomy during the peace talks; in Northern Ireland, this dialogue was largely absent from the formal peace negotiations.

In Chiapas, the demands discussed at the peace table were of a multidimensional nature, connecting the local dimension (land rights, indigenous rights, and indigenous autonomy) to the global fight against neoliberalism (Olesen, 2005); this allowed for the inclusion of women's demands in the aftermath of the armed conflict. In contrast, the focus in Northern Ireland on the ethno-national dimension of conflict fails to include women's voices and demands (Ashe 2012), which reinforces the private nature of sexual violence. Further, in Chiapas, the indigenous Zapatista communities continue to be autonomous spaces after the peace agreement, whereas in Northern Ireland, representatives of the republican communities form part of the power-sharing government. This leads, in the latter case, to a penetration of the community space by conservative gender images, which pushes women and their changed ethnic and gender perceptions to the margins. On the other hand, in Chiapas the community space remains dominated by changed gender images marked by women's participation in the public sphere.

This results in different outcomes of the mobilization and demobilization process at the micro level; first, contention in intimate partnerships, visible in reports about an increase in domestic violence (PSNI, 2012), often connected to an increase in alcoholism in Northern Ireland linked to the lack of reconciling "violent conflict masculinities" (Hamber 2007; Hamber et al., 2006). Second, we can observe in both cases a tendency toward an increasing distance between men and women, evident in many reported martial breakdowns in Northern Ireland and in Chiapas and the decisions of some women not to get married. However, in the latter case we can also see an adaption to changed gender images and powershifts in male-female relationships. These different directions of change are influenced by the way shifts in gender and ethnic perceptions occurring during conflict are addressed (Chiapas) or marginalized (Northern Ireland) in post-agreement politics in the public sphere. Directions of identity change are further impacted by the breadth of autonomous spaces for alliance building on women's shared gender interests across boundaries, which is wide in Chiapas and narrow in Northern Ireland.

In cases where ethnic identity formation develops from bridging differences (episode one of demobilization in Northern Ireland) to reaffirming differences (episode two of demobilization in Northern Ireland), challenges for changing unequal gender structures are high. In processes where the transition from armed conflict follows the direction from highlighting to bridging ethnic differences (Chiapas), obstacles for shifting symbolic and social gendered boundary processes are lower. The availability of independent space, which allows for the bridging of ethnic and class differences, plays a crucial role in the translation from intersubjective perceptions into social change. If and how these independent spaces open up is connected to the identity category being triggered and to the particular level (community, state, family) highlighted within the different episodes of contention and peace.

Episodes of contention open autonomous spaces for the shift in symbolic and social gender boundaries. However, a reengagement with these macro-level structures in peace processes brings revolutionary movements closer to the macro sphere of power. If macro-level processes lead to a reaffirmation of the ethnic boundary, changes at the gender boundary become obscured. The emphasis on changes in ethnic and gender identifications do not simply disappear but remain largely locked between the community and the private sphere. If the emphasis remains on ethno-national concerns at the state level, change in gender identity is not fully embraced in macro-level politics and structures, and the potential for contention increases in the private realm (Northern Ireland). In peace processes that not only focus on the ethnic boundary but which include a wider social justice agenda and a greater range of actors besides ethnic ones, changes in gender identity are better adapted at the micro level (Chiapas); this allows for addressing contention in intimate relationships.

Conclusion

As my comparative research has demonstrated, distinctions in mobilization and demobilization processes in Chiapas and in Northern Ireland reveal different directions of change at the symbolic and at the social level of boundary processes. It further shows centrality of spaces for building solidarity on women's gender interests across ethnic borders in peace and conflict situations for changes at both the symbolic and the social gender boundary.

Contextual differences between the two case studies reveal obstacles and opportunities to translate shifts in the way women perceive themselves as "women," and as part of their community (symbolic boundary), into changes in the gendered structure of the state, the community, and the family (social boundary). The perceptions of female activists from different ethnic and class backgrounds provide individual accounts of reimagining womanhood and show the unexpected dimensions of social change, which are not revealed by exploring ethno-national perspectives alone. Listening to women's voices contributes to breaking down essentialist notions of ethno-national conflict; it reveals the ways in which ethnic and gender identity change in conflict situations and the impact these changes have on women's everyday life in settlement processes. How women from marginalized communities form alliances and the way spaces for alliance formation across ethnic, class, gender, and other boundaries in peace and conflict situations open, brings to light the intersection of identity categories. These intersectional dynamics take on different forms and have different effects at the identity level, related to different modes of alliance building.

Although perceptions and positioning within each category differ, we can observe some general trends evolving from the analysis of female activists' collective identity narratives from Chiapas and Northern Ireland. Processes of deessentializing womanhood during conflict often collide with mechanisms that reaffirm unequal gender structures in societies in transition. If and how ethnic and gender identity changes occurring during social mobilizations become translated into structural changes in demobilization processes is influenced by the way ethnic identity is highlighted at the macro level. This translation is visible in the way in which ethnic distinctions become institutionalized in the state structure, in policymaking, in party-political agendas, and the like. On the other hand, increasing contention in the private realm stems from the lack of addressing gender and ethnic identity change in the aftermath of armed conflict.

6

Lessons Learned from Listening to Women's Voices in Peace and Conflict Situations

> *Realizing that I [as mestiza] can learn a lot from the indigenous women broke down a hierarchy I had in my head and allowed me to learn from the rich knowledge and experiences of the indigenous Zapatistas, their spirituality and the way they work with men. It taught me to understand that we need a constructive dialogue based on "differences and equality" to transform our society. As white or mestiza women we cannot create this change without our indigenous sisters, women cannot create change without getting men to accept this change. But we can only work together if we understand where we come from, our differences. Indigenous women have taught me to listen carefully, to listen, not only to talk, that's where we need to start.*
>
> Cristina, mestiza women's rights and community activist, San Cristóbal de las Casas, Chiapas[1]

In Chiapas and in Northern Ireland, women were actors in the ideological re-creation of the community and in the transformation of its culture. Shifts in women's ethnic and gender perceptions during conflict are interlinked with changes in the positioning of women toward the state, the community, and the family. However, in order to be widely accepted these shifts at the intersubjective level of identification need to be translated into objectified, social changes in demobilization processes. The opening of autonomous spaces for women to bridge boundaries and form alliances on shared interests has brought about transformations in both ethnic and gender identity, in Chiapas more than in Northern Ireland. This is evident in the visibility of shifts in women's image from being "silent symbols of resistance" to being "vocal agents of change" and in the translation of these shifts in perception into changes in gendered power structures. Ethnonational mobilizations against unequal power structures provide a space for the formation of shared gender interests amongst women within a certain ethnic category. However, the autonomous space available for extending this process of alliance formation beyond ethnic and class boundaries determines the potential for symbolic changes to become social reality; the way in which these shifts manifest at different levels of society (state, community, family) distinguishes Chiapas from Northern Ireland. A comparison of the two cases demonstrates how one-dimensional peace processes, which only highlight one boundary, namely the ethno-national, first, prevent new images of womanhood to penetrate the public sphere. Second, it shows that these processes lead to competition between traditional and shifted gender perceptions and structures at the community level and increase the potential for contention in male-female intimate partnerships at the micro level. Finally, peace processes solely focusing on the ethno-national boundary can bring challenges in alliance building on shared gender interests across different boundaries. These are general trends and tendencies evolving from this analysis, which do not encapsulate the diversity and complexity within each identity category evolving from the collective identity narratives. However, while I dedicated much space at the heart piece of this book, Chapters 3 and 4, for presenting these diverse voices, some general findings are important to enhance theory on intersectional identity and on gendered perspectives of ethno-national conflict and its aftermath.

This research shows that it is the private realm in which changes in gender identity become most significantly manifest in the aftermath of armed conflict. However, this micro level of society is largely ignored in peace processes, particularly in those processes that center solely on the regulation of ethno-national distinctions. Contemporary academic literature on ethno-national conflicts and policy analyses has tended to focus on the public sphere and to neglect the private realm. Failures of peace processes, but also significant opportunities to address gender inequality and gender based violence, often get overlooked through the focus on the macro-level of these processes.

Gender literature often emphasizes the poor representation of women in the public sphere, but does often not acknowledge shifts in women's perceptions and positioning in the private realm. In order to understand how women's participation in peace and conflict processes changes ethnic and gender identity, we need a multidimensional and multileveled approach in both policymaking and academic research, which places a particular emphasis on the private sphere. The micro level of analysis is important for revealing gender and ethnic boundary shifts during mobilization and for the translation of these shifts into structural changes in demobilization processes. Most research on post-conflict issues such as domestic violence, mental health issues, or alcoholism emphasizes regressive developments within the micro level in conflict settlement by focusing, for instance, on the increase in violence against women. Although it is of great importance to highlight failures of peace processes, it is also important to recognize shifts that have occurred in gender and other perceptions. The failure to acknowledge the intersection of changes in the ethnic and in gender identity does not allow a comprehensive understanding of the causal factors for contentious dynamics in the private sphere after episodes of armed conflict.

Studies of domestic violence in the transition from conflict to peace often portray women as victims or survivors of abuse, which reduces the agency developing out of the active participation of women from marginalized communities in ethno-national mobilization processes. This transforms the image of the subaltern woman from one of a "vocal agent for change," created during conflict, to that of a "silent victim of violence" and has a disempowering function. In order to avoid this, we need to dedicate more time and resources to investigating the complexity of intersecting changes in perceptions and positioning of both women and men in peace processes.

It is important to pay attention to the homogenizing incentive in academic scholarship, policymaking, and women's activism. While it is often used to achieve more clarity (academic research), or increase effectiveness and efficiency in policymaking and activism, it does not address the complexity of intersectional inequality and identity processes in peace and conflict situations. In order to understand how different dimensions of identity (gender, ethnicity, class, sexual orientation, and etc.) intersect in ethno-national mobilizations and demobilization processes, a multileveled approach that examines how different boundaries are formed, change, and converge at the macro (state), meso (community), and micro (family) level is required.

Female activists' collective identity narratives reveal that women's solidarity on shared gender interests is key to breaking down unequal gender structures and that it is important to acknowledge and respect difference within this process. An inclusive and effective feminist activism needs to acknowledge both the intersection of inequalities, which determine the positioning of women within society, and the way these intersectional inequalities inform how women perceive themselves as "woman," as "Catholic/indigenous," as "poor," as "of a certain age," and so on. To allow the different identifications of women to intersect in the development of women's solidarity on shared gender interests, this process needs to be based on a culture of respect to allow the creation of a dialogue of difference. Only that way feminist activisms can connect in autonomous spaces in which women can build strong alliances and convincingly target unequal power structures and perceptions that legitimize these inequalities.

A contemporary trend in women's activism is its incorporation into the structures that it sets out to break down. The availability of public funding often turns revolutionary feminist activism into a sector based in patriarchal macro-level structures. Certainly, the allocation of financial resources is important and is evidence of the public acknowledgment of the need for change in gendered structures. However, a critical evaluation of public funding intentions, structures, and requirements for the "women's sector" is essential and often not taken into account, as many women's organizations depend on these finances to guarantee their survival. This has not only a disempowering function but repeatedly results in the transformation of revolutionary feminisms into service provision. That way, women's work becomes about addressing the symptom rather than the cause for gender inequality. I do in no way take issue with this kind of women's community activism; it is essential. What I am arguing against is the way the financial dependency on government agencies can reduce feminist agency in women's community work. Dependency on government agencies combined with a misapprehension of "gender equality" can lead to regressive rather than progressive developments. Women's activism needs an autonomous space that allows for solidarity on shared interests across boundaries to develop. On the other hand, mechanisms need to be enhanced that open access for women and other marginalized groups to take active part in political decision making at all levels of society.

I also believe that working with men is crucial to breaking down unequal power structures, but first, we need to empower women and to address specific symptoms of their marginalized positioning in society, such as domestic violence. We can learn from indigenous and nonindigenous activists in Chiapas about the importance of "listening" and "understanding differences" in the formation of alliances on women's gender interests across boundaries. We can also learn from them about the need to create alliances with men. Women's community or grassroots activism contributes great experiences in this regard and provides an opportunity to learn if we listen to their voices. Community activism at the grassroots is a central space for transformation and those bottom-up dynamics based on respect for difference require more attention and support at the macro level of society without creating structures that curtail their transformative potential. That way, we can learn important lessons about the way women from marginalized communities create feminist agency by building bridges and negotiating women's issues in their communities and create spaces where women from different backgrounds can share their experiences and learn from each other.

By listening to women's voices from Chiapas and from Northern Ireland, I learned how social mobilizations against state-perpetrated injustice can open independent spaces for the formation of women's solidarity beyond boundaries. Female activists in both regions helped me to understand how a departure point based on "sameness" impacts negatively women's activism. The analysis of their narratives further allowed me to gain an insight into the way homogenous public peace processes, often based on power sharing of ethno-national groups, can significantly reduce autonomous spaces for women's activisms created during episodes of contention. A reaffirmation of contentious ethnic distinctions in peace processes and the depoliticization of ethnic, class, sexual, or other boundaries within women's movements limit this autonomous space. The structure of macro-level funding initiatives often negatively impact on women's activism, if they are designed to control and incorporate activism, rather than to strengthen it. An awareness of the ways in which macro-level dynamics reproduce unequal gender structures at the community level is crucial if financial support is to create agency for change and further solidarity amongst women, rather than contention.

Within this context, we need to reflect on the way we do academic research as well. Unfortunately, academic feminist research and theory development is often detached from feminist activism. Most work focuses on "studying" women in society, the way women engage in identity processes, how they experience inequality, and so on. Time, space, and funding constraints often do not allow academic researchers to work with women and listen actively to their experiences, perceptions, and perspectives. Furthermore, the false presumption of academic neutrality prevents many female academics from showing a political commitment with the "objects" of research as they are required to "neutralize" their feminist voice in order to have a credible voice in an often male dominated academic world; this is particularly true for subjects such as international relations, although scholars like Cynthia Enloe had a significant impact on the reframing of the discipline.

A multilevel approach, based on the acknowledgment and the respect for difference, is needed in research, policymaking, and activism in order to address the complexity of conflict and conflict settlement processes and enhance the development toward sustainable peace. Within this approach, it is important to listen to women's voices, to learn from their experiences of intersectional inequality, but also to actively support their work. Therefore, in order to ensure "respect for difference" in research practice and to create feminist agency, feminist research should not only focus on data gathering, but also on working *with* and *for the benefit* of women in order to give the objects of the study ownership of the project. My field research was restricted by time, space, and funding requirements. However, it was important for me to develop a bottom-up research approach, building on the activist work I have been involved in. Positioned as an academic researcher, activist, moderator, and facilitator of dialogues of difference, I set out to "listen" and to "learn" from the research participants, to enhance transformative learning processes, and to support women's activism in the respective post-conflict situations.

My research was informed by and engaged with women's activism in Chiapas by working with partners to create independent spaces for feminist activists to listen to and learn from each other's experiences and to create alliances for changing unequal power structures. By using an active-participatory approach involving the participants in the planning process of a two-day workshop and in the facilitation of the event, I learned about how our work can reaffirm unequal ethnic and class power structures, for instance, of positioning those who speak Spanish and have learned how to read and write over those who speak indigenous languages and are illiterate. Listening to the participants' advice to giving indigenous languages and Spanish the same space, we were able to address existing ethnic and class power hierarchies rather than affirming them.

The use of visual[2] and oral didactical methods such as the visualization technique and the theater of the oppressed enriched the exchange of experiences. It allowed me to adapt my pace to the pace of work of female activists from Chiapas as it encouraged us to slow down and to pay attention to the moment. I experienced how the slowing down and focusing fully on the moment brings the embodied "self" into the presence and allows for transformative learning. These processes were essentially emotional and imaginative rather than rational, conceptual, and linguistic. The creative tools we used in the workshop enabled us to find a way to communicate across language boundaries and fundamental differences in our ways of seeing the world or in our experiences. In order to provide continuity for the work started as part of this research, I created with collaborators of the two-day active-participative workshop resources to share with the participants. For instance, we videotaped the event and left copies of the video, along with the visual maps painted by participants, in their respective groups and communities. This information has been used by the participants in workshops they organized as follow up activities to further enhance dialogues about the Revolutionary Women's Law with men and women of their communities. Another outcome of this workshop was the formation of an alliance of indigenous and nonindigenous female activists that coordinated forces in the organization of a public forum and a march to highlight the problem of "violence against women."[3]

In Northern Ireland, I participated in and supported the organization of consultations with women affected by conflict from the Island of Ireland, from Liberia and from Timor L'Este. The consultation process was set up to feed into the development of a national action plan of the Irish government to implement the United Nations Security Council Resolution 1325 on "Women Peace and Security" in the Republic of Ireland. It opened a space not only for women to inform the process and have their voices included in this joint government and civil society initiative, but also provided a possibility for women to learn from each other, to support each other, and to create alliances as the workshops created safe spaces and an imaginative process geared toward the creation of a sustainable peace that is inclusive, participative, just, equal, and nonviolent.

This research project is part of a journey on which I have listened to and learnt from women about the way they engage in identity work and on how they have created and changed ethnic and gender boundaries in peace and conflict processes. The project brought in and built on my experiences as a feminist, human rights, and social justice activist. I set out to listen to the voices of the women who informed and formed part of this project and let those voices be heard within my work. Many voices have informed this research, voices of female activists from Chiapas and from Northern Ireland who participated in this project, those of academics who gave their advice and have published research on which I built, those of the many individual women and men I met on this journey. My journey will continue. I would like to conclude this part of my journey with the words of a friend who took part in this research and who tragically lost her life in the struggle for her rights as "indigenous," as "poor," and as a "woman":

> *My energy I gain from the others that made me the woman I am, I am not only a wife, a mother, a daughter, an aunt, I am someone who organizes in the community, I am a teacher, a food grower, I am also a grower of ideas and dreams, I am many women. I have to carry on growing food, growing dreams, growing ideas, growing hope, so I will not die.*
>
> Beatrice (Bety) Cariño,
> Indigenous Mixteca community and women's rights activist,
> Mexico[4]

Notes

1 Identity in Transition: Concept, Context, and Complexity

1. See, for instance, Cockburn (1998); Jayawardena (1986); Yuval-Davis (1997); and Yuval-Davis & Anthias (1989).
2. "Whiteness" was interpreted by women of color as part of the "essence" of womanhood that feminism represented (Conaghan, 2009, p. 23).
3. For a more detailed history, see, for example, Brah and Phoenix (2004).
4. For a further discussion on analytical issues in conceptualizing the intersectionality of social distinctions, see, for instance, Butler (1990), Yuval-Davis (2006).
5. For a further, in-depth elaboration on this aspect, see Jenkins (1996).
6. For an overview on different notions from the voluminous literature, see Brubaker and Cooper (2004).
7. For more detail, see, for instance, Cockburn (2000), Vickers & Druhvarajan (2002), Yuval-Davis (1997).
8. See Ashmore et al. (2004, p. 81), Fearon (1999, p. 13,16).
9. See Lamont (2012); Lamont & Molnar (2002); Pachucki et al. (2007); Todd (2005, 2010); Wimmer (2008).

2 Addressing Complexity and Difference in Research Methodology

1. For more information, please see, L. Alcoff & Potter (1993).
2. I will, in the following, refer to mixed-race women and mixed-race culture, state structures, and the like in Chiapas/Mexico by using the term mestiza (in relation to women)/mestizo (as regards to state).
3. For more information, please see http://www.sipaz.org/crono/proceng.htm accessed July 31, 2014.
4. The victims of the massacre in Acteal on December 22, 1997, were members of the pacifistic organization *Las Abejas* founded in 1992 to defend their basic human rights. Some 325 members of this organization were displaced to Acteal after having fled the violence perpetuated by paramilitary groups in their communities since mid-1997. According to witnesses, on December 22, 1997, a large group of paramilitaries, wearing police-like uniforms, entered the community and

started to shoot with high caliber weapons against the crowd, which at that moment was fasting and praying for peace. None of the victims was armed, and when the shooting started, they tried to flee. The result of this attack: 15 children, 21 women, and 9 men were killed and 25 wounded, some of them, seriously. "Fray Bartolomé De Las Casas' Human Rights Center, 'Acteal: Between Mourning and Struggle (Executive Summary)," http://www.frayba.org/archivo/informes/981201acteal_between_mourning_and_struggle_frayba.pdf, accessed May 26, 2011. For further information, see also, SIPAZ, "Impunity and the Responsibility of Mexican Authorities in the Acteal Case," http://www.sipaz.org/informes/vol13no1/vol13no1e.htm#ENFOQUE, accessed May 26, 2011. And Amnesty International, "Mexico: New Investigation into Acteal Massacre Is Essential," http://www.amnesty.org/en/for-media/press-releases/mexico-new-investigation-acteal-massacre-essential-20090813, accessed July 25, 2011.
5. On discussions of decolonization, please see, Hernández Castillo (2001), Mohanty (1992, p. 74–93), Speed (2006, p. 66–76), and Suárez & Hernández Castillo (2008).
6. I am consciously not using the work post-conflict here, as many female activists who participated in interviews or workshops felt uncomfortable or even rejected the use of the term.
7. My research has been granted ethical approval by the Human Research Ethics Committee in University College Dublin.
8. The Dublin workshop took place on November 17, 2010, in the Royal Irish Academy with 60 participants; the Derry workshop with 37 women took place in C.A.L.M.S. center on the December 2, 2010.
9. I am academic advisor to the consultancy and monitoring body for the implementation of UN Security Council Resolution 1325 in Ireland.
10. For instance, the event MujeresTrabajan con Mujeres with 41 mestiza and indigenous women's rights activists and academics took place in San Cristóbal de Las Casas on June 26, 2010.
11. The Revolutionary Women's Law is a key document of the Zapatista struggle entailing the specific demands of female Zapatista activists. Being the outcome of a consultation with indigenous Zapatista activists, the Women's Law from 1993 has impacted on women's activism both within and outside the Zapatista Movement. It was extended from 10 to 31 demands during the peace talks in 1996.
12. In November 2010, women from different organizations—including those who participated in the workshop—gathered at a forum in San Cristóbal de las Casas, in the highlands of Chiapas, to discuss the situations of violence experienced by women, and organized about 150 women, mostly from indigenous and peasant communities, as well as trade union members to march to address the issue of violence against women in Tuxtla Gutierrez, the Capital of Chiapas. The participants of our workshop took part in organizing these events and reported back to me that the workshop provided a space for feeding into the organization of the event.

13. This includes the following organizations: CIOAC (Central Independiente de Obreros Agrícolas y Campesinos), UNORCA (Unión Nacional de Organizaciones Regionales Campesinas Autónomas), and the ARIC-independiente (Asociación Rural de Interés Colectivo).
14. This includes the following organizations: Centro de los Derechos de la Mujer de Chiapas and the Diocesan Commission for Woman (CODIMUJ) in San Cristóbal de las Casas.
15. This includes the following organizations: SERAPAZ and the Centro de Derechos Humanos Fray Pedro Lorenzo de la Nada, both located in Ocosingo.
16. Due to issues of security and confidentiality, location and name of the community will not be mentioned in this research. It has been a community whose members have been involved in various mobilization processes: the farmers' movement, the Zapatista Movement, and some female members of the community define themselves as indigenous women's rights activists.

3 From the Margin to the Center: Female Narratives of Ethno-National Mobilization

1. Workshop "Women and the Conflict in Chiapas," Ocosingo (Chiapas), July 13 and July 14, 2010.
2. For more information on the history of Chiapas, please see, Olivera & Palomo (2005); Tobler (1994).
3. The mestizo/mixed race myth or the official narrative of Mexican national integration has its recorded origin in the colonial chronicle of Diaz De Castillo (1978).
4. The official founding date of the EZLN is November 17, 1983, but its roots go back to the indigenous and farmers' protests in the 1970s and 1980s (Kerkeling, 2003, p. 132).
5. For further information on the farmers' movement, please see, García De León (1985), González Esponda (1989).
6. Interview conducted on June 28, 2010, in San Cristóbal de las Casas, page 1, lines 7–11. Translation from Spanish to English by author.
7. Workshop organized on July 13 and July 14, 2010, in Ocosingo, Region Selva, Chiapas, page 3, line 22ff.
8. Article 27 was implemented in the Mexican Constitution after the Revolution in order to diffuse the existing of land concentration for the benefit of the small-scale farming, which benefits the small indigenous communities. For further details, see, Benjamin (1989).
9. Interview conducted on July 16, 2010, in San Cristóbal de las Casas, page 7, lines 17–22.
10. Interview conducted on July 16, 2010, in San Cristóbal de las Casas, page 12, lines 3–7.
11. President Lázaro Cárdenas passed the 1934 Agrarian Code and accelerated the pace of land reform.

12. A dynamic that formed part of the workshop organized on July 13 and July 14, 2010, in Ocosingo, Region Selva, Chiapas.
13. The Mayan founding myth is based on the following ideas: a) the whole cosmos is conceived of elements that balance against each other through their differences and create that way an equilibrium, this balance is constantly shifting, b) the earth is a person and it is sacred, a place of origins, a symbol that fuses with indigenous women's identity, c) the interconnectedness of all beings, and d) the heart is the center of all intellectual activities, it is not a reference to feelings or love, but to the origin of life, (Marcos, 2005, p. 81–112).
14. Interview conducted on July 2, 2010, in Tuxtla Gutierrez, page 2 line 4–5.
15. Many activists described the 70 years in which the Party of the Institutionalised Revolution was in power in Mexico as "dictatorship" (field notes, interviews).
16. Interview conducted on July 2, 2010, in Tuxtla Gutierrez, page 3, line 19ff.
17. Interview conducted on July 19, 2010, in San Cristóbal de las Casas, page 1, line 10–11.
18. Interview conducted on July 2, 2010, in Tuxtla Gutierrez, page 2 line 4–5.
19. Interview conducted on July 3, 2010, in San Cristóbal de las Casas, page 7, line 13–14.
20. Interview conducted on July 3, 2000, in San Cristóbal de las Casas, page 2 line 4.
21. Interview conducted on July 3, 2010, in San Cristóbal de las Casas, page 21, lines 19–22.
22. Article 27 was implemented in the Mexican Constitution after the Revolution in order to diffuse the existing of land concentration for the benefit of the small scale farming, which benefits the small indigenous communities. The change of Article 27 in 1992 has led to a reprivatization of indigenous land and again to an increase in land concentration in the hands of mestizas and multinational companies. See, for further details, Benjamin (1989).
23. Interview conducted on July 17, 2000, in San Cristóbal de las Casas, page 2, line 21.
24. Interview conducted on July 3, 2000, in San Cristóbal de las Casas, page 8, line 35.
25. Interview conducted on June 28, 2010, in San Cristóbal de las Casas, page 1, lines 7–11.
26. Interview conducted on June 28, 2010, in San Cristóbal de las Casas, page 1, line 14.
27. See interviews conducted on July 2, 2010, in Tuxtla Gutierrez, on July 11, 15, 16, and 19, 2010, in San Cristóbal de las Casas.
28. Interview conducted on July 2, 2010, in Tuxtla Gutierrez, page 8, lines 3–7.

29. Interview conducted on July 18, 2010, in San Cristóbal de las Casas, page 4, line 38ff.
30. Interview conducted on July 3, 2010, in San Cristóbal de las Casas, page 21, lines 3–4.
31. Interview conducted on July 17, 2010 in San Cristóbal de las Casas, page 15, line 4ff.
32. Workshop "Women and the Conflict in Chiapas," Ocosingo (Chiapas), July 13 and July 14, 2010, page 14, line 6.
33. The Revolutionary Women's Law is a key document of the Zapatista struggle entailing the specific demands of female Zapatista activists. Being the outcome of a consultation with indigenous Zapatista activists, the Women's Law of 1993 has impacted on women's activism both within and outside the Zapatista Movement.
34. Interview conducted on April 22, 2010, in Dublin, page 2, line 31.
35. Interview conducted on April 22, 2010, in Dublin, page 2, line 31.
36. Interview conducted on July 11, 2010, in San Cristóbal de las Casas, page 7, line 21.
37. Interview conducted on July 19, 2010, page 5, line 9.
38. Interview conducted on July 19, 2010, page 5, line 9.
39. Interview conducted on July 2, 2010, in Tuxtla Gutierrez, page 4, lines 30ff.
40. Interview conducted on July 2, 2010, in Tuxtla Gutierrez, page 4, lines 30ff.
41. Focus group, July 7, 2010, northern region of Chiapas, page 7, line 24.
42. Refer to note 13.
43. Focus group, July 7, 2010, northern region of Chiapas, page 7, line 24.
44. Interview conducted on July 16, 2010, in San Cristóbal de las Casas, page 8, lines 11–13.
45. A group of nuns—since 1992 known as CODIMUJ—started organizing indigenous women based on the idea to interpret with the indigenous women the bible with the mind, with the eyes, and through the heart of women—*con mente, ojo y corazón de mujer*. The group is active in the area of the dioceses of San Cristóbal de las Casas in Chiapas, Mexico, but has a network with indigenous women in other parts of Chiapas, Mexico, and also on an international level. Their work focuses on four pillars, mystic (*mística*), culture (*cultura*), gender (*genero*), and analysis (*análisis*).
46. References to the home as prison appear in interviews conducted on June 28, July 15, and July 17, 2010, in San Cristóbal de las Casas and in focus group discussion organized on July 7, 2010, in a rural indigenous village in the Selva region of Chiapas.
47. Interview conducted on June 28, 2010, in San Cristóbal de las Casas, page 5, line 30.
48. Focus group, July 7, 2010, northern region of Chiapas, page 7, lines 22–27.

49. Interview conducted on April 22, 2009, in Dublin, page 4, line 19ff.
50. These organizations include the, CODIMUJ, the Women's Rights Center of Chiapas (Centro de Derechos de Mujer de Chiapas), the Women's Group of San Cristóbal de las Casas (Grupo de Mujeres de San Cristóbal de las Casas, later renamed COLEM), the Center for Research and Action for Women (Centro de Investigación and Acción para la Mujer, CIAM), and other spaces of peace, women's, and human rights activism.
51. Focus group, July 7, 2010, in a rural indigenous village in the Selva region of Chiapas, page 6, line 4–6.
52. See references in interviews with indigenous women, such as interviews conducted on June 17, 2010, in Ocosingo, on June 28, July 15, and July 17, 2010, in San Cristóbal de las Casas, and in focus group organized on July 7, 2010, in a rural indigenous village in the Selva region of Chiapas.
53. Interview conducted on July 17, 2010, in San Cristóbal de las Casas, page 9, line 11.
54. Interview conducted on June 28, 2010, in San Cristóbal de las Casas, page 9, line 13.
55. There have been violent attacks post-peace agreement, but these events (from the start of the peace process in the early 1990s until 2010) form part of chapter 4.
56. Interview conducted on February 26, 2010, in Belfast, page 2, lines 7 and 8.
57. Interview conducted on February 26, 2010, in Belfast, page 2, lines 46–49.
58. Interview conducted on February 26, 2010, in Belfast, page 7, line 20.
59. Interview conducted on March 30, 2010, in Belfast, page 2, line 41–page 3, line 4.
60. All interview participants from republican background referred to the armed conflict in Northern Ireland as "war."
61. Interview conducted on March 8, 2010, in Belfast, page 1, lines 14 and 15.
62. Interview conducted on March 8, 2010, in Belfast, page 2, line 52–page 3, line 3.
63. Interview conducted on March 8, 2010, in Belfast, page 2, line 52–page 3, line 3.
64. Protestant area in West Belfast.
65. Protestant area in South Belfast
66. Interview conducted on March 8, 2010, in Belfast, page 1, lines 17–19.
67. Parades are an important part of Northern Irish culture. Although the majority of parades are held ostensibly by Protestant, unionist, or Ulster loyalist groups, nationalist, republican, and nonpolitical groups

also parade. For more information please see: http://cain.ulst.ac.uk/issues/parade/jarman.htm accessed on July 31, 2014.
68. Interview conducted on March 8, 2010, in Belfast, page 1 line 46ff.
69. Interview B conducted on March 8, 2010, in Belfast, page 2, line 52–page 3, line 3.
70. Interview B conducted on March 8, 2010, in Belfast, page 2, line 52–page 3, line 3.
71. Interview conducted on May 7, 2010, in Belfast, page 20, line 28.
72. Interview conducted on May 7, 2010, in Belfast, page 21, lines 7–8.
73. During August 12–17, 1969, Northern Ireland was rocked by intense political and sectarian rioting. There had been sporadic violence throughout the year arising from the civil rights campaign, which was demanding an end to discrimination against Irish Catholics and nationalists. Civil rights marches were repeatedly attacked by both Ulster Protestant loyalists and by the Royal Ulster Constabulary (RUC), a largely Protestant police force. Belfast saw by far the most intense violence of the August 1969 riots. Unlike Derry, where Catholic nationalists were a majority, in Belfast they were a minority and were also geographically divided and surrounded by Protestants and loyalists.
74. The Falls Curfew (also called the Battle of the Falls or the Rape of the Lower Falls) was a British Army operation during July 3–5, 1970, in an area along the Falls Road in Belfast, Northern Ireland. The operation started with a weapons search but quickly developed into rioting and gun battles between British soldiers and the official IRA. Women from the Falls Road developed a support structure in order to get food and other urgent supplies into their community.
75. Operation Demetrius (or internment as it is more commonly known) began in Northern Ireland on the morning of Monday, August 9, 1971. Operation Demetrius was launched by the British Army and RUC and involved arresting and interning (without trial) people accused of being paramilitary members.
76. Bloody Sunday took place on January 30, 1972, in the Bogside area of Derry, Northern Ireland, in which 26 unarmed civil rights protesters and bystanders were shot by soldiers of the British Army. The incident occurred during a NICRA march; the soldiers involved were the First Battalion of the Parachute Regiment.
77. Interview conducted on May 7, 2010, in Belfast, page 15, line 1ff.
78. Interview B conducted on March 8, 2010, in Belfast, page 15, line 3ff.
79. Interview conducted on March 8, 2010, in Belfast, page 7.
80. Interview A conducted on March 8, 2010, in Belfast, page 10, lines 46–49.
81. Interview B conducted on March 8, 2010, in Belfast, page 15, lines 5 and 6.
82. Interview conducted on May 7, 2010, in Belfast, page 15, line 1ff.
83. Interview conducted on May 7, 2010, in Belfast, page 16, line 40.
84. Interview conducted on May 30, 2010, page 7, line 7ff.

85. Interview B conducted on March 8, 2010, in Belfast, page 2, line 52–page 3, line 3.
86. Interview B conducted on March 8, 2010, in Belfast, page 2, line 52–page 3, line 3.
87. Interview B conducted on March 8, 2010, in Belfast, page 2, line 52–page 3, line 3.
88. Interview B conducted on March 8, 2010, in Belfast, page 2, line 52–page 3, line 3.
89. Interview conducted on May 13, 2010, in Belfast, page 7, line 32, page 8, lines 18 and 37–39.
90. Interview conducted on May 13, 2010, in Belfast, page 7, line 32, page 8, lines 18 and 37–39.
91. Interview conducted on May 13, 2010, in Belfast, page 7, line 32, page 8, lines 18 and 37–39.
92. Interview conducted on May 13, 2010, in Belfast, page 7, line 32, page 8, lines 18 and 37–39.
93. Interview conducted on May 13, 2010, in Belfast, page 7, line 32, page 8, lines 18 and 37–39.
94. Interview A conducted on March 8, 2010, in Belfast, page 3, line 5.
95. Interview A conducted on March 8, 2010, in Belfast, page 3, line 5.
96. Interview conducted on March 8, 2010, in Belfast, page 3.
97. Interview conducted on March 8, 2010, in Belfast, page 3.
98. Interview conducted on March 8, 2010, in Belfast, page 3.
99. Interview conducted on March 30, 2010, page 7, lines 3–7.
100. Interview conducted on March 30, 2010, page 6, line 27.
101. Interview conducted on March 30, 2010, page 7, lines 9–11.
102. Interview conducted on February 26, 2010, in Belfast, page 3, lines 11ff.
103. Interview conducted on February 26, 2010, in Belfast, page 3, line 9.
104. Interview conducted on March 24, 2010, in Belfast, page 5, lines 13–15.
105. Interview conducted on March 24, 2010, in Belfast, page 5, lines 13–15.

4 THE MEANING OF CONTENTIOUS PEACE: A MULTILAYERED APPROACH TO CONFLICT SETTLEMENT

1. Taking into account the critique of female activists on the term "post-conflict" in interviews I conducted, I will use the term "post-agreement" instead of referring to the episode after the signing of peace agreements.
2. With dissident women I am referring to women who are organized and participate actively in the promotion of state-perpetrated injustice and gender injustice.
3. The peace accords of San Andres are based on five principles: basic respect for the diversity of the indigenous population, the conservation of the natural resources within the territories used and occupied by indigenous peoples, a greater participation of indigenous communities in the decisions and control of public expenditures, the participation of

indigenous communities in determining their own development plans, and the autonomy of indigenous communities and their right of free determination in the framework of the State. The COCOPA (Comisión de Concordia y Pacificación) initiative by the federal congress' monitoring body responsible for overseeing talks between the two groups started an attempt to convert the original San Andres Accords into legislation, a proposal that was accepted by the EZLN, but was first rejected by the Mexican government under President Zedillo. http://www.globalexchange.org/countries/americas/mexico/SanAndres.html accessed August 1, 2014.

4. Two-and-a-half million Mexican citizens (over 90 percent of all participants) confirmed the political legitimacy of the Zapatista demands in the second national consultation (consulta nacional), which was conducted on March 21, 1999, in all parts of the country by 5,000 Zapatistas—2,500 male and 2,500 female Zapatista activists. Kerkeling (2003, p. 271).

5. The peace accords of 1996 focus on "indigenous rights," including the preservation of natural resources occupied by indigenous peoples, autonomy of indigenous peoples over their development, control over public expenditure, and the right to participate in state affairs. For further information on the content of the San Andres Peace Accords, please see, Aubry (2003, p. 219–41).

6. The 2001 Law of Indigenous Rights and Culture is much weaker in terms of indigenous self-determination, recognition of collective rights to land, territory, and natural resources, and the right of indigenous communities to regional affiliation, among other points.

7. Servicio Internacional para la Paz (International Service for Peace—SIPAZ), an international NGO based in San Cristóbal, defines low-intensity warfare as the "modality of counterinsurgency war against organized peoples" that uses psychological, military, religious, and informational tools to disarticulate movements that challenge the status quo and "destroy the support bases of the EZLN" (SIPAZ, 2006). For further information on the low-intensity warfare in Chiapas, please see, Johnston (2000); Swords (2007); and Castro Apreza (1999).

8. "Las Abejas" is a Christian, pacifist group in the highlands of Chiapas. They have the same demands like the Zapatistas, but do not support their armed resistance.

9. The violent paramilitary attack on the Christian pacifist group Las Abejas resulted in the killing of 45 civilians, 15 children, 21 women, and 9 men. "Fray Bartolomé De Las Casas," Human Rights Center, "Acteal: Between Mourning and Struggle (Executive Summary)." http://www.frayba.org/archivo/informes/981201acteal_between_mourning_and_struggle_frayba.pdf, accessed May 26, 2011. For further information, see also, SIPAZ, "Impunity and the Responsibility of Mexican Authorities in the Acteal Case," http://www.sipaz.org/informes/vol13no1/vol13no1e.htm#ENFOQUE, accessed May 26, 2011. And http://www.amnesty.org/en/for-media/press-releases

/mexico-new-investigation-acteal-massacre-essential-20090813, accessed May 26, 2011.
10. For instance, the daily national Mexican newspaper *La Jornada*, who provided a public platform for Zapatista demands, particularly in the special editions "La Jornada Sin Fronteras," for example, January 6, 2004, March 20, 2004, January 17, 2004, January 15, 2004, and December 31, 2003.
11. See, for instance, Hermann Bellinghausen (1999) or Luis Hernandez Navarro (2003).
12. The so-called caracoles are the regional coordination of the autonomous communities; the result of an internal reorganization of the relationship between the political arm of the movement—the autonomous communities—and the military wing, the EZLN, and between the movement and its external supporters. The "Juntas de Buen Gobierno" (JBG) are the formal representation of the autonomous communities, which from a part of the "caracol" (snail house). It is organized on the basis of democracy; its representatives rotate every few weeks. They are the point of connection of external supporters with the Zapatista Movement and coordinate the distribution of the material support the movement receives from outside.
13. On the June 28, 2005, the Zapatistas declared in their Sixth Declaration of the Lacandon Jungle, short "la sexta," their principles and vision on both a national and an international base. It reiterates the support for the indigenous peoples and extends the cause to include "all the exploited and dispossessed of Mexico." It further expresses the movement's sympathy to the international alter-globalization movement, and offers support for people suffering and fighting neoliberal globalization in Cuba, Bolivia, Ecuador, and elsewhere, with whom they share common cause. The declaration ends with an exhortation for all who have more respect for humanity than for material values to join with the Zapatistas in the struggle for social justice both in Mexico and abroad. The declaration called for an alternative national campaign (the other campaign) as an alternative to the presidential campaign of 2005. The other campaign remains post-2005 as element of diffusion and brokerage of the Zapatista remobilization. For more information, please see: Aguirre (2007); Anguiano, A. (2006); Rey & Barrera (2007).
14. Interview conducted on July 9, 2010, in Ocosingo, Chiapas, page 4, lines 24–45.
15. Interview conducted on April 22, 2009, in Dublin, page 2, lines 31ff.
16. Story shared in workshop dynamic "theatre of the oppressed," July 13 and 14, 2010, Ocosingo, Chiapas (Mexico), page 19.
17. Interview conducted on July 2, 2010, in Tuxtla Gutierrez, page 11, line 11.
18. Interview conducted on July 19, 2010, in San Cristóbal de las Casas, page 4, line 17.
19. Interview conducted on July 9, 2010, in Ocosingo, Chiapas, page 4, line 52–53.

20. Oportunidades is the principal antipoverty program of the federal Mexican government. Founded in 1997, the original name of the program was Progresa; the name was changed in 2002. It is directed at women and funds are distributed monthly in accordance with the number of children. The money is for the purpose of attending medical consultations and sessions on preventative medicine. Albeit praised by World Bank and academics and imitated by other governments, the program is criticized, in particular among indigenous women for, being overbearing in its encouragement of birth control or sterilization right after or even during birth; in some cases sterilizations on indigenous women are carried out without their consent. It is considered a factor of the internal divisions in rural communities, as opposition groups such as the Zapatistas refuse to accept these funds. (Field notes, in particular of an encounter of feminist community activists and academics [mestiza, indigenous, and international] "Encuentro de mujeres trabajando con mujeres," June 25 and 26, 2010, in San Cristóbal de las Casas, Chiapas). For more information on the program, please see, Smith-Oka (2009); Gutierrez (2010).
21. Interview conducted on July 16, 2010, in San Cristóbal de las Casas, page 9, lines 18–21.
22. (Programa de Certificación de Derechos Ejidales y Titulación de Solares Urbanos); for more details, please see, DeVos (2002).
23. Interview conducted on July 19, 2010, in San Cristóbal de las Casas, page 12, lines 10–13.
24. Indigenous women often use the term wordless as synonym for worthless ("no tengo palabras") in reference to their disadvantaged life situation.
25. These phrases as quoted in the text occur in various interviews I conducted with indigenous women in Chiapas, in particular, in the order I use them here, in the interview with Carmen, an indigenous women's activist, conducted on June 28, 2010, in San Cristóbal de las Casas, Chiapas.
26. "Being able to read and write" and to communicate and "construct a dialogue in their indigenous language and in Spanish."
27. For more details, please see, DeVos (2002).
28. Interpretation of a visual map positioning men and women in an "ideal community"; the map was created by female activists during the workshop "Women and the Conflict in Chiapas," July 13 and 14, 2010, Ocosingo, Chiapas (Mexico), page 5ff.
29. Interview conducted on July 3, 2010, San Cristóbal de las Casas, Chiapas, page 29, lines 8–12.
30. Interview conducted on July 3, 2010, San Cristóbal de las Casas, Chiapas page 32, lines 35–36.
31. For more details, please see, Centro De Derechos Humanos Fray Bartolomé De Las Casas (2011).
32. The Revolutionary Women's Law is a key document of the Zapatista struggle entailing the specific demands of female Zapatista activists. Being the outcome of a consultation with indigenous Zapatista activists,

the Women's Law from 1993, extended in 1996, has impacted on women's activism both within and outside the Zapatista Movement.
33. In May 2014, the head of the Zapatista rebels in southern Mexico, known as Subcomandante Marcos, has announced that he is leaving the group's leadership.
34. Please see note 13. In preparation for this alternative campaign, the Zapatistas invited to their territory over 600 national leftist organizations, indigenous groups, and nongovernmental organizations in order to listen to their claims for human rights and social justice in a series of biweekly meetings that culminated in a plenary meeting on September 16, 2005, the day Mexico celebrates its independence from Spain. In this meeting, Subcomandante Marcos requested official adherence of the organizations to the Sixth Declaration, and detailed a six-month tour of the Zapatistas through all 31 Mexican states that took place concurrently with the electoral campaign starting January 2006. The other campaign remains post-2005 an element of diffusion and brokerage of the Zapatista remobilization.
35. Interview conducted on June 17, 2010, in Ocosingo, page 12–13.
36. Interview conducted on June 17, 2010, in Ocosingo, page 9–11.
37. Both the women's forum/assembly and the march had been organized in November 2010, the women's assembly took place in San Cristóbal de las Casas, while the march was organized in Tuxtla Gutierrez, the capital of Chiapas: both events brought together many women from different ethnic communities, class backgrounds, and sexualities in solidarity against violence against women.
38. Interpretation of an "activism" map outlining the planning of activities to promote gender equality provided during the workshop 'Women and the Conflict in Chiapas," July 13 and 14, 2010, in Ocosingo, Chiapas (Mexico), page 31.
39. Interview conducted on July 17, 2010, in San Cristóbal de las Casas.
40. Interview conducted on July 19, 2010, in San Cristóbal de las Casas.
41. Interview conducted on July 19, 2010, in San Cristóbal de las Casas.
42. Interview conducted on July 19, 2010, in San Cristóbal de las Casas.
43. Interview conducted on June 28, 2010, in San Cristóbal de las Casas, page 4, lines 23–24
44. Interview conducted on July 17, 2010, in San Cristóbal de las Casas, page 7, lines 18–19.
45. Interview conducted on July 17, 2010, in San Cristóbal de las Casas, page 7, lines 18–19.
46. Interview conducted on June 28, 2010, in San Cristóbal de las Casas, page 9, lines 17–19.
47. Interview conducted on July 17, 2010, in San Cristóbal de las Casas, page 7, lines 18–19.
48. Interview conducted on July 17, 2010, in San Cristóbal de las Casas, page 18, lines 21–23.
49. Interview conducted on July 17, 2010, in San Cristóbal de las Casas, page 8 line 1.

50. Interview conducted on June 27, 2010, in San Cristóbal de las Casas, page 26, lines 30–31.
51. Conferences organized were, for instance, in 1995, by the European Women's Platform in Northern Ireland and the National Women's Council in Ireland.
52. Interview conducted on March 24, 2010, in Belfast.
53. Interview conducted on March 30, 2010, in Derry, page 18, lines 28–31.
54. Interview conducted on March 24, 2010, in Belfast, page 7, line 32–page 8, line 2.
55. Interview conducted on May 7, 2010, in Belfast, page 5, line 38.
56. Interview conducted on March 24, 2010 in Belfast.
57. Interview conducted on March 24, 2010, in Belfast, page 2, line 3ff.
58. Interview conducted on March 30, 2010, in Belfast, page 14, line 14.
59. Interview conducted on March 30, 2010, in Belfast, page 14, lines 15–16.
60. Interview conducted on March 30, 2010, in Belfast, page 19, line 43.
61. The Opsahl Commission was an independent public inquiry into ways forward for Northern Ireland, which took place from 1992–93; the commission was entirely separate from government and state authorities. For more information on the Opsahl Commission, please see, Elliott (2013); Guelke (2003); Opsahl (1993).
62. Interview conducted with women's rights and community activist May 30, 2010, in Derry, page 10, lines 11–14.
63. Interview conducted on March 30, 2010, in Belfast, page 14, line 14.
64. Interview conducted on March 30, 2010, in Belfast, page 14, lines 23ff.
65. Interview conducted on March 30, 2010, in Belfast, page 16, lines 40–41.
66. Interview conducted on February 26, 2010, in Belfast, page 10, line 1.
67. Interview conducted on March 24, 2010, in Belfast, page 9, line 1.
68. Interview conducted on February, 26, 2010, in Belfast, page 10, lines 3–4.
69. Interview conducted on February, 26, 2010, in Belfast, page 10, lines 11–12.
70. Either "parallel consent," defined as a "majority of those members present and voting, including a majority of the Unionist and Nationalist designations" or a so called weighted majority of 60 percent of "members present and voting, including at least 40 percent of each of the Nationalist and Unionist designations present and voting," is required for key decisions in the devolved Northern Ireland Assembly. Assembly members (MLAs) must designate themselves as Nationalist, Unionist, or "other" on important decisions, in order to measure cross-community support. Such decisions include, for instance, the election of the chair of the assembly and the first minister and deputy first minister, standing orders, and budget allocations. Northern Ireland Act, 1998, http://www.opsi.gov.uk/Acts/acts1998/ukpga_19980047_en_1, accessed July 31, 2011.

71. Four episodes of suspension of the assembly followed the devolution of powers from Westminster (the longest from October 2002 until May 2007).
72. Interview conducted on March 16, 2010, in Belfast page 3, lines 6–13.
73. Refer to note 66.
74. Interview conducted on March 24, 2010, in Belfast, page 8, line 13–23.
75. Interview conducted on March, 24, 2010, in Belfast, page 7, line 15–21.
76. Interview conducted on March, 24, 2010, in Belfast, page 10, line 27.
77. Interview conducted on March 26, 2010, in Belfast, page 7, lines 1–5.
78. Interview conducted on May 7, 2010, in Belfast, page 5, line 36.
79. Interview conducted on May 7, 2010, in Belfast, page 3, line 2.
80. Interview conducted on March 8, 2010, page 9, line 46.
81. Interview conducted on May 7, 2010, in Belfast, page 24, lines 19–20.
82. Interview conducted on March 26, 2010, in Belfast, page 7, lines 21–22.
83. Interview conducted on May 13, 2010, in Belfast, page 6, lines 3–5.
84. Interview conducted on May 13, 2010, in Belfast, page 5, line 32.
85. Interview conducted on May 13, 2010, in Belfast, page 6, line 11.
86. Interview conducted on May 13, 2010, in Belfast, page 9, lines 9–10.
87. Interview conducted on March 24, 2010, in Belfast, page 11, line 24–page 12, line 2.
88. Interview conducted on March 24, 2010, in Belfast, page 11, line 24–page 12, line 2.
89. Interview conducted on May 13, 2010, in Belfast, page 5, line 32.
90. Interview conducted on May 13, 2010, in Belfast, page 6, lines 3–5.
91. Interview conducted on March 8, 2010, page 9, line 46.
92. Interview conducted on May 13, 2010 in Belfast.
93. Interview conducted on May 7, 2010, in Belfast, page 24, line 17.
94. Interview conducted on March 24, 2010, in Belfast, page 9, line 30
95. Interview conducted on March 24, 2010, in Belfast, Page 8, lines 3–5.
96. Interview conducted on March 8, 2010, in Belfast, page 6, line 14.
97. Interview conducted on March 26, 2010, in Belfast, page 6, lines 10–17.
98. Interview conducted on March, 30, 2010, in Derry, page 10, lines 11–14.
99. Interview conducted on March 30, 2010, in Derry, page 5, lines 14–20.
100. Interview conducted on March, 3, 2010, in Belfast, page 12, lines 11–14.
101. Interview conducted on March 30, 2010, in Derry, page 5, line 17.
102. Interview conducted on March, 30, 2010, in Derry, page 10, line 8.
103. Interview conducted on March 26, 2010, in Belfast, page 3, lines 25–26, page 5, lines 10–14, page 9, line 13, and page 10, lines 14–15.

104. Interview conducted on March 16, 2010, in Belfast, page 9, lines 16–17.
105. Interview conducted on March 26, 2010, in Belfast, page 2, line 28.
106. Interview conducted on March 26, 2010, in Belfast, page 2, line 32, page 8, lines 7–8, and page 10, line 30.
107. Field notes taken during an event organized on women, peace, and security with women affected by conflict on the island of Ireland, reference from a grassroots activist from Northern Ireland.
108. Interview conducted on March 26, 2010, in Belfast, page 10, line 30.
109. Interview conducted on May 7, 2010, in Belfast, page 23, lines 11–18.
110. Interview conducted on March 26, 2010, in Belfast, page 5, line 24.
111. Interview conducted on May 7, 2010, in Belfast, page 23, lines 21–22.
112. Interview conducted on May 7, 2010, in Belfast, page 20, lines 11–12.
113. See, for instance, Hamber 2007, Hamber et al. 2006.
114. Interview conducted on March 8, 2010, page 7, line 6ff. Visible also in other interviews with female community activists, conducted on March 8, 9, 24, 26, and 30, 2010, and May 7, 2010.

5 Connecting Boundary Processes during Episodes of Mobilization and Demobilization

1. See, for example, Della Porta (2013) and Mahoney & Thelen (2009).
2. For more on section 75 of the Good Friday Agreement, see chapter 4.
3. For critical feminist discussion of women and the military, see, for instance, Enloe (1983, 2000), Yuval-Davis (1997).
4. For more in-depth studies on female combatants, please see, Alison (2009); Ruddick (1989).
5. This development is visible in the impact of female indigenous activists in the work of independent women's groups such as the Women's Rights Centre in Chiapas or the Feminist Collective in San Cristóbal and in academic-activist initiatives like "women working with women."
6. References appear in interviews with independent women's activists from Northern Ireland.
7. For further critique on the tendency to institutionalize ethnic divisions in consociational peace agreements, please see, Finlay (2011, p.3); Horowitz (1985, p. 575); McGrattan (2010, pp. 181–97).
8. The Revolutionary Women's Law of 1993 consists of ten demands, among which are the right of indigenous women to political participation and leadership positions, the right to a life free of sexual and domestic violence, the right to decide how many children to have and to raise, the right to a fair salary, the right to choose a marriage partner, and the right to good health and education services. For further details, please see, S. Speed, A. R. Hernández Castillo, and L. M. Stephen (eds.), *Dissident Women. Gender and Cultural Politics in*

Chiapas (Austin: University of Texas, 2006) page 3ff. The demands have been extended to 31 in 1996 (Kerkeling, 2003, p. 148).
9. For instance, the civil unrest in San Salvador Atenco in 2006, the foundation of the Autonomous Municipality of San Juan Copala in 2006, mass mobilization after Andrés Manuel López Obrador loses elections in 2006, and so on.
10. With Monica McWilliams and Mary Blood, only two NWCI candidates participated in the 1996 Forum/Peace Negotiations. See, Fearon (1999, p. 168).
11. Visible in the evolution of the *Andersonstown News* from a newssheet for the Andersonstown Central Civil Resistance Committee in 1972 to a privately owned media group of locally influential newspapers, see, Bean (2007).
12. See, for example, Porter (1998, p. 45ff); Ward (1983); Ward and McGivern (1980, pp. 66–72).
13. In their Revolutionary Women's Law, indigenous women were dividing the negative traditions that define women as "assets" or "property" from those perceived as positive and empowering for themselves as women and as indigenous peoples (traditional dress, knowledge of traditional medicine, juridical system, spiritual practices, and etc.) (Blackwell, 2008, p. 121).
14. Images of female Zapatista commanders presenting the Mexican flag at the peace table and speaking in the Mexican parliament on behalf of the movement are evidence of changes at the macro level.

6 Lessons Learned from Listening to Women's Voices in Peace and Conflict Situations

1. Interview conducted on July 19, 2010, in San Cristobal de las Casas, page 5, lines 11ff.
2. Female activists were painting maps of the community and positioning themselves within this setting. The methodology is based on the "Rural Participative Diagnostic," which provides tools for an individual diagnostic, planning, and development processes. For more details, see, Expósito Verdejo (2003).
3. In November 2010, women from different organizations and backgrounds gathered at a forum in San Cristobal to discuss the situations of violence experienced by women from different backgrounds. They also organized about 150 women, mostly from indigenous and peasant communities, as well as union members to march in the Chiapas capital, Tuxtla Gutierrez. The organizations represented in the workshop were part of the organization committee of the event and told me that our workshop provided a space for feeding into the organization of the event.
4. Recorded personal conversation that took place during Latin American Week event in April 2009 in Dublin.

BIBLIOGRAPHY

Aguirre, F. G. (2007). Ante la imposible geometría del poder y la democracia bárbara: La Otra Campaña zapatista. *Perspectivas: Revista de Ciências Sociais*, 30(2), 33–54.

Alcoff, L., & Potter, E. (Eds.). (1993). *Feminist Epistemologies*. New York: Routledge.

Alison, M. H. (2009). *Women and Political Violence: Female Combatants in Ethno-National Conflict*. London: Routledge.

Alsop, R., Fitzsimons, A., & Lennon, K. (2002). *Theorizing Gender*. Oxford: Polity.

Alvarez, S. E. (1990). *Engendering Democracy in Brazil: Women's Movements in Transition Politics*. Princeton: Princeton University Press.

Amnesty International. (February 28, 2005). *Mexico: Justice Fails in Ciudad Juarez and the City of Chihuahua*. Retrieved July 15, 2011, from http://goo.gl/1Swq6V

———. (March 1, 1996). *Overcoming Fear: Human Rights Violations against Women in Mexico*. Retrieved July 15, 2011, from http://goo.gl/0kSmXg

———. (August 13, 2009). *Mexico: New Investigation into Acteal Massacre is Essential*. Retrieved July 25, 2011, from http://goo.gl/LwJ4ra

Anderson, M. (2011). *Identity Change and Powershift: The Case of Loyalism in Northern Ireland* (Unpublished doctoral dissertation). University College Dublin.

Anguiano, A. (2006). La Sexta Declaración, la irrupción de La Otra Campaña y el miedo de la clase política. *Bajo el Volcán*, 6(10), 23–30.

Anthias, F. (2006). Belongings in a Globalising and Unequal World: Rethinking Translocations. In N. Yuval-Davis, K. Kannabiran, & U. Vieten (Eds.), *The Situated Politics of Belonging* (pp. 17–31). London: Sage.

Anthias, F., & Yuval-Davis, N. (1983). Contextualising Feminism—Gender, Ethnic and Class Divisions. *Feminist Review*, 15, 62–75.

Aretxaga, B. (1997). *Shattering Silence. Women, Nationalism and Political Subjectivity in the North*. Princeton: Princeton University Press.

Arzipe, L., & Botey, L. (1986). Las Políticas de Desarrollo Agrario y su Impacto sobre la Mujer Campesina en México. In M. León & C. D. Deere (Eds.), *La Mujer y la Política Agraria en América Latina* (pp. 67–83). Bogotá: Siglo XXI-ACEP.

Ashe, F. (2006). Gendering the Holy Cross School Dispute. Women and Nationalism in Northern Ireland. *Political Studies*, 54(1), 147–64.
———. (2012). Gendering War and Peace: Militarized Masculinities in Northern Ireland. *Men and Masculinities*, 15(3), 230–48.
Ashmore, R. D., Deaux, K., & McLaughlin-Volpe, T. (2004). An Organizing Framework for Collective Identity: Articulation and Significance of Multidimensionality. *Psychological Bulletin*, 130(1), 80–114.
Aubry, A. (2003). Autonomy in the San Andres Accords. In J. Rus, R. A. Hernandez Castillo, & S. L. Mattiace (Eds.), *Mayan Lives, Mayan Utopias. The Indigenous Peoples of Chiapas and the Zapatista Rebellion* (pp. 219–42). Oxford: Rowman & Littlefield Publishers.
Baldez, L. (1997). Primaries vs. Quotas: Gender and Candidate Nominations in Mexico. *Latin American Politics and Society*, 49(3), 69–96.
Bardon, J. (1992). *A History of Ireland*. Belfast: Blackstaff.
Barritt, D.P., & Carter, C.F. (1962). *The Northern Ireland Problem: A Study in Group Relations*. London: Oxford University Press.
Bartolomé, M. A. (1995). Movimientos etnopolíticos y autonomías indigenas en México. *América Indígena*, 1–2, 361–82.
Beale, J. (1986). *Women in Ireland: Voices of Change*. Basingstoke: MacMillan.
Bean, K. (2007). *The New Politics of Sinn Fein*. Liverpool: Liverpool University Press.
Beckett, J.C. (1981). *The Making of Modern Ireland 1603–1923*. London and Boston: Faber & Faber.
Belausteguigoitia, M. (2002). The Colour of the Earth: Indigenous Women before the Law. *Development*, 45(1), 47–53.
Bell, C. (1998). Women, Equality and Political Participation. In J. Anderson & J. Goodman (Eds.), *Dis/Agreeing Ireland: Contexts, Obstacles, Hopes* (pp. 211–231). London: Pluto Press.
Bell, C., & Ní Aoláin, F. (2005). Forward: Women's Rights in Transitioning and Conflicted Societies. In C. O'Rourke (Ed.), *Women and the Implementation of the Good Friday/Belfast Agreement*. Magee Campus: Transitional Justice Institute, University of Ulster.
Bellinghausen, H. (March 11, 1999). La Sociedad Civil, Protagonista en la Búsqueda de un País Mejor. *La Jornada*.
Benjamin, T. (1989). *A Rich Land a Poor People. Politics and Society in Modern Chiapas*. Albuquerque: University of New Mexico Press.
Berger, M. T. (2001). Review Essay: Romancing the Zapatistas International Intellectuals and the Chiapas Rebellion. *Latin American Perspectives*, 28(2), 149–170.
Berger, P., & Luckmann, T. (1966). *The Social Construction of Reality: A Treatise in the Sociology of Knowledge*. London: Penguin.
Bew, P. (1994). *Ideology and the Irish Question: Ulster Unionism and Irish Nationalism*. Oxford: Clarendon Press.
Blackwell, M. (2006). Waving in the Spaces. In S. Speed, A. R. Hernández Castillo, & L. M. Stephen (Eds.), *Dissident Women. Gender and Cultural Politics in Chiapas* (pp. 115–54). Austin: University of Texas Press.

———. (2011). *Chicana Power! Contested Histories of Feminism in the Chicano Movement*. Austin: University of Texas Press.
Boal, A. (1979). *The Theatre of the Oppressed*. London: Pluto.
Bourdieu, P. (1977). *Outline of a Theory of Practice*. Cambridge: Cambridge University Press.
———. (1984). *Distinction: A Social Critique of the Judgment of Taste*. Cambridge MA: Harvard University Press.
Brah, A., & Phoenix, A. (2004). Ain't I A Woman: Revisting Intersectionality. *Journal of International Women's Studies*, 5(3), 75–86.
Brubaker, R. & Cooper, F. (2004). Beyond Identity. In R. Brubaker (Ed.), *Ethnicity Without Groups*. Cambridge: Harvard University Press.
Brubaker, R., Feischmidt, M., Fox, J., & Grancea, L. (2006). *National Politics and Everyday Ethnicity in a Transylvanian Town*: Princeton: Princeton University Press.
Buckland, P. (1979). *The Factory of Grievances: Devolved Government in Northern Ireland*. Dublin: Gill and Macmillan.
———. (1981). *A History of Northern Ireland*. Dublin: Gill and Macmillan.
Burguete Cal y Mayor, A. (2005). 'Una Década de Autonomías de facto en Chiapas (1994–2004): Los Limites. In P. Dávalos (Ed.), *Pueblos Indígenas, Estado y Democracia* (pp. 239–78). Buenos Aires: CLACSO.
Burton, F. (1978). *The Politics of Legitimacy: Struggles in a Belfast Community*. London: Routledge.
Butler, J. (1990). *Gender Trouble. Feminism and the Subversion of Identity*. New York: Routledge.
Byrne, S. (2009). Women and the Transition from Conflict in Northern Ireland: Lessons for Peace-Building in Israel/Palestine. IBIS Working Papers. Retrieved from http://irserver.ucd.ie/bitstream/handle/10197/2416/89_byrne.pdf?sequence=1
Cameron Commission (1969). *Disturbances in Northern Ireland: Report of the Commission appointed by the Governor of Northern Ireland*. Norwich: Her Majesty's Stationery Office.
Campaign for Social Justice in Northern Ireland (1969). *Northern Ireland: the Plain Truth*. Dungannon: Campaign for Social Justice in Northern Ireland.
Centro de Derechos Humanos Fray Bartolomé de Las Casas, A. C. (2011). *Gobierno crea y administra Conflictos para el Control Territorial en Chiapas. Informe Especial*. San Cristóbal de las Casas: Centro de Derechos Humanos Fray Bartolomé de Las Casas, A. C.
Chambers, E. (2000). Applied Ethnography. In N.K. Denzin & Y.S. Lincoln (Eds.), *The SAGE Handbook of Qualitative Research* (pp. 851–69). London: Sage.
Cho, S., Williams Crenshaw, K., & McCall, L. (2013). Toward a Field of Intersectionality Studies. Theory, Applications, and Praxis. *Signs*, 38(4), 785–810.
Choo, H. Y., & Marx Ferree, M. (2010). Practicing Intersectionality in Sociological Research: A Critical Analysis of Inclusions, Interactions

and Institutions in the Study of Inequality. *Sociological Theory*, 28, 129–49.
Coakley, J. (2007). National Identity in Northern Ireland: Stability or Change? *Nations and Nationalism*, 13(4), 573–97.
Cockburn, C. (1998). *The Space between Us. Negotiating Gender and National Identities in Conflict*, London: Zed Books.
———. (2000). The Anti-Essentialist Choice: Nationalism and Feminism in the Interaction between two Women's Projects. *Nations and Nationalism*, 6(4), 611–29.
———. (2001). The Gendered Dynamics of Armed Conflict and Political Violence. In C. Moser & F.C. Clark (Eds.), *Gender, Armed Conflict and Political Violence* (pp. 13–24). London: Zed Books.
Cohen, J. L. (1985). Strategy or Identity: New Theoretical Paradigms and Contemporary Social Movements. *Social Research*, 52(4), 663–716.
Cohn, C. (1998). Gays in the Military: Texts and Subtexts. In M. Zalewski & J. Parpart (Eds), *The Man Question in International Relations* (pp. 129–49). Boulder, CO: Westview Press.
———. (2013). *Women and Wars*. Cambridge: Polity Press.
Cohn, C., & Ruddick, S. (2004). A Feminist Ethical Perspective on Weapons of Mass Destruction. In S. H. Hashmi & S. P. Lee (Eds.), *Ethics and Weapons of Mass Destruction: Religious and Secular Perspectives* (405–435). Cambridge: Cambridge University Press.
Cohn, C., & Jacobson, R. (2013). Women and Political Activism in the Phase of War and Militarization. In C. Cohn (Ed.), *Women and Wars* (102–23). Cambridge: Polity Press.
Collier, G. (1994). Roots of the Rebellion in Chiapas. *Cultural Survival Quarterly*, 18(1), 14–18.
Collier, G. & Lowery Quaratiello, E. (1999). *Basta! Land and the Zapatista Rebellion in Chiapas*. Oakland CA: Institute for Food and Development Policy.
Comisión Económica para América Latina y el Caribe. (2005). *Objetivos de Desarrollo de Milenio: Una Mirada desde América Latina y el Caribe*. Mexico City: Comisión Económica para América Latina y el Caribe.
Compton, P. (1989). The Changing Religious Demography of Northern Ireland: Some Political Considerations. *Irish Political Studies*, 78(312), 393–402.
Conaghan, J. (2009). Intersectionality and the Feminist Project in Law. In E. Grabham, et al. (Eds.), *Intersectionality and Beyond. Law, Power and the Politics of Location* (pp. 49–76). New York: Routledge Cavendish.
Connor, W. (1994). *Ethno-Nationalism: The Quest for Understanding*. Princeton: Princeton University Press.
Coogan, T. P. (1980). *On the Blanket: The H-Block Story*. Dublin: Ward River Press.
Corcoran, M. (2006). *Out of Order. The Political Imprisonment of Women in Northern Ireland 1972–1998*. Portland, Oregon: Willan Publishing.

Cormack, R.J., & Osborne, R.D. (1983). *Religion, Education and Employment: Aspects of Equal Opportunity in Northern Ireland*. Belfast: Appletree.

Cormack, R.J., Gallagher, A.M., & Osborne, R.D. (1993). *Fair Enough? Religion and the 1991 Population Census*. Belfast: Fair Employment Commission for Northern Ireland.

Cornell, S. (1996). The Variable Ties that Bind. *Ethnic and Racial Studies*, 19(2), 265–89.

Cortes, F., et al. (2003). *Perfiles de la Pobreza en Chiapas*. Mexico City: Secretaria de Desarrollo Social (Gobierno de Chiapas), El Colegio de México.

Coulter, C. (1993). *The Hidden Tradition: Feminism, Women and Nationalism in Ireland*, Cork: Cork University Press.

Courbage, Y. (1997). The Demographic Factor in Ireland's Movement Towards Partition (1607–1921). *Population: An English Selection*, 9, 169–190.

Crawford, B. (1998). The Causes of Cultural Conflict: An Institutional Approach. In B. Crawford & R.D. Lipschutz (Eds.), *The Myth of "Ethnic Conflict": Politics, Economics, and "Cultural" Violence* (pp. 3–43). Berkeley: International and Area Studies, University of California at Berkeley.

Crenshaw, K. (1991). Mapping the Margins: Intersectionality, Identity Politics, and Violence against Women of Color. *Stanford Law Review*, 43(6), 1241–99.

Cullen, L. M. (1981). *The Emergence of Modern Ireland 1600–1900*. London: Batsford Academic and Educational.

Cullen Owens, R. (2005). *A Social History of Women in Ireland 1870–1970*. Dublin: Gill & Macmillan.

Cunningham, W., & Cos-Montiel, F. (2002). *Las Encrucijadas del Género y la Cultura: Impedimentos para el Desarrollo Económico en Oaxaca, Chiapas y Guerrero*. New York: World Bank.

Cusack, T. (2000). Janus and Gender: Women and the Nation's Backward Look. *Nations and Nationalism*, 6(4), 546–60.

Deere, C. D. (2008). Pobreza Activos y la Desigualdad de Género. *IX Encuentro Internacional de Estadísticas de Género*. Aguascalientes, México.

Deere, C. D., & Leon, M. (2000). *Genero, Propiedad y Empoderamiento. Tierra, Estado y Mercado en America Latina*. Bogota: Tercer Mundo Facultad de Ciencias Humanas, Universidad National de Colombia.

della Porta, D. (2008). Comparative Analysis: Case-Oriented versus Variable-Oriented Research. In D. della Porta & M. Keating (Eds.), *Approaches and Methodologies in the Social Sciences* (198–222). Cambridge: Cambridge University Press.

———. (2013). *Clandestine Political Violence* (Cambridge: Cambridge University Press).

Delphy, C. (1993). Rethinking Sex and Gender. *Women's Studies International Forum*, 16(1), 1–9.

Department for Learning and Employment of Northern Ireland (2008). *School Leavers Survey*. Belfast: Department for Employment and Learning Northern Ireland.

Devine, P., Kelly, G., & Robinson, G. (2011). An Age of Change? Community Relations in Northern Ireland. *ARK Research Update*, 72.

DeVos, J. (2002). *Una Tierra para sembrar Sueños. Historia reciente de la Selva Lacandona 1950–2000*. Mexico City: CIESAS-FCE.

Diaz de Castillo, B. (1978). *The Conquest of New Spain*. (J. M. Cohen, Trans.). Marmondsworth: Penguin Books. (Original work published).

Diaz Polanco, H. (1998). 'La Autonomía, Demanda Central de los Pueblos Indigenas: Significado e Implicaciones. In V. Alta (Ed.). *Pueblos Indigenas y Estado en America Latina* (pp. 213–18). Quito: Universidad Andina Simon Bolivar.

Dietz, G. (1996). Indianische Bewegungen und "Zapatismo" im ländlichen Mexiko. Vom Assistenialismus zur Regionalautonomie. *Lateinamerika. Analysen–Daten–Dokumentationen*, 24, 67–88.

Dirkx, J. (2000). After the Burning Bush: Transformative Learning as Imaginative Engagement with Everyday Experience. *Proceedings of the Third International Transformative Learning Conference* (pp. 247–52). New York: Teachers College Columbia University.

Donnelly, C., Mc Keown, P., & Osborne, R. D. (2006). *Devolution and Pluralism in Education in Northern Ireland*. Manchester: Manchester University Press.

Eber, C. (1999). Seeking Our Own Food: Indigenous Women's Power and Autonomy in San Pedro Chenalho, Chiapas, 1980–1998. *Latin American Perspectives*, 26(3), 6–36.

Eber, C., & Kovic, C. (Ed.). (2003). *Women in Chiapas. Making History in Times of Struggle and Hope*. New York: Routledge.

Edgerton, L. (1986). Public Protest, Domestic Acquiescence: Women in Northern Ireland. In R. Ridd & H. Callaway (Eds.), *Caught up in Conflict: Women's Responses to Political Strife* (pp. 61–79). London: Macmillan.

Edwards, R. D. (1973). *An Atlas of Irish History*. London: Methuen.

Eibenschutz, C. T. (2008). Desigualdad y Políticas Sociales Erróneas producen Inequidad en México. *Revista de salud pública*, 10(1), 119–32.

Elliott, M. (2013). The Role of Civil Society in Conflict Resolution: The Opsahl Commission in Northern Ireland, 1992–93. *New Hibernia Review*, 17(2), 86–102.

Elliott, S. (1971). *The Electoral System in Northern Ireland since 1920*. Belfast: Queen's University Press.

Elshtain, J. B. (1981). *Public Men, Private Women: Women in Social and Political Thought*. Princeton: Princeton University Press.

Enloe, C. (1980). *Ethnic Soldiers: State Security in Divided Societies*. Harmondsworth: Penguin.

———. (1983). *Does Khaki become You?* London: Pluto.
———. (2000). *Maneuvers: The International Politics of Militarizing Women's Lives*. Berkeley: University of California Press.
———. (2002). Demilitarization—Or more of the Same. Feminist Question to Ask in the Post-War Moment. In C. Cockburn & D. Zarkovic (Ed.), *The Post-War Moment: Militaries, Masculinities and International Peacekeeping* (pp. 22–32). London: Lawrence and Wishart.
Epstein, C. F. (1988). *Deceptive Distinctions. Sex, Gender, and Social Order*. New Haven, CT: Yale University Press.
Erikson, E. H. (1968). *Identity: Youth and Crisis*. New York: Norton.
Escárcega, S. (2003). *Indigenous Intellectuals and Activists: From Social Justice to Human Rights*. Paper presented at Meeting of the Latin American Studies Association, Dallas, Texas (March 27–29, 2003).
Espinosa Damián, G. (2005). *Entre el Cuerpo y la Política: Cuatro vertientes del feminismo en México: diversidad de rutas y cruce de caminos*. PhD Dissertation, National School of Anthropology and History, (ENAH), Mexico City.
Espinoza Cortez, L. M. (1995). Aproximación a la Producción Agropecuaria en Chiapas. In R. Miranda-Ocampo (Ed.), *Chiapas el Regreso a la Utopía* (pp. 63–80). Chilpancingo: Universidad Autónoma de Guerrero/México: Editorial Comuna.
Estados Unidos de Mexicanos (1963). VII Censo General de Populación—1960. Mexico City: Secretaria de Industria y Comercio.
Esteva, G. (2001). The Meaning and Scope in the Struggle for Autonomy. *Latin American Perspectives*, 28(2), 243–70.
Eversley, D. (1989). *Religion and Employment in Northern Ireland*. London: Sage.
Expósito Verdejo, M. (2003). *Diagnostico Rural Participativo. Una Guía Práctica*. Santo Domingo: Centro Cultural Poveda.
Fair Employment Agency. (1977). *An Industrial and Occupational Profile of the two Sections of the Population in Northern Ireland: An Analysis of the 1971 Population Census*. Belfast: Fair Employment Agency (FEA).
Falls Women's Centre, Herstory, (2009). *The Falls Women's Centre 1982–2008*. Belfast: The Falls Women's Centre.
Fearon, J. D. (1999). *What Is Identity (As We Now Use the Word)?* Retrieved March 31, 2014, from http://goo.gl/mh2LaE
Fearon, K., & McWilliams, M. (2000). Swimming against the Mainstream: The Northern Ireland Women's Coalition. In C. Roulston & C. Davies (Ed.), *Gender, Democracy and Inclusion in Northern Ireland* (pp. 117–37). New York: Palgrave.
Finlay, A. (2011). *Governing Ethnic Conflict: Consociation, Identity and the Price of Peace*. New York: Routledge.
Fitzgerald, V., Stewart, F., & Wang, M. (2001). An Overview of the Case Studies. In F. Stewart & V. Fitzgerald (Eds.), *War and Underdevelopment 2: Country Experience* (pp. 104–148). Oxford: Oxford University Press.

Fitzpatrick, B. (1988). *Seventeenth Century Ireland: The Wars of Religion*. Dublin: Gill and Macmillan.

Flood, M. (1994). Changing Patterns of Interdependence: The Effects of Increasing Monetarization on Gender Relations in Zinacantan, Mexico. *Research in Economic Anthropology*, 15, 145–73.

Flores-Macías, G. (2013). Mexico's 2012 Elections: The Return of the PRI. *Journal of Democracy*, 24(1), 128–141.

Fortier, A. M. (2000). *Migrant Belongings: Memory, Space, Identities*. Oxford: Berg.

Freyermuth, G. (2003). *Las Mujeres del Humo. Morir in Chenalhó*. Mexico D.F.: CIESAS.

———. (2008). Realidad y Disimulo: Complicidad e Indiferencia Social en Chiapas frente de la Muerte Femenina. In M. Olivera (Ed.), *Violencia Feminicida en Chiapas. Razones Visibles y Ocultas de nuestras Luchas, Resistencias y Rebeldías* (pp. 129–202). Tuxtla Gutierrez: UNACH.

Gallagher, F. (1957). *The Indivisible Island: the Story of the Partition of Ireland*. London: Gollancz.

Gallagher, A. M., Osborne, R.D., & Cormack, R.J. (1995). *Fair Shares? Employment, Unemployment and Economic Status*. Belfast: Fair Employment Commission.

Galligan, Y., & Wilford, R. (1999). Women's Political Representation in Ireland. In Y. Galligan, E. Ward, & R. Wilford (Eds.), *Contesting Politics: Women in Ireland, North and South* (pp. 130–48). Boulder, Colorado: Westview Press.

Galligan, Y., Ward, E., & Wilford, R. (Eds.). (1999). *Contesting Politics: Women in Ireland, North and South*. Boulder, CO: Westview Press.

Garcia de Leon, A. (1985). *Resistencia y Utopia. Memorial de Agravios y Crónica de Revueltas y Profecías Acaecidas en la Provincia de Chiapas durante los últimos 500 años de su Historia*. México: Ediciones Era.

Garland Thomson, R. (1997). *Extraordinary Bodies: Figuring Physical Disability in American Culture and Literature*. New York: Colombia University Press.

Garza Caligaris, A. M. (1999). *El Genero entre Normas en Disputa. Pluralidad Legal y Normas en San Pedro Chenalho*. Tuxtla Gutiérrez: Universidad Autónoma de Chiapas.

———. (2000). El Movimiento de Mujeres en Chiapas. *Haciendo Historia: Anuario de Estudios Indigenas VIII* (pp. 109–35).Tuxtla Gutierrez, Chiapas: Instituto de Estudios Indigenas, UACH.

———. (2002). *Genero, Interlegalidad y Conflicto en San Pedro Chenalho*. Tuxtla Gutierrez, San Cristobal de las Casas: UNAM, UNACH.

Garza, A. M., and Freyermuth, G. (2000). Problemas de la Antropología frente a la Muerte. Genero y Muerte Materna en los Altos de Chiapas. In C. Stern & C.J. Echarri (Eds.), *Salud Reproductiva y Sociedad. Resultados de Investigación* (pp. 363–92). Mexico City: El Colegio de Mexico.

George, A. L., & Bennett, A. (2005). *Case Studies and Theory Development in the Social Sciences*. London: MIT Press.

Gerson, J. M., & Peiss, K. (1985). Boundaries, Negotiation, Consciousness: Reconceptualising Gender Relations. *Social Problems*, 32, 317–31.

Gilland L. K., & Farrington, C. (2006). Alternative Ulster? Political Parties & the Non-Constitutional Policy Space in Northern Ireland. *Political Studies*, 54(4), 715–42.

Gilligan, C. (1983). *In a Different Voice: Psychological Theory and Women's Development*. Cambridge, MA: Harvard University Press.

Glantz, M (2001). *La Malinche, Sues Padres y Sues Hijos*. Mexico: Taurus.

Glenn, E. N. (2002). *Unequal Freedom: How Race and Gender Shaped American Freedom and Labor*. Cambridge, MA: Harvard University Press.

Goldring, M. (1991). *Belfast: From Loyalty to Rebellion*. London: Lawrence and Wishart.

Gonzales Rivas, M. (2009). Chiapas, the South, and Mexico's Regional Inequality in the Context of Trade Openness. *Working Paper Series*. New York: Mario Einaudi Center for International Studies.

Gonzalez Esponda, J. (1989). *Movimiento Campesino Chiapaneco 1974–1984*. Tuxtla Gutierrez: UNACH.

Guelke, A. (2003). Civil Society and the Northern Irish Peace Process. *Voluntas: International journal of Voluntary and nonprofit Organizations*, 14(1), 61–78.

Gurr, T. R. (1993). *Minorities at Risk: A Global View of Ethnopolitical Conflicts*. Washington, DC: United States Institute of Peace Press.

Gurr, T. R., & Moore, W. H. (1997). Ethnopolitical Rebellion: A Cross-Sectional Analysis of the 1980s with Risk Assessments for the 1990s. *American Journal of Political Science*, 41(4), 1079–103.

Gutierrez Chong, N. (1995). Miscegenation as Nation-Building: Indian and Immigrant Women in Mexico. In D. Stasilius & N. Yuval-Davis (Eds.), *Unsettling Settler Societies. Articulations of Race, Ethnicity and Class* (pp. 161–87). London: Sage.

———. (1999). *Nationalist Myths and Ethnic Identities. Indigenous Intellectuals and the Mexican State*. Lincoln, London: University of Nebraska Press.

———. (2001). The Study of National Identity. In A. Dieckhoff & N. Gutierrez (Eds.), *Modern Roots: Studies of National Identity* (pp. 53–82). Aldershot: Ashgate.

———. (2007). Symbolic Violence and Sexualities in the Myth Making of Mexican National Identity. *Ethnic and Racial Studies*, 31(3), 524–42.

Gutierrez, J. C (2010). *The Oportunidades of México*. Retrieved June 15, 2011, from http://goo.gl/xwH2vD

Gutiérrez, M., & Palomo, N. (2000). A Women's Eye View of Autonomy. In A. Burguete Cal y Mayor (Ed.), *Indigenous Autonomy in Mexico* (pp. 53–82). Copenhagen: International Working Group on Indigenous Affairs).

Gutiérrez, N. (2007). Symbolic Violence and Sexualities in the Myth Making of Mexican National Identity. *Ethnic and Racial Studies*, 31(3), 524–42.

Hackett, C. (1995). Self-Determination: The Republican Feminist Agenda. *Feminist Review*, 50, 111–16.

———. (2004). Narratives of Political Activism from Women in West Belfast. In L. Ryan & M. Ward (Eds.), *Irish Women and Nationalism. Soldiers, New Women and Wicked Hags* (pp. 145–66). Dublin: Irish Academic Press.

Hale, C. R. (2006). Activist Research v. Cultural Critique: Indigenous Land Rights and the Contradictions of Politically Engaged Anthropology. *Cultural Anthropology*, 21(1), 96–120.

Hall, P. A., & Lamont, M. (2013). Why Social Relations Matter for Politics and Successful Societies. *Annual Review of Political Science*, 16, 49–71.

Hamber, B. (2007). Masculinity and Transitional Justice: An Exploratory Essay. *International Journal of Transitional Justice*, 1(3), 375–90.

Hamber, B., Hillyard, P., Maguire, A., McWilliams, M., Robinson, G., Russell, D., & Ward M. (2006). Discourses in Transition: Re-Imagining Women's Security. *International Relations*, 20(4): 487–502.

Hamilton, S. (2002). Neoliberalism, Gender and Property Rights in Rural Mexico. *Latin American Research*, 37(1), 119–43.

Hansen, T.B. (2001). *Wages of Violence: Naming and Identity in Postcolonial Bombay*. Princeton: Princeton University Press.

Harbom, L., Högbladh, S., & Wallensteen, P. (2006). Armed Conflict and Peace Agreements. *Journal of Peace Research*, 43(5), 617–31.

Harvey, N. (1994). Rebellion in Chiapas: Rural Reforms, Campesino Radicalism, and the Limits to Salinismo. *Transformation of Rural Mexico Series*, 5, 1–43.

———. (1998). *The Chiapas Rebellion*. London: Duke University Press.

Hepburn, A. C. (1983). Employment and Religion in Belfast, 1901–1951. In R. J. Cormack & R. D. Osborne (Eds.), *Religion, Education and Employment: Aspects of Equal Opportunity in Northern Ireland* (pp. 42–63). Belfast: Appletree.

Her Majesty's Stationery Office. (1983). Northern Ireland Census 1981: Economic Activity Report. Belfast: Her Majesty's Stationery Office.

Hernández Castillo, R. A. (1997). Between Hope and Adversity. The Struggle of Organised Women in Chiapas since the Zapatista Uprising. *Journal of Latin American Anthropology*, 3(1), 102–20.

———. (1998). Indigenas y religiosas en Chiapas: ¿Una nueva teología india desde las mujeres? *Cristianismo y Sociedad*, 35(137), 32–55.

———. (2001). *La Otra Frontera: Identidades Múltiples en el Chiapas Poscolonial*: Mexico City: CIESAS.

———. (2006). Between Feminist Ethnocentricity and Ethnic Essentialism. The Zapatistas' Demands and the National Indigenous Women's Movement. In S. Speed, R. A. H. Castillo, & L. M. Stephen (Eds.), *Dissident Women. Gender and Cultural Politics in Chiapas* (pp. 57–74). Austin: University of Texas Press.

———. (2008). Diálogos e Identidades Políticas: Génesis de los Procesos Organizativos de Mujeres Indigenas en México, Guatemala y Colombia.

In R. A. H. Castillo (Ed.), *Etnographias e Historias de Resistencia. Mujeres Indigenas, Procesos Organizativos y Nuevas Identidades Políticas* (pp. 45–126). Mexico City: Publicaciones de la Casa Chata.

———. (2010). The Emergence of Indigenous Feminism in Latin America. *Signs*, 35(3), 539–45.

Hernández Millán, A. (1998). *Los Hijos más pequeños de la Tierra*. Mexico City: Plaza y Valdez Editores.

Hernández Navarro, L. (2003). El zapatismo, fuente de inspiración para los movimientos altermundistas. *La Jornada*, December 29.

Hernández Valdez, A. (2000). Las Causas Estructurales de la Democracia Local en México, 1989–1998. *Política y Gobierno*, 7(1), 101–24.

Hill Collins, P. (1990). *Black Feminist Thought: Knowledge, Consciousness and the Politics of Empowerment*. Boston: Unwinhyman.

———. (2006). *From Black Power to Hip Hop. Racism, Nationalism and Feminism*. Philadelphia: Temple University Press.

Hill, M., & Ward, M. (2010). Conflicting Rights: The Struggle for Female Citizenship in Northern Ireland. In E. Breitenbach & P. Thane (Eds.), *Women and Citizenship in Britain and Ireland in the Twentieth Century* (pp. 113–37). London, New York: Continuum.

Hinds, B., Hope, A., & Whitaker, R. (1997). *From the Margins to the Mainstream: Working towards Equality, Development and Peace*. Belfast: Northern Ireland UN Beijing Coordinating Committee and Northern Ireland Women's European Platform.

Hoewer, M. (2002). *Bericht zur aktuellen Lage im mexikanischen Bundesstaat Chiapas*. Mexico City: Friedrich Ebert Stiftung in Mexico, FESMEX.

———. (2013). Women, Violence, and Social Change in Northern Ireland and Chiapas. *International Journal of Conflict and Violence*, 7(2), 216–231.

———. (2014). Beyond the Ethno-National Divide: Intersecting Identity Transformations during Conflict, Identities. Global Studies in Culture and Power. Published online February 17, 2014. DOI: 10.1080/1070289X.2013.868353.

hooks, B. (1981). *Ain't I a Woman: Black Women and Feminism*. Boston: South End Press.

Horowitz, D. L. (1985). *Ethnic Groups in Conflict*. Berkeley: University of California Press.

Howard, P., & Homer-Dixon, T. (1996). Environmental Scarcity and Violent Conflict: The Case of Chiapas, Mexico. Occasional Paper Project on Environment, Population and Security Washington, DC.

Huffschmid, A. (2004). *Diskursguerrilla. Waffenergreifung und Widersinn*. Heidelberg: Synchron Publishers.

Human Rights Center: Fray Bartolomé de Las Casas (2011). Acteal: Between Mourning and Struggle (Executive Summary). Retrieved May 26, 2011, from, http://goo.gl/9ZxiPB

Human Rights Watch, (2011). World Report 2011. Mexico. Retrieved July 7, 2011, from http://goo.gl/hoO7xR

Hunter, R. (1996). Deconstruction of the Subjects of Feminism: the Essentialist Debate in Feminist Theory and Practice. *Australian Feminist Law Journal* 6, 135–62.

Inglis, T. (1987). *Moral Monopoly: The Catholic Church in Modern Irish Society.* Dublin: Gill and Macmillan.

INI & UNDP (2001). La migración indígena en Mexico: Estado del Desarrollo Económico y Social de los Pueblos Indígenas de México. *Estudios sobre las Culturas Contemporaneas*, 7 (13), 157–161.

Instituto Nacional de Estadística y Geografía, (1990). Censo Nacional de Población y Vivienda. In Instituto Nacional de Estadística y Geografía (Ed.), *Geografía e Informática* (pp. 50–79). Mexico City: Instituto Nacional de Estadística.

———. (1991). Censo Nacional de Población y Vivienda. In Instituto Nacional de Estadística y Geografía (Ed.), *Geografía e Informática*, Mexico City: Instituto Nacional de Estadística.

———. (2001). Indicadores Sociodemográficos de México (1930–2000). In Instituto Nacional de Estadística y Geografía (Ed.), *Geografía e Informática*. Mexico City: Instituto Nacional de Estadística.

———. (2005a). Sociodemografía y género. In Instituto Nacional de Estadística y Geografía (Ed.), *Geografía e Informática*. Mexcio City: Instituto Nacional de Estadística.

———. (2005b). Encuesta Nacional de Ocupación y Empleo. In Instituto Nacional de Estadística y Geografía (Ed.), *Geografía e Informática*. Mexico City: Instituto Nacional de Estadística.

Inter-American Commission for Human Rights. (2003). *The Situation of the Rights of Women in Ciudad Juarez, Mexico. The Right to be Free from Violence and Discrimination.* Washington, DC: Inter-American Commission on Human Rights. Retrieved July 15, 2011, from http://goo.gl/UVHDSg

International Work Group for Indigenous Affairs, (2001). We Want to Be Both Indigenous and Mexican. *Indigenous Affairs*, 2, 61–66.

Ita, A. D. (2006). Land Concentration in Mexico after PROCEDE. In P. Rosset, R. Patel, & M. Courville (Eds.), *Promised Land: Competing Visions of Agrarian Reform* (pp. 148–164). Oakland, CA: Food First Books.

Jacobi, T. (2006). From the Trenches: Dilemmas of Feminist IR Fieldwork. In B. A. Ackerly, M. Stern, & J. True (Eds.), *Feminist Methodologies for International Relations* (pp. 153–173). Cambridge: Cambridge University Press.

Jayawardena, K. (1986). *Feminism and Nationalism in the Third World.* London: Zed Books.

Jenkins, R. (1996). *Social Identity.* London: Routledge.

———. (2008). *Rethinking Ethnicity.* London: Sage.

Jervis, R. (1978). Cooperation under the Security Dilemma. *World Politics*, 30, 167–214.

Johnston, J. (2000). Pedagogical guerrillas, armed democrats, and revolutionary counter publics: Examining paradox in the Zapatista uprising in Chiapas Mexico. *Theory and Society*, 29(4), 463–505.

Kampwirth, K. (2004). *Feminism and the Legacy of Revolution. Nicaragua, El Salvador, Chiapas.* Ohio University: Ohio University Press.
Karl, M. (1995). *Women and Empowerment. Participation and Decision Making.* London: Zed Books.
Kelleher, M. (1997). *The Feminisation of the Famine: Expressions of the Inexpressible?* Cork: Cork University Press.
Kenney, M. (1991). Neighbourhoods and Parades: The Social and Symbolic Organisation of Conflict in Northern Ireland (Unpublished doctoral dissertation). University of Michigan.
Kerkeling, L. (2003). *La lucha sigue! EZLN—Ursachen und Entwicklungen des zapatistischen Aufstands.* Münster: UNRAST.
K'inal A. (1995). *Mujeres Indigenas de Chiapas: Nuestros Derechos, Costumbres y Tradiciones.* Mexico City: San Cristobal de Las Casas.
Kinghan, N. (1975). *United We Stood: The Official History of the Ulster Women's Unionist Council 1911–1974.* Belfast: Appletree Pres.
Kronsell, A., & Svedberg E. (Ed.). (2012). *Making Gender, Making War. Violence, Military and Peacekeeping Practices.* New York: Routledge.
Kumar, K.. (2000). Nation and Rmpire: English and British National Identity in Comparative Perspective. *Theory and Society*, 29(5), 575–608.
Lagunes, L. (1999). A Propósito de Chiapas. In S. Lovera & N. Palomo (Ed.), *Las Alzadas* (pp. 110–04). Mexico City: CIMAC.
Lamas, M. (1986). La antropología feminista y la categoría de género, *Nueva Antropologia*, 8(30), 173–222.
Lamont, M. (1992). *Money, Morals and Manners: The Culture of the French and American Upper-Middle Class.* Chicago: University Press.
———. (2000). *The Dignity of Working Men: Morality and the Boundaries of Race, Class, and Immigration.* New York: Harvard University Press, Russell Sage Found.
———. (2012. How has Bourdieu Been Good to Think With? The Case of the United States. *Sociological Forum*, 27(1), 238–44.
Lamont, M., & Molnar, V. (2002). The Study of Boundaries in the Social Sciences. *Annual Review of Sociology*, 28, 167–95.
Leigh, D. (2009). Colonialism, Gender and the Family in North America: For a Gendered Analysis of Indigenous Struggles. *Studies in Ethnicity and Nationalism*, 9(1), 70–88.
Lenkersdorf, C. (1996). *Los hombres verdaderos: voces y testimonios tojolabales: lengua y sociedad, naturaleza y cultura, artes y comunidad cósmica.* Mexico, DF: Siglo xxi.
Leyva Solano, X. (1998). The New Zapatista Movement. Political Levels, Actors and Political Discourses in Contemporary Mexico. In V. Napolitano & X. Leyva Solano (Eds.), *Encuentros Antropológicos. Power, Identity and Mobility in Mexican Society* (pp. 35–55). London: Institute of Latin American Studies.
———. (2001). Chiapas es México. Autonomías Indigenas: Luchas Políticas con una Gramática Moral. *ICONOS Revista de Ciencias Sociales*, 11, 110–25.

Leyva Solano, X. (2005). Indigenismo, Indianismo y "Ciudadanía Étnica" de Cara a las Redes Neo-zapatistas. In P. Dávalos (Ed.), *Pueblos Indígenas, Estado y Democracia* (pp. 279–309). Buenos Aires: CLASCO.

———. (2008). Nuevos Procesos Sociales y Políticos en América Latina. In R. Hoetmer (Ed.), *Repensar la Política desde América Latina: Política, Cultura, Democracia Radical y Movimientos Sociales* (pp. 109–31). Lima: Programa Democracia y Transformación Global.

———. (2010). ¿Academia versus Activismo? Repensarnos desde y para la Práctica-Teórico Política. Retrieved July 1, 2011, from http://goo.gl/EFlPmc

Leyva Solano, X., & Ascencio Franco, G. (1996). *Lacandonia al Filo de Agua*. Mexico City: CIESAS.

Leyva Solano, X., & Speed, S. (2008). Hacia la investigación descolonizada: nuestra experiencia de co-labor. In X. Leyva Solano, A. Burguete, & S. Speed (Ed.), *Gobernar (en) la diversidad: experiencias indígenas desde América Latina. Hacia la investigación de co-labor* (pp. 65–107). Mexico City: CIESAS-FLASCO.

Lijphart, A. (1975). The Comparable Case Strategy in Comparative Research. *Comparative Political Studies*, 8, 158–77.

Lozano, R., et al. (2001). México: Marginality, Need, and Resources Allocation at the County Level. In R. Lozano, et al. (Eds.), *Challenging Inequities in Health. From Ethics to Action* (pp. 13–23). Oxford: Oxford University Press.

Luccisano, L. (2004). Mexico's Progresa Program (1997–2000): An Example of Neo-Liberal Poverty Alleviation Programs Concerned with Gender, Human Capital Development, Responsibility and Choice. *Journal of Poverty*, 8(4), 31–57.

Mahoney, J., & Thelen, K. (Eds.). (2009). *Explaining Institutional Change: Ambiguity, Agency and Power* (Cambridge: Cambridge University Press.

Marcos, S. (2005). The Borders within: The Indigenous Women's Movement and Feminism in Mexico. In M. Wallner & S. Marcos (Eds.), *Dialogue and Difference. Feminisms Challenge Globalization* (pp. 81–112). New York: Palgrave Macmillan

Marx Ferree, M. (2009). Inequality, Intersectionality and the Politics of Discourse. In E. Lombardo, O. Meier, & M. Verloo (Eds.), *The Discursive Politics of Gender Equality: Stretching, Bending and Policy-Making* (pp. 86–104). London: Routledge.

Mattiace, S.L. (2003). *To See with Two Eyes. Peasant Activism and Indigenous Autonomy in Chiapas, Mexico*. Albuquerque: University of New Mexico Press.

Mc Laughlin, E., & Baker, J. (2007). Equality, Social Justice and Social Welfare: A Road Map the New Egalitarianisms. *Social Policy and Society*, 6(1), 53–68.

McAdam, D., Tarrow, S., & Tilly, C. (2001). *Dynamics of Contention*. Cambridge: Cambridge University Press.

———. (2008). Methods of Measuring Mechanisms of Contention. *Qualitative Sociology*, 31, 307–31.
McCall, L. (2005). The Complexity of Intersectionality. *Signs*, 30(3), 1771–800.
McClintock, A. (1993). Family Feuds: Gender, Nationalism and the Family. *Feminist Review*, 44, 61–80.
McCoy, G. (2000). Women, Community and Politics in Northern Ireland. In C. Roulston & C. Davis (Eds.), *Gender, Democracy and Inclusion in Northern Ireland* (pp. 3–23). New York: Palgrave.
McGarry, J., & O'Leary, B. (1995). *Explaining Northern Ireland: Broken Images*. Oxford: Blackwell.
McGrattan, C. (2010). Explaining Northern Ireland? The Limitations of the Ethnic Conflict Model. *National Identities*, 12(2), 181–97.
McWilliams, M. (1993). Women in Northern Ireland: An Overview. In E. Hughes (Ed.), *Culture and Politics in Northern Ireland: 1960–1990* (pp. 81–100). Milton Keynes: Oxford University Press.
———. (1995). Struggling for Peace and Justice: Reflections on Women's Activism in Northern Ireland. *Journal of Women's History*, 6(4), 13–39.
Melaugh, M. (2013). Draft List of Deaths Related to the Conflict in 2008. Retrieved July 25, 2011, from http://goo.gl/toctA5
Mihesuah, D. A. (2003). *Indigenous American Women: Decolonization, Empowerment, Activism*. Lincoln: University of Nebraska Press.
Millán Moncayo, M. (2002a). Indigene Frauen in der neuen Politik. In U. Brand and A. E. Cecena (Eds.), *Reflexionen einer Rebellion. 'Chiapas' und ein anderes Politikverständnis* (pp. 198–213). Münster: Westphälisches Dampfboot.
———. (2002b). *Chiapas y sus Mujeres Indigenas: de su Diversidad y Resistencia*. Retrieved Feburuary 2011, from http://goo.gl/IuQzrh
———. (2006). Indigenous Women and Zapatismo. New Horizons of Visibility. In S. Speed, R. A. H. Castillo, & L.M. Stephen (Eds.), *Dissident Women. Gender and Cultural Politics in Chiapas* (pp. 75–96). Austin: University of Texas Press.
Miller, B. (1992). Collective Action and Rational Choice: Place, Community, and the Limits to Individual Self-Interest. *Economic Geography*, 68(1), 22–42.
Miller, R., Wilford, R., & Donoghue, F. (1996). *Women and Political Participation in Northern Ireland*. London: Avebury.
Mitchell, C. (2006). *Religion, Identity and Politics in Northern Ireland*. Aldershot: Ashgate.
Mohanty, C. T. (1992). Feminist Encounters: Locating the Politics of Experience. In M. Barrett & A. Phillips (Eds.), *Destabilizing Theory: Contemporary Feminist Debates* (pp. 74–93). Cambridge: Polity.
Molyneux, M. (1985). Mobilization without Emancipation? Women's Interests, the State, and Revolution in Nicaragua. *Feminist Studies*, 11(2), 227–54.

Molyneux, M. (2001). *Women's Movements in International Perspective. Latin America and Beyond*. New York: Palgrave.

Morrison, E. (2009). The Bureau of Military History and Female Republican Activism, 1913–23. In M. G. Valilius (Ed.), *Gender and Power in Irish History* (pp. 59–83). Dublin: Irish Academic Press.

Munck, R., & Rolston, B. (1987). *Belfast in the Thirties: An Oral History*. Belfast: Blackstaff.

Murray, D. (1985). *Worlds Apart. Segregated Schools in Northern Ireland*. Belfast: Appletree.

Nash, J. (2003). The War of the Peace: Indigenous Women's Struggle for Social Justice in Chiapas, Mexico. In S. Eckstein & T.P. Wickham-Crowley (Eds.), *What Justice? Whose Justice?* (pp. 285–312). University of California Press.

National Union for Public Employees. (1992). *Women's Voices: Oral History of Women's Health in Northern Ireland (1900–90)*. Dublin: Attic Press.

Newdick, V. (2005). The Indigenous Woman as Victim of Her Culture in Neoliberal Mexico. *Cultural Dynamics*, 17 (1), 73–92.

Nigh, R. (2003). Demographische Entwicklung, Migration und Ökologie im Hochland von Chiapas und der Selava Lacandona. In U. Köhler (Ed.), *Chiapas. Aktuelle Situation und Zukunftsperspektives für die Krisenregion im Südosten Mexicos* (pp. 101–48). Frankfurt am Main: Vervuert.

Northern Ireland Act. (1998). Retrieved May 17, 2011, from http://goo.gl/C5yji6

Northern Ireland Assembly, Research and Information Service. (2007). *Northern Ireland Assembly Elections 2007*. Belfast: Northern Ireland Assembly, Research and Information Service.

Northern Ireland Judicial Appointments Commission. (2011). *Annual Report and Accounts 2009–2010*. London: Her Majesty's Stationery Office.

O'Dowd, M. (2005). *A History of Women in Ireland. 1500–1800*. Harlow: Pearson Education Limited.

O'Keefe, T. (2006). Menstrual Blood as a Weapon of Resistance. *International Feminist Journal of Politics*, 8(4), 535–56.

O'Neill, E. (2005). Holding Flames. Women Illuminating Knowledge of Self Transformation (Unpublished doctoral dissertation). University of Toronto.

Oakley, A. (1985). *Sex, Gender and Society*. Aldershot: Arena.

Olesen, T. (2005). *International Zapatismo. The Construction of Solidarity in the Age of Globalization*. London: Zed Books.

Olivera, M. (2004). Una larga Historia de Discriminaciones y Racismos. In M. Olivera (Ed.), *De Sumisiones, Cambios y Rebeldías. Mujeres Indigenas de Chiapas 1* (pp. 56–91). Tuxtla Gutiérrez: UNICACH.

———. (2005). Discriminación Étnica y Genérica de las Indigenas en el Siglo XIX. In M. Olivera & M. D. Palomo (Eds.), *Chiapas: De la Independencia a la Revolución* (pp. 163–98). Mexico City: CIESAS y COCyTECH.

———. (2008a). Violencia Feminicidia en México: Expresión de la Crisis Estructural. In M. Olivera (Ed.), *Violencia Feminicidia en Chiapas. Razones Visibles y Ocultas de nuestras Luchas, Resistencias y Rebeldías* (pp. 29–44). Tuxtla Gutiérrez, San Cristóbal de las Casas: UNICACH, Centro de Derechos de la Mujer de Chiapas.

———. (Ed.). (2008b). *Violencia Feminicidia en Chiapas. Razones Visibles y Ocultas de nuestras Luchas, Resistencias y Rebeldías*. Tuxtla Gutierrez, Chiapas: UNACH.

Olivera, M., & Cardenas, G. (1998). *Violencia Estructural hacia las Mujeres'. Reclamo de las Mujeres ante la Violencia, la Impunidad y la Guerra*. San Cristóbal de las Casas: CDMDC.

Olivera, M., & Palomo, M. D. (Eds.). (2005). *Chiapas: De la Independencia a la Revolución*. Hidalgo, Tuxtla Gutiérrez: CIESAS, COCyTECH.

Oonagh, M. (1994). Women's Agenda for Peace. In *Clar na mBan Conference Report, 9*. Belfast: Clar na mBan Publication.

Opsahl, T. (1993). *A Citizens' Inquiry: The Opsahl Report on Northern Ireland*. Dublin: Lilliput Press.

Ortleib, M. (2004). Applications of Anthropology 1: Professional Anthropology in the C21-Seminar Report. *Anthropology in Action*, 11(1), 24–26.

Osborne, R. D., & Cormack, R. J. (1987). *Religion, Occupations and Employment. Research Paper 11*. Belfast: Fair Employment Agency.

Osborne, R. D., & Murray, R. C. (1978). *Educational Qualifications and Religious Affiliation in Northern Ireland: An Examination of G.C.E. 'O' and 'A' Levels, Research Paper No. 3*. Belfast: Fair Employment Agency.

Osborne, R. D., & Shuttleworth, I. (2004). *Fair Employment in Northern Ireland. A Generation on*. Belfast: Blackstaff Press.

Pachucki, M. A., Pendergrass, S., & Lamont, M. (2007). Boundary Processes: Recent Theoretical Developments and New Contributions. *Poetics*, 35, 331–51.

Parra, M., & Diaz, B. M. (1997). *Los Altos de Chiapas: Agricultura y Crisis Rural*. Mexico City: El Colegio de la Frontera Sur.

Patrinos, H., & Panagides, A. (1994). Poverty and Indigenous People in Mexico. *Akwe:kon—Journal of Indigenous Issues*, 11(2), 71–77.

Patterson, H. (1989). *The Politics of Illusion: Republicanism and Socialism in Modern Ireland*. London: Hutchinson Radius.

Piel, J. (1993). Naciones Indoamericas o Partías de Criollo?. In A. Escobar (Ed.), *Indio, Nación y Comunidad en el México del Siglo XVI* (pp. 19–30). Mexico City: Centro de Estudios Mexicanos y Centroamericanos and CIESAS.

Pollak, A. (Ed.). (1993). *A Citizen's Enquiry: The Opsahl Report on Northern Ireland*. Dublin: Lilliput Press.

Porter, E. (1998). Identity, Location, Plurality: Women Nationalism and Northern Ireland. In R. Wilford & R. L. Miller (Eds.), *Women Ethnicity and Nationalism. The Politics of Transition* (pp. 3–61). London and New York: Routledge.

Porter, E. (2000). Participatory Democracy and the Challenge of a Dialogue across Difference. In C. Roulston & C. Davis (Eds.), *Gender, Democracy and Inclusion in Northern Ireland* (pp. 141–63). New York: Palgrave.

Posen, B. (1993). The Security Dilemma and Ethnic Conflict. In M.E. Brown (Ed.), *Ethnic Conflict and International Security* (pp. 103–24). Princeton: Princeton University Press.

Przeworski, A., & Teune, H. (1970). *The Logic of Comparative Social Inquiry.* New York: Wiley-Interscience.

PSNI—Police Service of Northern Ireland. (2012). *Domestic Abuse Incidents and Crimes Reported by the Police in Northern Ireland: Quarterly Update to 31 March 2012. PSNI: Northern Ireland Statistic and Research Agency.* Retrieved from http://www.psni.police.uk/quarterly_domestic_abuse_bulletin_apr-mar_11_12.pdf

Purdie, B. (1990). *Politics in the Streets: The Origins of the Civil Rights Movement in Northern Ireland.* Belfast: Blackstaff.

Ramírez Barreto, A. C. (2007). Eréndira on Horseback: Variations on a Tale of Conquest and Resistance. In Natividad Gutiérrez Chong (Ed.), *Women, Ethnicity and Nationalism* (pp. 113–30). Aldershot: Ashgate.

Report of the Commission Appointed by the Governor of Northern Ireland (1969). Belfast: Her Majesty's Stationery Office.

Rey, J., & Barrera, M. (2007). El andar zapatista y la Otra Campaña. *Intersticios. Revista sociológica de pensamiento crítico,* 1(2), 127–37.

Rojas, R. (1994). *Chiapas: Y las Mujeres Que?* Mexico City: La Correa Feminista.

Ronfeld, D., J. Arquilla, G. E. Fuller, & M. Fuller. (1998). *The Zapatista Social Netwar in Mexico.* Santa Monica and Washington DC: RAND.

Rooney, E. (1995a). Women in Political Conflict. *Race and Class,* 37(1), 51–66

———. (1995b). Political Division, Practical Alliance: Problems for Women in Conflict. *Journal of Women's History,* 4(1), 40–48.

———. (2000). Women in Northern Irish Politics. In C. Roulston & C. Davis (Eds.), *Gender, Democracy and Inclusion in Northern Ireland* (pp. 164–86). New York: Palgrave.

Rose, K. (1994). *Diverse Communities: The Evolution of Lesbian and Gay Politics in Ireland.* Cork: Cork University Press.

Rose, R. (1971). *Governing without Consensus. An Irish Perspective.* London: Faber and Faber.

Rose, W. (2000). The Security Dilemma and Ethnic Conflict: Some New Hypotheses. *Security Studies,* 9(4), 1–51.

Roulston, C. (1996). Equal Opportunities for Women. In A. Aughey & D. Morrow (Eds.), *Northern Ireland Politics* (pp. 45–58). London: Longman.

———. (1997a). Gender, Nation, Class: the Politics of Difference in Northern Ireland. *Scottish Affairs,* 18(Winter). Retrieved August 20, 2011, from http://goo.gl/Rs1Yca

———. (1997b). Women on the Margin. The Women's Movement in Northern Ireland. In L.A. West (Ed.), *Feminist Nationalism* (pp. 45–58). London: Routledge.
Rovira, G. (1997), *Mujeres de maíz*. Mexico City: Ediciones Era.
Ruane, J. & Todd, J. (1996). *The Dynamics of Conflict in Northern Ireland: Power, Conflict, and Emancipation*. Cambridge: Cambridge University Press.
———. (2001). The Politics of Transition? Explaining Political Crises in the Implementation of the Belfast Good Friday Agreement. *Political Studies*, 49, 923–40.
———. (2003). The Roots of Intense Ethnic Conflict May Not In Fact be Ethnic: Categories, Communities and Path Dependence. *ISSC Discussion Paper Series*, Working Paper 2003/17.
Rubin, G. (1975). The Traffic in Women: Notes on the Political Economy of Sex. In R. Reiter (Ed.), *Towards an Anthropology of Women* (pp. 157–210). New York: Monthly Review Press.
Ruddick, S. (1989). *Maternal Thinking: Towards a Politics of Peace*. Boston: Beacon Press.
Rus, D. (1990). *La Crisis Económica de la Mujer Indígena: el Caso de Chamula (Chiapas)*. San Cristóbal de las Casas, Mexico: Instituto de Asesoría Antropológica para la Región Maya.
Rus, J. (1983). Whose Caste War? Indios, Ladinos and the Chiapas "Cast War" of 1869. In M. J. MacLeod & R. Wasserstorm (Eds.), *Spaniards and Indians in South-Eastern Mesoamerica. Essays on the History of Ethnic Relations* (pp. 127–168). London: University of Nebraska Press.
Rus, J., Mattiace, S., & Hernández Castillo, A. R. (Eds.). (2002). *El Movimiento Zapatista en Chiapas: La Gente Indígena y el Estado*. Copenhagen and Mexico City: The International Work Group on Indigenous Affairs and El Centro de Investigaciones Superiores en Antropología Social.
Sales, R. (1997). *Women Divided. Gender Religion and Politics in Northern Ireland*. London: Routledge.
Schmidt-Eule, M. (2002). *Chiapas 1994–2001. Analyse eines Konfliktes im Süden Mexikos*. Frankfurt am Main: Europäischer Verlag der Wissenschaften.
Scott, Joan (1986). Gender: A Useful Category of Historical Analysis. *American Historical Review*, 91, 1035–75.
Schoene, B. (2002). The Union and Jack. In G. Norquay & G. Smith (Eds.), *Across the Margins: Identity and Chance in the Atlantic Archipelago* (pp. 83–98). Manchester: Manchester University Press.
Seawright, J., & Gerring, J. (2008). Case Selection Techniques in Case Study Research: A Menu of Qualitative and Quantitative Options. *Political Research Quarterly*, 61, 294–308.
SEPI (Secretaria de Pueblos Indios). (2006). *Indicadores de Identidad Sociocultural y Territorial de los Pueblos Indios de Chiapas*. San Cristóbal de las Casas: Secretaria d Pueblos Indios.

Secretaría de Salud. (1992). *Recursos y Servicios. Boletín de Información Estadística, No 12.* Mexico City: Secretaría de Salud.

———. (1995). *Recursos y Servicios. Boletín de Información Estadística, No.15.* Mexico City: Secretaría de Salud.

Shannon, C. B. (2002). From House Rights to Civil Rights 1963–68. In Angela Bourke et al. (Eds.), *The Field Day Anthology of Irish Writing* (pp. 379–81). New York: New York University Press.

Shirlow, P., & Murtagh, B. (2006). *Belfast: Segregation, Violence and the City.* London: Pluto.

Sideris, T. (2001). Rape in War and Peace: Social Context, Gender, Power and Identity. In S. Meintjes, A. Pillay, & M. Turshen (Eds.), *The Aftermath. Women in Post-Conflict Transformation* (pp. 142–143). London, New York: Zed Books.

Sinn Fein. (October 22, 2007). Sinn Féin Support Assembly Debate on Abortion. Retrieved July 18, 2011, from http://goo.gl/v2SKZp

Web Not Found. (2006). "Glosario." SIPAZ. http://www.sipaz.org/glosario/glosesp.htm. Accessed April 3, 2014.

———. (2011a). Servicio International para la Paz "Brief History of the Conflict in Chiapas: 1994–2007." http://www.sipaz.org/crono/proceng.htm. Accessed July 25, 2011.

———.(2011b), "Impunity and the Responsibility of Mexican Authorities in the Acteal Case." http://www.sipaz.org/informes/vol13no1/vol13no1e.htm#ENFOQUE. Accessed May 26, 2011.

———. (2011c). Oaxaca/Chiapas: Latent Conflict in Chimalapas, with Risk of Confrontation. Retrieved May 10, 2011, from http://goo.gl/fyTnx

———. (2014). ANALYSIS: First Year of Enrique Peña Nieto, with Contradictory Perceptions of the "Mexican Moment." Retrieved April 3, 2014, from http://goo.gl/MFVQhN

Skeggs, B. (1994). Situating the Production of Feminist Ethnography. In M. Maynard & J. Purvis (Eds.), *Researching Women's Lives from a Feminist Perspective* (pp. 79–92). New York: Taylor and Francis.

Sluga, G. (2000). Female and National Self-Determination. A Gender Re-Reading of the Apogee of Nationalism. *Nations and Nationalisms*, 6(4), 495–521.

Smith, A. (1995). Education and the Conflict in Northern Ireland. In S. Dunne (Ed.), *Facets of the Conflict in Northern Ireland* (pp. 166–173). London: Macmillan.

Smith, D. C., & Chambers, G. (1991). *Inequality in Northern Ireland.* Oxford: Clarendon Press.

Smith-Oka, V. (2009). Unintended Consequences: Exploring the Tensions between Development Programs and Indigenous Women in Mexico in the Context of Reproductive Health. *Social Science and Medicine*, 68/11, 2069–2077.

Smyth, A. (1995). Paying our Disrespects to the Bloody States We're in: Women, Violence, Culture, and the State. *Journal of Women's History*, 7(1), 190–215.

Somers, M. (1994). The Narrative Construction of Identity: A Relational and Network Approach. *Theory and Society*, 23, 605–49.
Sommerhoff, G., & Weber, C. (1999). *Mexico*. Darmstadt: Wissenschaftliche Buchgesellschaft.
Speed, S. (2003). Action Speak Louder than Words: Indigenous Women and Gendered Resistance in the Wake of Acteal. In C. Eber & C. Kovic (Eds.), *Women of Chiapas. Making History in Times of Struggle and Hope* (pp. 47–65). New York and London: Routledge.
———. (2006). At the Crossroads of Human Rights and Anthropology: Toward a Critically Engaged Activist Research. *American Anthropologist*, 108 (1), 66–76.
Speed, S., & Reyes, A. (2002). " In Our Own Defense": Rights and Resistance in Chiapas. *PoLAR: Political and Legal Anthropology Review*, 25(1), 69–89.
———. (2005). Rights, Resistance, and Radical Alternatives: The Red De Defensores Comunitarios and Zapatismo in Chiapas. *Humboldt Journal of Social Relations*, 29(1), 47–82.
S. Speed, R. A. H. Castillo, & L. M. Stephen (Eds.) (2006). *Dissident Women. Gender and Cultural Politics in Chiapas*. Austin: University of Texas Press
Stasilius, D., & Yuval-Davis, N. (Eds.). (1995). *Unsettling Settler Societies. Articulations of Gender, Race, Ethnicity and Class*. London: Sage.
Stephen, L. (2001). Gender, Citizenship, and the Politics of Identity. *Latin American Perspectives*, 28(6), 54–69.
Stephen, L. M. (2002). *Zapata Lives! Histories and Cultural Politics in Southern Mexico*. Berkeley: University of California Press.
Stewart, F. (Ed.). (2008). *Horizontal Inequalities and Conflict. Understanding Group Violence in Multiethnic Societies*. Houndmills, Basingstoke, Hampshire: Palgrave Macmillan.
Stewart, F. (2010). Horizontal Inequalities: A Neglected Dimension of Development, *Working Paper No. 1*. Retrieved January 9, 2010, from http://goo.gl/YO46nM
Suárez, L., & Hernandez Castillo, R. A. (2008). *Descolonizando el Feminismo*. Madrid: Ediciones Cátedra.
Swords, A. C. (2007). Neo-Zapatista Network Politics Transforming Democracy and Development. *Latin American Perspectives*, 34(2), 78–93.
Tello Díaz, C. (1995). *La Rebelión de las Cañadas*. Mexico City: Aguilar, León y Cal.
Thomas, J. (1993). *Doing Critical Ethnography: Qualitative Research Methods Series 26*. Newbury Park: Sage Publications.
Tilly, C. (1998). *Durable Inequality*. Berkeley: University of California Press.
Tobler, H. W. (1994). *La Revolución Mexicana. Transformación Social y Cambio Político, 1876–1940*. Mexico D.F.: UNAM.

Todd, J. (1990). Northern Irish Nationalist Political Culture. *Irish Political Studies*, 5, 31–44
———. (2005). Social Transformation, Collective Categories, and Identity Change. *Theory and Society*, 34, 429–63.
———. (2007). Introduction: National Identity in Transition? Moving out of Conflict in (Northern) Ireland. *Nations and Nationalism*, 13(4), 1–7.
———. (2010). Symbolic Complexity and Political Division: The Changing Role of Religion in Northern Ireland. *Ethnopolitics*, 9(1), 85–102.
Toledo Tello, S. (1996). *Fincas, Poder y Cultura en Simojovel: 1975–1985*. Tuxtla Gutierrez: Universidad Autónoma de Chiapas.
Toledo Tello, S., & Garza Caligaris, A. M. (2006). Gender and Stereotypes in the Social Movements in Chiapas. In S. Speed, R. A. H. Castillo, & L. M. Stephen (Eds.), *Dissident Women. Gender and Cultural Politics in Chiapas* (pp. 97–114). Austin: University of Texas Press.
Tonge, J. (2002). *Northern Ireland. Conflict and Change*. Harlow, Essex: Pearson Education Limited.
Trejo, G., & Jones, C. (1998). Political Dilemmas of Welfare Reform: Poverty and Inequality in Mexico. In S. Kaufman Purcell & L. Rubio (Eds.), *Mexico Under Zedillo* (pp. 67–101). Lynne: Rienner.
Turshen, M. (2001). Engendering Relations of State to Society in the Aftermath. In S. Meintjes, A. Pillay & M. Turshen (Eds.), *The Aftermath. Women in Post-Conflict Transformation* (pp. 78–94). London, New York: Zed Books.
United Nations Commission on Human Rights (August 10, 2010). Indigenous Issues in Chiapas, Mexico. Retrieved July 15, 2011, from http://goo.gl/a7uApZ
Urquhart, D. (2000). *Women in Ulster Politics 1890–1940*. Dublin: Irish Academic Press.
Vickers, J., & Druhvarajan, V. (2002) *Gender, Race and Nation: A Global Approach*. Toronto: University of Toronto Press.
Villafuerte Solis, D. (2002). *La Tierra en Chiapas. Viejos Problemas Nuevos*. Mexico D.F.: Fondo De Cultura Económica.
Villafuerte Solis, D., García Aguitar, M. d. G. (1994). Los Altos de Chiapas en el Contexto del Neoliberalismo. Causas y Razones del Conflicto Indígena. In S. Soriano Hernández (Ed.), *A Propósito de la Insurgencia en Chiapas* (pp. 83–119). Mexico City: Asociación para el Desarrollo de la Investigación Científica y Humanística en Chiapas.
Ward, M. (1983). *Unmanageable Revolutionaries: Women and Irish Nationalism*. London: Pluto Press.
———. (2004). Times of Transition: Republican Women, Feminism and Political Representation. In L. Ryan & M. Ward (Eds.), *Irish Women and Nationalism. Soldiers, New Women and Wicked Hags* (pp. 184–201). Dublin: Irish Academic Press.
Ward, M., & McGivern, M. (1980). Images of Women in Northern Ireland. In R. Kearney (Ed.), *The Crane Bag 4* (pp. 66–72). Dublin: Blackwater Press.

Ward, M., & McMinn, J., (1987). A Difficult, Dangerous Honesty in 10 Years of Feminism in Northern Ireland. A Discussion. Belfast: Women's News.

Wasserstrom, R. (1978). Population Growth and Economic Development in Chiapas 1524–1975, *Human Ecology*, 6(2), 127–43.

Watermann, P. (1998). *Globalisation, Social Movement and the New Internationalisms*. London: Mansell.

———. (1999). Of Saints, Sinners and Compañeras: Institutionalised Lives in the Americas Today. In *Institute of Social Studies, Working Papers Series* 286.

Waylen, G. O. (2000). Gender and Democratic Politics: A Comparative Analysis of Consolidation in Argentina and Chile. *Journal of Latin American Studies*, 32(3), 765–93.

Wendt, A. (2004). The State as Person in International Theory. *Review of International Studies*, 29, 289–316.

White, B. (1969). One Man, One Vote—Who would Gain? *Belfast Telegraph*, January 30, 1969.

Whyte, J. H. (1983). How Much Discrimination Was There in the Unionist Regime? In T. Gallagher and Connell (Eds.), *Contemporary Irish Studies* (pp. 1–35). Manchester: Manchester University Press.

———. (1990). *Interpreting Northern Ireland*. Oxford: Clarendon Press.

Wilford, R. (1996). Women in Politics in Northern Ireland. *Parliamentary Affairs*, 49(1), 41–54.

———. (1996). Women and Politics in Northern Ireland. In J. Lovenduski & P. Norris (Eds.), *Women in Politics* (pp. 169–84). Oxford: Clarendon Press. Wilford, R. & Wilson, R. (August 2003). A Route to Stability: The Review of the Belfast Agreement. *Democratic Dialogue*. Retrieved August 20, 2011, from http://goo.gl/c6B2bk

Wimmer, A. (2008). The Making and Unmaking of Ethnic Boundaries: A Multi-Level Process Theory. *American Journal of Sociology*, 113(4), 970–1022.

Wittig, M. (1992). *The Straight Mind*. New York: Beacon.

Wolcott, Harry F. (1994). *Transforming Qualitative Data: Description, Analysis, and Interpretation*. California: Sage Publications.

Wolff, R. D., & Resnick, S. A. (1987). *Economics: Marxian versus Neoclassical*. Baltimore: Johns Hopkins University Press.

Womack, J. (1965). *Land and Freedom. Zapata and the Mexican Revolution*. New York: Alfred A. Knopf.

———. (1999). *Rebellion in Chiapas: An Historical Reader*. New York: New York Press.

Wright, F. (1987). *Northern Ireland. A Comparative Analysis*. Dublin: Gill and Macmillan.

Wright, M. (2001). The Dialectics of Still Life: Murder, Women, and the Maquiladoras. In J. Comaroff & J. Comaroff (Eds.), *Millennial Capitalism and the Culture of Neoliberalism* (pp. 125–46). Durham: Duke University Press.

Yin, Robert K. (1984), *Case Study Research: Design and Methods.* Beverly Hills: Sage Publications.

Yuval-Davis, N. (1997). *Gender and Nation.* London: Sage.

———. (2006). Intersectionality and Feminist Politics. *European Journal of Women's Studies,* 13(3), 193–209.

———. (2011). *The Politics of Belonging. Intersectional Contestations.* London: Sage.

———. (2012). Dialogical Epistemology—An Intersectional Resistance to the "Oppression Olympics." *Gender & Society,* 26(1), 46–54.

Yuval-Davis, N., & F. Anthias. (Eds.). (1989). *Woman-Nation-State.* Basingstoke, UK: Palgrave Macmillan.

Zetterberg, P. (2009). Do Gender Quotas Foster Women's Political Engagement? Lessons from Latin America. *Political Research,* 62(4), 715–30.

Index

abortion, 86, 129, 140
Acteal massacre, 33, 100–1, 179n4
activism
   alliances and, 47–8, 68–9, 87–8, 95, 169–78
   autonomy and, 91–2, 134
   Catholics and, 85–8, 150
   Chiapas and, 31–2, 47, 115–19
   community, 77–9, 83–4, 89, 91–2, 94, 117, 124–7, 133–4, 137–9, 156–60, 171, 174–5
   conflict settlement and, 123–36
   family and, 26, 39, 47, 86, 163
   feminism and, 48, 64, 71, 89–90, 93–4, 124–7, 154–7, 166–8
   grassroots, 131–6
   identity and, 48–90, 149, 174
   intersectionality and, 97
   neoliberalism and, 105, 108, 158
   Republican Movement and, 85–9, 131–3, 150, 160–2
Aguirre, F. G., 188n13
Alison, M. H., 166
alliance formation
   alternative space for building, 108–14
   Chiapas and, 68–9, 90, 94–5, 99–102, 105–14
   community and, 92
   conflict settlement and, 97–102, 125–6, 129, 131, 138, 142, 144
   farmer's protests and, 55–8
   gender issues and, 88, 90, 129, 144, 150
   identity and, 88
   Northern Ireland and, 87–8, 122, 125–6, 129
   social mobilization and, 24–5, 155–61, 169–70
   women's activism and, 47–8, 68–9, 87–8, 95, 169–78
Alsop, R., 8, 16, 21
Alvarez, S. E., 12
Andersonstown News, 194n11
Anthias, F., 8, 16, 19, 162
anti-essentialism, 11
Aretxaga, B., 70, 76, 84, 93
ARIC-Independiente, 115, 181n13
artwork, 39
Ashe, F., 70, 125, 127, 168
Ashmore, R. D., 17–18, 37
Aubry, A., 187n5
autonomy
   activism and, 91–2, 134
   alliances and, 171–2
   autonomous zones, 103
   Chiapas and, 99–111, 142–3, 153–4, 156, 168–9
   community structures and, 108–10
   farmers' protests and, 56
   indigenous women and, 34, 51, 56, 95, 105–11, 142–3, 153–4, 159
   Northern Ireland and, 86, 121, 128, 139
   San Andres Peace Accords and, 159, 168–9
   women and, 85–6, 174–5
   Zapatistas and, 38, 41, 91, 99–103, 110–11, 121

Bardon, J., 72
Bartolomé, M. A., 55
Beale, J., 80, 93
Bean, K., 194n11
Belausteguigoitia, M., 99
Bell, C., 122, 125, 160
Bellinghausen, H., 113
Benjamin, T., 181n8, 182n22
Berger, M. T., 113
Blackwell, M., 11, 113, 194n13
Bloody Sunday, 76, 185n76
Boal, A., 39
Bourdieu, P., 17, 23–4
Brah, A., 179n3
British Abortion Act (2007), 129
brokerage, 25, 151, 155, 162
  see also alliance formation
Brubaker, R., 18–19, 21, 25, 48
Burguete Cal y Mayor, A., 111
Burton, F., 76
Butler, J., 13, 179n4
Byrne, S., 125

Campaign for Social Justice, 71
campesinos, 42
caracoles, 101, 188n12
Cárdenas, Lázaro, 54
Catholics
  Chiapas and, 12
  community and, 78, 138
  feminist activism and, 85–8, 150
  identity and, 10, 12, 74–7, 93, 138, 140, 144, 161–5, 174
  indigenous women and, 10–12
  marginalization and, 70, 77, 144
  Northern Ireland and, 12, 20, 71–8, 128–9, 131
  Protestants and, 129
  women and, 10–12, 71–8, 80, 90, 131
Chiapas
  alliances and, 55–8, 68–9, 90, 94–5, 99–102, 105–14
  Catholics and, 12
  collective identity narratives, 48–51
  conflict settlement and, 8
  ethno-national conflict in, 15, 22, 29–30
  family and, 57, 66–7
  farmer's protests, 55–8, 114–15
  female activism and, 31–2, 47, 115–19
  female symbols of protest in, 62–5
  feminism in, 65–9
  identity and, 20, 26, 48–51, 90–5, 162–5
  indigenous women in, 10, 12, 51–5, 57–8
  mestizas, 55–7
  mobilization and, 29–30, 90–5, 149–51
  Northern Ireland and, 32–5
  peace process and, 141–6
  private realm and, 119–21, 165–9
  public sphere and, 102–8
  research on, 37–8, 41–4
  social change and, 152–4
  solidarity, 155–62
  women's narratives and, 1–3, 47–51, 97–8, 171–2, 175–8
  women's perceptions and positioning in, 99–121
  Zapatista Movement and, 58–65, 110–14
child care, 82, 90, 121, 138–9
Cho, S., 10, 12–13
Choo, H. Y., 14
civil rights, 34, 41–2, 70–4, 85–91, 94, 150, 154–6, 161
Clár na mBan (Women's Agenda for Peace), 122, 124–5, 157–8, 160
Cockburn, C., 89, 122
Cohn, C., 7–8, 21, 24, 157
co-labor, 32, 36
Collier, G., 120
Commander Esther, 102–4, 154
Commander Ramona, 63, 93, 103–4
Conaghan, J., 179

conflict settlement
  alternative space for building new community structures and alliances, 108–10
  demobilization process in Northern Ireland, 121–41
  farmers' organizations and, 114–15
  feminist dialogue across borders, 115–19, 136–41
  grassroots activism and, 131–6
  intersecting boundary processes in peace processes, 141–6
  overview, 97–9
  private realm in transition, 119–21
  public sphere and, 102–8
  women's activism and, 123–31
  women's perceptions and positioning in "post-conflict" Chiapas, 99–101
  Zapatista communities and, 110–15
connectedness, 18, 48
Connor, W., 20
Coogan, T. P., 84
Corcoran, M., 84, 87
Cornell, S., 18
Coulter, C., 76
Crawford, B., 15
Crenshaw, K., 9, 26
Cumann na d'Teachtaire (League of Women Delegates), 122
Cusack, T., 21

della Porta, D., 2, 30
DeVos, J., 101
Diaz de Castillo, B., 181n3
Diaz Polanco, H., 95
Diocesan Council of Women (Coordinadora Diocesana de Mujeres, CODIMUJ), 65–7, 181n14, 183n45, 184n50
Dirkx, J., 39
domestic violence, 51, 53, 60, 81–2, 90, 108, 111, 130, 133, 141, 145, 166, 168, 173, 175

Eber, C., 56
Edgerton, L., 93
education, 40, 50, 52–4, 56, 60, 64, 67, 74, 103, 107–9, 132, 134, 136–7
ejidos, 52, 54, 56, 106
Elliott, M., 191n61
Elshtain, J. B., 79
Emiliano Zapata Peasant Organization (Organización Campesina "Emiliano Zapata," OCEZ), 50
Enloe, Cynthia, 7, 15, 24, 176
Epstein, C. F., 13
Equality Commission for Northern Ireland, 128
Erikson, E. H., 17
Espinosa Damián, G., 119, 158
Esteva, G., 108
ethics, 2, 35, 48
Expósito Verdejo, M., 194n2
EZLN
  see Zapatista Army of National Liberation

Falls Road Curfew, 75–6, 185n74
Falls Women's Centre, 80, 91, 157
family
  Chiapas and, 57, 66–7
  community and, 77–82
  conflict settlement and, 97–8, 141, 171–2, 174
  female activism and, 26, 39, 47, 86, 163
  gender and, 145, 155
  identity and, 19, 41, 145
  indigenous women and, 51–2, 57, 66–7, 106, 108
  Northern Ireland and, 70–1, 74–82, 86, 92–5
  positioning and, 39, 41, 167
  private realm and, 119, 121, 138–41, 163
  solidarity and, 155
Fearon, J. D., 17
Fearon, K., 122, 126

feminism
  activism and, 48, 64, 71, 89–90, 93–4, 124–7, 154–7, 166–8
  agency, 174–6
  anti-essentialism and, 11
  civil rights and, 71
  conflict settlement and, 97–8
  contentious dialogue across borders, 136–41
  differing spaces of, 65–9
  ethno-national theories and, 8, 20, 34–5
  field research and, 35–6
  identity and, 7–13, 19–20, 22, 168, 174, 178
  indigeneity and, 10, 56, 64, 66–8, 94, 113–15
  intersectionality and, 9–12, 26
  mestizas and, 66–8, 102, 112–14
  nationalism and, 19–22
  NGOs and, 67
  participatory research approach, 29–30
  politics and, 102, 104, 152
  postcolonial research and, 22
  Republican Movement and, 77–85, 122–3, 136, 163, 166
  social movements and, 56
  solidarity, 143–5, 151, 155–61
  standpoint theory, 30–2
  toward a constructive cross-border dialogue of, 115–19
  women's rights and, 85–9, 113–14
finca system, 49, 53–4, 56
Finlay, A., 193n7
Flores-Macías, G., 160
Fortier, A. M., 152
free trade agreements, 59, 101, 156

Galligan, Y., 88, 122
Garza, A. M., 53
Garza Caligaris, A. M., 51, 67, 114–15
gender equality, 10, 24, 64, 78–9, 103, 106, 108, 114–17, 123, 130–1, 133, 139–40, 168, 174

Gerson, J. M., 13
Gilland, L. K., 129
Gilligan, C., 79
Glantz, M., 68
globalization, 1, 113, 156, 188n13
Good Friday/Belfast Peace Agreement (1998), 121, 127–31, 135, 158–60, 165
Guelke, E., 191n61
Gutierrez, J. C., 50, 189n20
Gutiérrez Chong, Natividad, 22, 53, 68

Hackett, C., 80, 122–3, 125, 139
Hale, C. R., 32
Hall, Peter A., 2, 29
Hamber, B., 146, 168
Hansen, T. B., 15
Harbom, L., 99
health care, 53
Hernández Castillo, R. A., 67, 99, 111–12, 119, 158
Hill Collins, P., 9, 26
Hinds, B., 126
homosexuality, 89
hooks, bell, 11
Horowitz, D. L., 8, 16, 29, 193n7
Huffschmid, A., 62, 93
Human Rights Watch, 11
Hunter, R., 11

identity
  activism and, 48–90, 149, 174
  boundaries and categories of, 22–6
  Catholics and, 10, 12, 74–7, 93, 138, 140, 144, 161–5, 174
  collective, 2–3, 14, 17–19, 22, 27, 37, 39–40, 43, 141, 172, 174
  Chiapas, 48–69
  Northern Ireland, 69–90
  concept of, 16–19
  de-essentializing, 19–22
  explained, 14–16
  feminism and, 7–13, 19–20, 22, 168, 174, 178

group story, 18
intersectionality and, 2, 20, 26, 32, 50, 157, 170–4
marginalization and, 162–4
mobilization and, 18–22, 24, 29–30, 33
Republican Movement and, 12, 20, 91–4, 162–5
transformation of, 152, 155, 162
Zapatistas and, 162–5
Independent Confederation of Agricultural Workers and Peasants (CIOAC), 50, 181n13
indigenous autonomy, 34, 51, 56, 91, 95, 99–100, 108, 110–11, 142–3, 154, 156, 159, 168
Inglis, T., 84
international relation (IR) studies, 35
internment, 76, 78, 87, 145, 185n75
intersectionality
 analysis of, 26, 29
 difference and, 9–14
 ethnicity and, 50
 identity and, 2, 20, 26, 32, 50, 157, 170–4
 indigenous women in Chiapas and, 51–5
 inequality and, 51–5, 92, 97, 139, 143
 Northern Ireland and, 139, 176
 peace process and, 149
 research on, 8–9
 social change and, 152, 157
 women's activism and, 97
Irish Republican Army (IRA), 75, 77–8, 80, 82–5, 132–3, 135, 138, 185n74

Jacobi, T., 35
Jacobson, R., 8, 157
Jayawardena, K., 8
Jenkins, R., 17–18
Jervis, R., 15
Johnston, J., 187n7
Juntas de Buen Gobierno (JBG), 188n12

Kampwirth, Karen, 41, 57, 157
Kenney, M., 76
Kerkeling, L., 107, 111, 181n4, 187n4
K'inal Antzetik, 111
kinship, 19–20
 see also family
Kronsell, A., 7

Lamas, M., 119
Lamont, Michele, 2, 9, 23–4, 26, 29, 153
land ownership, 52, 54, 60, 106–8, 143
land rights, 34, 50, 91, 155, 168
Las Abejas, 100, 179n4, 187n8
Leigh, D., 10, 30
Lenkersdorf, C., 101
Leyva Solano, Xochitl, 32, 36, 41, 53, 95, 111, 113, 161

macho behavior, 119
marches, 56, 70–3, 101, 103, 112, 115, 157, 177
Marcos, S., 53, 65, 164, 182n13
marginalization
 Catholics and, 70, 72–3, 77
 community and, 12, 155–6
 gender and, 12–13, 39, 168–70, 173, 175
 identity and, 162–4
 indigenous culture and, 50–4, 92, 113, 150, 159
 mobilization and, 1
 Northern Ireland and, 70, 72–3, 77, 91–2, 150
 Zapatistas and, 113
Marron, Oonagh, 112
Martínez Veloz, Jaime, 100
Marx Ferree, M., 12
Marxism, 56

masculinity, 7, 9, 21, 24, 168
massacres, 33, 100–1, 179n4
Mattiace, S. L., 59, 95, 111
Mayan Cosmovision, 52, 55, 65–6, 182n13
Mazariegos, Diego, 56
McAdam, D., 16–19, 24–5, 29, 33, 35, 152, 155
McCall, L., 9–10, 13–14
McClintock, A., 22, 152
McCoy, G., 86
McGivern, M., 80, 93, 194n12
McGrattan, C., 193n7
McLaughlin-Volpe, T., 17, 37
McWilliams, Monica, 84, 122, 126, 194n10
Melaugh, M., 33, 70
mental health, 173
mestizo culture, 22, 31, 42, 49–50, 53–8, 60–3, 65–9, 92, 94, 102, 104–8, 112, 114–19, 143, 171
Mihesuah, D. A., 12
Millán Moncayo, 51, 57, 64, 105, 111
Miller, B., 15
Miller, R., 122
Mitchell, C., 7, 140
mobilization
    alliances and, 24–5, 155–61, 169–70
    Chiapas and, 29–30, 90–5, 149–51
    demobilization, 2, 27, 29–30
    ethno-national boundary and, 1, 8, 31, 74–7
    identity and, 18–22, 24, 29–30, 33
    mechanisms of, 25–7
    Republican Movement and, 74–7
    study of, 39–43
    women and, 33–5
    Zapatistas and, 56–7
    see also social mobilization
Mohanty, C. T., 11, 180n5
Molyneux, M., 10, 12, 157
motherhood, 8, 19, 68, 80, 85, 93, 120, 135, 138–40, 145, 178

national identity, 8, 21, 31, 69, 72, 78, 91, 94, 128, 137
nationalism, 8, 16, 22, 68–9, 78, 81, 86–7, 93, 95, 99, 111, 122–3, 126, 129, 136, 163, 166
neoliberalism
    indigenous autonomy and, 34, 91–2, 156, 158
    modernization and, 54, 59
    Other Campaign, 144
    peace negotiations and, 158, 168
    privatization and, 54, 101
    women's activism and, 105, 108, 158
    Zapatista Movement and, 49–51, 59, 91–2, 101, 112–13, 144
nonengagement, 104
North Atlantic Free Trade Zone, 101
Northern Ireland
    civil rights and, 70–4
    collective identity narratives, 69–70
    different spaces and pathways of activism, 89–90
    ethno-national boundary, 74–7
    from family making to community making, 77–82
    feminism and, 85–9
    IRA and, 82–5
    mobilization and identity formation, 90–5
    women's re-inventions of Republicanism, 77–85
    see also Republican Movement
Northern Ireland Civil Rights Association (NICRA), 71, 185n76
Northern Ireland Women's Coalition (NIWC), 122–3, 125–9, 143, 153–4, 158, 160

O'Keefe, T., 84, 93
Olesen, T., 59, 91, 100, 112–13, 118, 159, 168

Olivera, M., 106
O'Neill, E., 39
Operation Demetrius, 185n75
   see also internment
Oportunidades, 106, 108, 189n20
Opsahl Commission, 126, 191n61
Other Campaign, 101, 113, 144
otherness, 13, 22–3, 31, 40–1,
   49, 61, 73, 76, 88, 92, 94,
   118–19, 156, 162

Pachucki, M. A., 23
patriarchal structures, 87–9, 127,
   129, 161–3, 174
PIRA, 71
Plan de Ayala National Council
   (CNPA), 50
pogroms, 76
Porter, E., 89, 94, 194n12
Posen, B., 15
postcolonial study, 22, 34
poverty, 49, 53–4, 56, 65, 67, 89, 94,
   108, 158, 174, 178, 189n20
PRI (Partido Revolucionario
   Institucional), 55–6, 101, 159
privatization, 52, 54, 101, 106
PROCEDE program, 106, 108
proportional representation with
   single transferable vote
   (PRSTV), 131
Protestants, 70, 72–6, 78, 86, 92,
   127–9, 131, 164

racism, 10, 22, 103
Ramírez Barreto, A. C., 68
rebellion, 54, 56, 63
reproductive rights, 140
Republican Movement
   civil rights and, 70–4
   commitment and, 82–5
   community and, 77–82, 133–41,
      150
   conflict settlement and, 97,
      122–33, 141–5
   different spaces and pathways of
      activism, 89–90

feminist activism and, 85–9, 150,
   160–2
grassroots activism and, 131–3
identity and, 12, 20, 91–4, 162–5
interviewees from, 41–2
IRA and, 82–5
mobilizing ethno-national
   boundary, 74–7
NIWC and, 124–7, 160
private realm between transition
   and tradition, 138–41,
   166–8
solidarity and, 152–8
state and, 33, 151
women's re-invention of, 77–82
   see also Northern Ireland
Revolutionary Women's Law, 40,
   62–5, 68, 91, 93, 111, 143,
   156, 159, 163, 177
Rey, J., 188n13
Reyes, A., 101
Rojas, R., 117
Ronfeld, D., 52, 159
Rooney, E., 89, 127
Rose, K., 89
Rose, W., 15
Roulston, C., 87, 89, 94
Rovira, G., 104
Ruane, J., 69, 91
Ruddick, S., 8, 21, 157
Ruiz, Don Samuel, 56, 66
Rus, J., 111

Salazar Mendiguchía, Pablo, 104
Sales, R., 87, 161
sameness, 10, 12, 16, 19, 25, 84,
   175
San Andres Accords on Indigenous
   Rights and Culture (1996),
   99–100, 112, 159
San Cristóbal de las Casas, Chiapas,
   38, 42, 56, 171
Scott, Joan, 21
secession, 151
SERAPAZ, 38, 181n15
sexism, 10, 77, 80–1, 83–4, 107

Shannon, C. B., 71
Sideris, T., 151
silence, 21, 55, 62, 71, 74, 103–4, 164
"silent resistance," 104, 171
Sinn Fein, 80–1, 85, 91, 124–6, 129, 156, 160–1
Sixth Declaration of the Selva Lacandona, 113, 188n13, 190n34
Skeggs, B., 35, 40
Sluga, G., 9
Smith-Oka, V., 189n20
social justice, 31–2, 34, 50, 55–7, 60, 67, 70–1, 74, 85–6, 89, 109, 134, 142, 154–60, 167–9, 178
social mobilization, 10–11, 13–14, 18, 20, 22, 24–6, 33–4, 43, 48, 51, 58, 68–9, 77, 90–1, 97, 112, 121, 130, 149, 152–3, 155, 159, 167, 170, 175
Somers, M., 16
Speed, S., 32, 36, 64, 101, 111
Stasilius, D., 50
Stephen, L., 99, 104, 111
strategic gender interests, 12–13, 35, 47, 79–81, 89, 91, 97, 144, 146, 157
strategic political action, 58–69
Suárez, L., 180n5
Subcomandante Marcos, 113, 190n32

Tello Diaz, C., 50, 52, 54, 56
theater of the oppressed, 39, 177
Thomas, J., 34
Tilly, C., 16, 25, 29, 152, 155
Todd, J., 7–8, 16–18, 20, 23, 25–6, 29, 69, 76, 78, 91
Toledo Tello, S., 51, 53, 67, 114–15
Tonge, J., 160
Turshen, M., 166
Tuxtla Gutierrez, Chiapas, 180n12, 190n37, 194n3

United Nations (UN)
  Commission on Human Rights, 11
  Security Council Resolution (UNSCR) 1325, 38, 178, 180n9
  Zapatista Movement and, 102
United States, 87, 101, 106

Velasco, Manuel, 100
Vicenta, Compañera, 114
Villafuerte Solis, D., 52, 54, 56
visualization, 177

Ward, M., 80, 88, 93–4, 122
Watermann, P., 118
Waylen, G. O., 8
welfare programs, 106, 129
Wendt, A., 8, 16
whiteness, 179n2
Wilford, R., 88, 122, 129
Wimmer, A., 17
Wolcott, Harry F., 40
Women against Imperialism, 79, 87
Women's Coalition (NIWC), 22–3, 122, 125–9, 131, 143, 153–4, 158, 160
"wordless," 106, 189n24

Yin, Robert K., 35
Yuval-Davis, N., 8–11, 13, 19, 26, 50, 152, 156, 162, 167

Zapatista Army of National Liberation (EZLN)
  alliance building and, 69, 144
  background of conflict with government, 33, 50
  community and, 110–15, 145
  female leadership, 62
  feminist activism and, 65–9, 150, 155–7
  founding of, 50, 181n4
  identity and, 162–5
  indigeneity and, 50–1

indigenous women and, 50–2, 56–61, 91–4, 116–19, 143, 154–9
international dimension of protests, 101
mobilization in 1980s, 56–7
Other Campaign and, 144
peace settlements and, 99–101, 107, 143, 145
political action, 58–62
private realm and, 119–21, 166–8
public sphere and, 102–8, 145
research on, 38, 41–2
Revolutionary Women's Law and, 62–5, 180n11, 183n33
SERAPAZ and, 38
state and, 107, 151, 154, 161